WORK AND EMPLOYMENT IN A GLOBALIZED ERA:
AN ASIA PACIFIC FOCUS

STUDIES IN ASIA PACIFIC BUSINESS
1369-7153

Editors: Robert Fitzgerald, Chris Rowley and Paul Stewart

Management in China: The Experience of Foreign Businesses
Edited by Roger Strange

Greater China: Political Economy, Inward Investment and Business Culture
Edited by Chris Rowley and Mark Lewis

Beyond Japanese Management: The End of Modern Times?
Edited by Paul Stewart

Human Resource Management in the Asia Pacific Region:
Convergence Questioned
Edited by Chris Rowley

Korean Businesses: Internal and External Industrialization
Edited by Chris Rowley and Johngseok Bae

China's Managerial Revolution
Edited by Malcolm Warner

Managed in Hong Kong: Adaptive Systems, Entrepreneurship and Human Resources
Edited by Chris Rowley and Robert Fitzgerald

Globalization and Labour in the Asia Pacific Region
Edited by Chris Rowley and John Benson

Work and Employment in a Globalized Era

An Asia Pacific Focus

Editors

Yaw A. Debrah and Ian G. Smith

Cardiff Business School, University of Wales

R Routledge
Taylor & Francis Group

LONDON AND NEW YORK

First published in 2001 by
FRANK CASS PUBLISHERS

This edition published 2013 by Routledge
2 Park Square, Milton Park, Abingdon, Oxon, OX14 4RN
711 Third Avenue, New York, NY 10017

Routledge is an imprint of the Taylor & Francis Group, an informa business

Copyright © 2001 Frank Cass & Co. Ltd.

British Library Cataloguing in Publication Data

ISBN 0 7146 5135 4 (cloth)
ISBN 0 7146 8162 8 (paper)
ISSN 1369-7153

Library of Congress Cataloging-in-Publication Data

Work and employment in a globalized era : an Asia Pacific focus /
editors, Yaw A. Debrah, Ian G. Smith
   p. cm. – (Studies in Asia Pacific business, ISSN 1369-7153)
   Includes bibliographical references (p.) and index.
   ISBN 0-7146-5135-4 – ISBN 0-7146-8162-8
   1. Labour market–Pacific Area. 2. Labour market–Australia.
3. Industrial relations – Pacific Area. 4. Personnel management–Pacific
Area. 5. International economic integration. I. Debrah, Yaw A., 1956–
II. Smith, Ian G. III. Title. IV. Series.
   HD5850.43.A6 W67 2001
   331.12'095–dc21   00-012259

This group of studies first appeared in a special issue of
Asia Pacific Business Review [ISSN 1360-2381], Vol.7, No.1 (Autumn 2000)
published by Frank Cass and Co. Ltd.

Contents

Introduction: Globalization and the   YAW A. DEBRAH
Workplace in Pacific Asia   and IAN G. SMITH   1

Globalization and Confrontation: PETER WARING,
The Transformation of the   DUNCAN MACDONALD
Australian Coal Industry   and JOHN BURGESS   21

Australian Trade Unions' Responses   PETER HOLLAND,
to Human Resource Management   LINDSAY NELSON
Initiatives in a Globalized Era   and CATHY FISHER   46

Labour Responses to Globalization:
The Australian Experience   BERNARD McKENNA   71

Cross-Cultural Diversity,   DIANNE LEWIS,
Leadership and Workplace   ERICA FRENCH
Relations in Australia   and THIPAPHONE PHETMANY   105

Expatriate Academics in a Globalized Era:
The Beginnings of an Untold Story?   JULIA RICHARDSON   125

Globalized New Public Management and
its Impact on Scientific Research Activity
in New Zealand   STEVE McKENNA   151

Globalization, Economic Crisis and
Employment Practices: Lessons from a   PAWAN BUDHWAR
Large Malaysian Islamic Institution   and KHAIRUL FADZIL   171

Global Competitive Pressures, Labour
Market and Employment Issues in the
Japanese Service Sector   YOKO SANO   199

Globalization, Economic Development and
the Reliance on *Guanxi* as a Job Search
Strategy for Chinese Students   CHENG SOO MAY 215

Conclusion: Globalization, Work and
Employment – Asia Pacific Experiences   IAN G. SMITH
in Retrospect   and YAW A. DEBRAH 239

Notes on Contributors   255

Index   259

1

Introduction:
Globalization and the Workplace
in Pacific Asia

YAW A. DEBRAH and IAN G. SMITH

The economic successes, in the 1980s and early 1990s, of the East Asian Newly Industrializing Economies (NIEs) of Singapore, South Korea, Hong Kong and Taiwan (the four *tiger economies*), Malaysia, Indonesia and Thailand (the three *dragon economies*), China and Japan, set off debates in both Australia and New Zealand on the need to extend the export market into Asia to enjoy the benefits of its booming economies. After much soul searching both Australia and New Zealand realized the benefits of tying their economic futures to that of East Asia and, as a result, are now key economic players in East Asia. In fact, some Australian and New Zealand companies have established subsidiaries in East Asia. Equally, some companies from East Asia have followed the Japanese example of setting up subsidiaries in Australia and New Zealand and, indeed, in other countries in the region.

For many years the economic boom fostered more economic integration in the region but, towards the end of the 1990s, East Asia was suddenly thrust into a recession. This economic bust has had negative effects not only on the economies of the region but also the global economy. This was, perhaps, inevitable in view of the interlinkages in global capitalism. Beginning in an ASEAN country, the financial crisis triggered by the devaluation of the Thai baht, in 1997, soon produced a powerful domino effect in the Asian markets and, like a tidal wave, soon engulfed Japan and South Korea. Asian economic observers have suggested that the Asian financial crisis was mainly due to the region's excessive reliance on export demand and volatile foreign capital (Montagnon, 1999). Similarly, Kelly and Olds (1999) attributed the cause of the crisis not to domestic regulatory imperfections but rather to the level of globalization to which Asian economies have exposed themselves. On the links between the Asian economic crisis and the global economy, Wagstyl (1998:I) similarly comments that:

> If the business world needed a reminder that globalization brings risks as well as rewards, it has come in the shape of the economic crisis in East Asia. The region, which has acted as an engine of global growth for decades, has slowed suddenly, shaking almost everybody on board.

As the Asian financial crisis unfolded, the world witnessed the far-reaching effects of economic globalization. In a sense, the financial crisis was a rude reminder of the downside of economic globalization; the dangers involved in the increasing integration of the global economy. Economic globalization here implies the growing interdependence of regional and national economies. This involves the increasing importance of regional and global trading arrangements, more influential roles for international financial institutions and MNCs, and the rapid acceleration in global financial transactions (Wiseman, 1998).

Before the Asian crisis, the Asia Pacific region was often described as a *miracle economy* flourishing in the Pacific Century (Islam and Chowdhury, 1997). The crisis dented such confident proclamations, but recent months have witnessed a flurry of economic activity in the region, which now appears to be experiencing both a resurgence and expansion of global corporate activity and, hence, a reassertion of its global influence. Indeed the current importance of the Asia-Pacific region to global business cannot be overemphasized. On this issue, Lehmann (1998:2) comments that *without East Asia, globalization cannot take place.* He further asserts that globalization ultimately entails having a presence in the Asia-Pacific region as well as in Europe and North America.

In spite of this realization, very little empirical research has been conducted on the broad HRM, employment and workplace implications of economic globalization in the Asia-Pacific region: existing research having focused mainly on the globalization of Japanese companies and other western MNCs operating in the region. Such an approach ignores the increasingly important globalizing activities of MNCs from the emerging Asian economies. In an interesting analysis of economic globalization of business firms from emerging economies, Yeung (1999) shows that MNCs from Asian countries have become global players in international business and have created employment in many countries. These MNCs, together with other companies in the region, have significant impacts on work and employment and are reshaping employment relations.

Undoubtedly, employers, governments, employees and trade unions have all, in various ways and over time, responded to the impacts of MNCs and domestic companies on HRM, work, employment and workplace policies and practices. Thus, in an attempt to illuminate our understanding of the complexities and multiple impacts of economic globalization on industrial relations in East Asia, Frenkel and Peetz (1998) have conducted an empirical study based on China, Malaysia and Korea. They show that economic globalization heightens competitiveness both at the firm and national level. Hence, both managers and the state adopt strategies designed to enhance labour productivity. Frenkel and Peetz (1998) argue that while, in all three countries, there is increased pressure for more flexibility in labour use, the outcome is constrained by cultural norms valuing hierarchy and security. Moreover, the strategies adopted by the various governments vary with respect to historical circumstances, resource endowments, and internal political dynamics, which include the influence of trade unions. Thus, the authors conclude that the extent and impact of globalization vary between countries, resulting in similar preoccupations by policy makers, yet leading to variable responses and industrial relations outcomes.

This volume attempts to bring to the fore the diverse impacts of globalization on work and employment in the Asia-Pacific region. In this regard, some of the contributions explore new dimensions of the familiar debates in the literature, but others deal with what can be considered as overlooked or unconventional influences, impacts and implications of economic globalization. In a sense, the essays in this volume contribute to the debates on both the impacts of globalization on HRM, work, the workplace and employment, and the responses of individual employees, trade unions and employers. In so doing, the contributions explore globalization and workplace human resource issues in unionized as well as non-unionized organizations and in MNCs as well as non-MNCs. This has been done through original research conducted in Australia,

New Zealand, Singapore, Malaysia and China. We have used the term Asia-Pacific region broadly to cover East and South East Asia, Australia and New Zealand.

Before attending to a review of the main issues covered by the contributors, it is necessary to provide a broad overview of the impact of globalization on the workplace and employment.

GLOBALIZATION, WORKPLACE AND EMPLOYMENT

With the advent of the new millennium and the emergence of the *new economy*, organizations need to actively develop strategies to deal with the impacts of economic globalization. In the management literature and business media we are constantly reminded of the forces of economic globalization and the consequent competitive pressures facing organizations. In fact, the management literature is replete with discussions and examples of how globalization and competitive pressures impact on our lives.

In discussing the diverse impacts of economic globalization on work and employment, Knights and Lee (1996) begin from the position of the forces driving it. Presumably, if we understand its driving forces we would be able to perceive how they are changing work and employment in contemporary society. These driving forces include: (a) the pervasive adaptation of free market ideology worldwide; (b) economic expansion in developing countries and the associated worldwide wave of economic liberalization, including the lowering of tariff and other barriers to international trade; (c) advances in communication technology, which have lowered the costs of doing international business; and (d) the promotion of capital and knowledge transfer. Supposedly, the increase in cross-borders financial flows have increased the demand and encouragement for foreign investment and resulted in the rapid growth in world trade. Also, it is asserted that the deregulation of capital transfers and financial markets, arising from the privatization of public enterprises, has also accelerated the adoption of global perspectives in business practices. These, then, are the main manifestations of the increasing globalization of the world economy (Lee, 1996), and they have resulted in the emergence of the transnational economy which has far-reaching implications for work, the workplace and employment relations.

According to Horton (1998), the transnational economy has been the characteristic mode of economic globalization since the 1960s. Economic globalization has spread through the expansion of international trade, financial flows and the activities of MNCs. Such activities minimize barriers between countries and foster closer economic integration. Through foreign direct investment (FDI) MNCs are able to carry out production activities outside the country of origin.

One of the consequences of pursuing such policies by MNCs is the constantly changing location of production and employment. Wiseman (1998) comments that, with declining transport and communication costs, many MNCs make decisions on the location of plants purely on the basis of costs of production rather than by physical location. Such decisions result in changes at the workplace and in employment relations.

With the emergence of the transnational economy, there is an increasing realization that organizations need to operate in a global market, hence even domestic organizations are now beginning to locate themselves in a globally competitive environment. In this regard, organizations now develop global strategies pertaining to customers, products, finance capital, intellectual capital and production processes. One of the issues emerging out of the persuance of such policies is outsourcing. Organizations, both domestically based and MNCs, are now increasingly outsourcing some elements of their production to areas where labour costs are cheaper or taxes lower (Wiseman, 1998). Many such organizations are now scanning the globe for the best materials and services at the best price. Leading companies focus resources on core competencies and outsource everything else. Thus, with the emergence of the transnational economy, firms no longer restrict themselves to purchasing in the domestic market. Rather firms conduct global searches for the best price, technology, delivery and quality. Reasons for sourcing globally include: (a) cheaper labour rates; (b) more uniform quality; (c) better access to technology; (d) better access to innovation and new ideas; (e) better access to local markets; (f) greater economies of scale due to consolidated production; (g) lower taxes and duties; (h) market pressure for a local presence; (i) the ability to leverage spot deals; and (j) less pressure from labour unions (Pyke, 1998).

Pyke (1998) argues that the benefits of global sourcing clearly outweigh the costs. If we accept this argument then it means that globalization is transforming business practices with tremendous consequences for the traditional workplace, HRM and employment practices. For workers, these consequences include rising workloads, increased stress, declining job security, downsizing and rising unemployment as companies adopt labour flexibility strategies to reduce labour costs. As Wiseman (1998: 36) succinctly puts it:

> For workers it [globalization] simply means that their competition is the world. It will not be enough to be the best in Melbourne or indeed Australia. Workers will have to be world class, for a global corporation will seek out the most effective place in the world to perform a task.

Thus, while globalization undoubtedly creates opportunities for both organization and employees it, at the same time, poses a threat to the job security of employees.

In relation to employees, Lee (1996:486) identifies, among other things, the following anxieties pertaining to economic globalization:

(a) the fear in industrialized countries that globalization is unleashing a new international competition from newly industrialized countries that they cannot withstand and which is causing unemployment and falling relative wages among skilled workers;

(b) a similar fear in developing countries that liberalization will lead to job losses and rising wage inequality;

(c) a fear that the globalization of the labour market is leading to a race to the bottom with respect to wages and labour standards.

Lee (1996) discusses the sources of anxiety over the implications of globalization on unemployment in the industrialized countries. These fears revolve around the increasing volume of imports from low-wage to high wage countries. Here, the main arguments are that such imports have resulted in: (a) the destruction of manufacturing jobs, especially in labour intensive sectors; (b) the rise of wage inequality in some industrialized countries; and (c) the erosion of labour-intensive jobs, which have also resulted in a decline in the demand for unskilled labour which in turn has resulted in a decline in their earnings relative to the more skilled.

Another source of concern relates to the impact of the increasing outflows of FDI to low-wage economies, mainly due to the attraction of lower costs. As Lee (1996) points out, the impact of this process is similar to that of increasing imports from low-income countries. It amounts to the *export* of low-skilled work from high wage to low wage countries through relocation. Over time, this has the effect of depressing the demand for low-skilled workers in the industrialized world and reinforcing the effects of increasing competition.

At another level there is some concern that globalization has also lead to the development of a global labour market. This concern revolves around the fact that an increasing proportion of the world labour force is involved in work linked to international trade and capital flows. Thus, the growing exchange of labour services effected through trade, investment flows and international subcontracting of production is forging closer links between markets (Lee, 1996).

With the emergence of such a global labour market employers can, potentially, actively drive down labour cost. On this issue, Donahue (1994:47) notes that:

> The world has become a huge bazaar with nations peddling their workforces in competition against one another, offering the lowest price for doing business.

Such developments perhaps justify the fear that economic globalization will lead to increased income inequality both in developing and developed countries.

It is against this backdrop that trade union leaders have argued that the increase in global competition will be detrimental to the interest of workers as it will generate pressures to lower wages and labour standards. It is argued that, in an environment of heightened competition, both domestic based companies and MNCs tend to resort to cost-minimization strategies which, in turn, have negative effects on wages and conditions of employment in those organizations. Under severe competitive pressures organizations tend to adopt restructuring, downsizing, hardened resolve in collective bargaining and relocation of operations to lower cost foreign countries, as avenues to achieve their cost-minimization objectives. It is argued that this is made easier by the attendant weakening of the bargaining position of labour in many countries. As such, employers can more easily substitute foreign for domestic workers by relocating production abroad. This strengthens the bargaining position of employers either by actually choosing this option or by merely threatening to do so (Lee, 1996). Thus, trade unions and workers have to settle for less or moderate their demands during wage negotiations. In an attempt to tackle such negative impacts of economic globalization on workers, some trade unions have developed strategies on economic globalization.

But, with more resources at their disposal, it is managers who have capitalized on the opportunities offered by globalization to restructure their HRM, workplace and employment systems. In a study based on the pharmaceutical industry, Frenkel and Royal (1998) provide an interesting analysis of the management role in changing workplace relations in subsidiaries of global companies. They argue that, in recent years, MNCs have been repositioning and reorganizing as natural trade barriers come tumbling down and global competition intensifies. These developments have far-reaching consequences for work organization and labour/employee relations globally. But it is not only MNCs that are influencing workplace changes, domestic companies in their responses to globalization are equally restructuring work and employment practices.

GLOBALIZATION AND WORKPLACE CHANGES IN THE ASIA PACIFIC REGION

Kelly and Olds (1999) contend that so much of the theoretical discourse on globalization has emerged from Western contexts and yet the processes and the tonic of globalization have arguably worked with most transformative power in the Asia-Pacific region. In East Asia globalization fostered growth while, at the same time, impacting on employee relations and employment systems. It also, however, played a significant role in the financial crisis.

But Lasserre and Schutte (1995) point out that countries in the Asia-Pacific region cannot be considered as a homogeneous economic or political system. National and business cultures vary significantly and macro-economic data show extreme differences. In the Asia Pacific region there are advanced industrialized countries, newly industrializing economies and developing

countries. Hence, it is possible that economic globalization will
have different workplace and employment implications and effects
in different countries in this part of the world. It is also possible
that there will be some commonality in the impact of economic
globalization on all countries.

In terms of the commonality of the impact of globalization in
the region, Frenkel and Peetz assert that globalization is changing
previously stable workplace systems in East Asia. They cite the
ongoing changes in the paternalistic workplace relationships
founded on unchallenged hierarchies which provided long-
term/permanent employment and some form of non-wage
welfare/benefits for employees. In recent years, increasing pressure
arising from globalization is forcing organizations in East Asia to
make changes to the traditional form of employment relations,
with consequent uncertainty and job insecurity for workers.

Nowhere is this more evident than in Japan. Harukiyo and
Hook (1998), for instance, show how Japanese business
management is being restructured for low growth and
globalization. The authors maintain that the major elements of
Japanese-style management – lifetime employment, seniority
promotion system, enterprise unions, *keiretsu* and sub-contracting
relations, developed primarily in response to rapid and high
economic growth during the post-war industrialization period – are
undergoing some fundamental transformations. In effect,
globalization is forcing Japanese companies to pursue a drastic
restructuring of work organization and employment practices,
causing large-scale departures from established management
norms. In fact, the traditional employment structures are
fragmenting and creating unemployment unprecedented in recent
Japanese history (Graham, 1998). In particular, the core of
employees of Japanese companies who were guaranteed annual
salary increases in return for life-long loyalty to the company are
now struggling, just as the companies are, to cope with the changes.
On this, Graham (1998:v) comments that:

> Increasingly, the core of life-timers is being cut down –
> which has reduced the total number of employees. It has
> also led to an increase in the number of temporary
> workers as companies try to fill their staffing needs with
> cheaper, low maintenance alternatives to life-time

workers. Meanwhile, older workers are being encouraged to volunteer for early retirement.

These changes are taking place against a backdrop of increasing technology and, hence, higher skill requirements at the workplace. In recent years, the increasing technology at the workplace is changing radically the types of skills required of Japanese workers. The need for computer-literate staff and specialists in various types of advanced technological equipment are making employers willing to boycott the lifetime employment system to hire the staff they require, often from temporary agencies. Companies are now outsourcing more activities and relying more on temporary employees. Alexandra (1999) notes that, for a country famous for providing lifetime employment, this is a major transformation. These changes are fundamental and have long-term implications at the workplace.

The intensification of global competition also makes it increasingly unaffordable for Japanese companies to wait for their employees to develop over many years. This and other factors are thus hastening the death of the lifetime employment system. Other factors relate to the conditions underpinning the lifetime employment system, namely: strong corporate profitability, easy bank lending terms, and a steady supply of graduates committed to one company. These are disappearing fast and with them the lifetime employment system (Harney, 2000).

These changes are by no means limited to Japan. In the whole of East and South East Asia, such fundamental changes are occurring at the workplace as a result of globalization. As mentioned earlier, Frenkel and Peetz (1998) provide empirical evidence on the effects of globalization on industrial relations in China, Malaysia and South Korea. They explored the impact of globalization on industrial relations procedures – that is, the way labour market institutions and rules for setting wages and conditions of employment have changed. They also examined the substantive changes in industrial relations, especially earnings levels, labour use and industrial conflict. The study shows that globalization has affected most sectors in all three countries. Equally, Taiwan, Singapore, Malaysia, Hong Kong, Indonesia and Thailand have all, in the last few years, made changes to their HRM, workplace and employment practices in response to globalization (Low, 1998; Yeung 1999a; Debrah *et al.*, 2000; Kamoche, 2000). This is also the case in Australia and New Zealand.

OVERVIEW OF THE VOLUME

All the papers in this issue were presented at the 14th Annual Employment Research Unit Conference at Cardiff Business School, University of Wales, UK in September 1999, under the conference theme of Globalization, Workplace and Employment: Responses for the Millennium. The contributions presented here were drawn from the best papers on the Asia-Pacific region.

Waring *et al.*'s contribution systematically examines how globalization is transforming workplace organization and impacting on the strategies of Australian managers and trade unions and industrial relations in coal mining firms. In addition, it explores the defensive and global strategies adopted by the trade unions in order to maintain rights and conditions, respond to the growing power of managers and counter the anti-union actions of the federal government.

The authors argue that, like other industries of the Australian economy, the coal sector has undergone some institutional and structural changes over the last decade. These changes include: (a) the shift towards export sector production; (b) the removal of export price controls; (c) increasing foreign ownership; (d) a reduction in the number of producers through acquisitions and industry exits; (e) the shift towards workplace based enterprise bargaining; (f) changes to the institutional arrangements governing employment relations; (g) the shift away from underground to open cut production; and (h) shifts in both domestic and international product market conditions.

It is maintained that these changes have been precipitated by economic globalization. As such, Waring *et al.* provide an analysis of how competitive pressures are being generated through the successive deregulation of domestic and foreign product markets, especially electricity, together with the downward pressure on prices flowing from the recent Asian economic downturn. It is asserted that the situation has been exacerbated by export buyers using monopsonistic power to exert downward pressure on coal prices whilst employing a range of market tactics to stimulate excess capacity. The authors argue that this view is generally not shared by transnational producers who simply contend that Australian mines must compete with low-cost mines in developing countries. Hence, recent price reductions negotiated by Asian buyers have had a significant impact on workers. In particular, firms have attempted to recover profits lost through market negotiations by cutting back on labour costs. Consequently, this has resulted in the retrenchment of approximately 25 per cent of the industry's workforce in the last two years and, in addition, has led to work intensification and large-scale industrial disputes.

Furthermore, it is reported that global competitive pressures in recent years have generated significant changes to labour process strategies at the workplace level. Hence, aggressive managers, particularly those in the transnational mining corporations, are selectively attempting to transform working practices and labour deployment and, at the same time, reduce the application of industry awards and the influence of trade unions.

Waring *et al.* outline those changes and developments, from the organization of coal production through to the management of the export chain, that are impacting on the workplace organization and the industrial relations of the Australian coal industry. In particular, they highlight the attempts and strategies of management to increase productivity, realize functional and numerical flexibilities in the deployment of labour and deregulate employee relations. But trade unions are in a weakened position to resist such management labour flexibility strategies because they are facing institutional, legal and global competitive pressures to accept the new managerial style. Consequently, there have been persistent and sporadic outbreaks of industrial conflict in the midst of the erosion of employment conditions and a shift towards greater managerial control of the labour process.

Changes in the legislative arena have constrained the Australian trade unions' ability to organize and engage in industrial action at the workplace. At the same time the power of management has been enhanced through legislative provisions that curb the right to strike and facilitate non-union agreements and individual employment contracts. In the view of the authors, this is a manifestation of a global trend towards the *American model*, whereby individual bargaining replaces collective arrangements, HRM policies are put in place of industrial agreements and long-standing employment conditions are pushed aside for efficiency reasons.

In another contribution, Holland *et al.* analyse Australian trade unions' responses to employment practices and policies of companies operating at greenfield sites. The study contends that the internationalization of business and communication and increasing mergers and alliances means that, increasingly, the location of these greenfield organizations is incidental. Thus, globalization has generated something akin to inter-state, national and regional beauty contests where governments vie to attract inward investments, particularly to the more regionally depressed areas, with generous incentives.

The essay shows that, in the Australian context, deregulation of the work environment, by means of decentralized bargaining, has made it possible for organizations to initiate more innovative approaches to employee relations. In such an environment, organizations tend to adopt a unitarist framework in employee relations. History, traditional work patterns, custom and practice within a pluralist and collectivist approach to employee/industrial relations do, however, provide a significant legacy in opposition to the unimpeded implementation of sophisticated and comprehensive employee relations underpinned by a human resource philosophy. In the view of Holland *et al.*, the study of greenfield sites provides a unique opportunity to examine what an organization's key decision-makers perceive as the most desirable human resource policies, practices and initiatives when given the opportunity of an organizational *tabula rasa*, but in circumstances where, externally, unions, if no longer encouraged, are at least tolerated. It also allows for an examination of trade union responses to this situation.

Using a qualitative case study approach, involving semi-structured interviews with HR managers and trade union representatives, the contribution discusses issues relating to human resources management and employee relations at greenfield sites within the context of HRM and its unitarist underpinnings. In so doing, the contribution also discusses how globalization affects the achievement of trade union objectives.

Bernard McKenna's contribution explores the responses of Australian trade unions to globalization. It uses the Australian experience to critically examine the triumphalist claims made by the proponents of globalization. In particular, it delves into the experience of the Australian trade union movement when it entered into a corporatist consensus with the Australian government regarding trade liberalization, privatization, enterprise bargaining and globalization. The essay argues that, by shedding their traditional labourist discourse, the Australian trade union movement has permitted a complete neo-liberal, technocratic hegemony to arise which has increased social inequity and driven Australia dangerously close to a Brazilian or Asian-style economic crisis. After a short description of Australian political economy, from 1983 to the present, the author provides a critical, discursive analysis of globalization as a neo-liberal technocratic discourse and ends the piece with a brief re-appraisal of globalization in the context of contemporary hypercapitalism.

Lewis *et al.* assess the transformation of Australia from a *white only* country and, consequently, a homogeneous workplace, to a multicultural society and workplace. They trace the origins of the term *multiculturalism*, which came into popular usage in Australia in the 1980s and the liberalization of immigration policies which have allowed non-whites to immigrate, live and work in Australia. Demographic analysis reveals that increasing numbers of people living in Australia were born overseas and a significant number come from non-English speaking backgrounds. In fact, the Australian government's point system for selecting skilled and professional immigrants to Australia has increased the ethnic mix in Australia.

Lewis *et al.* contend that while the changing ethnic composition has enriched Australian society, it has also created a number of employment issues for Australian managers and the Australian workforce in general. Thus, multiculturalism poses challenges for managers as they have to adapt to the increasing cultural diversity in the workplace, not least of which is cross-cultural management. This contribution thus examines the relationship between perceived leadership behaviour and subordinate job satisfaction in two different cultural groups. This is done by means of an empirical case study carried out in four Australian manufacturing organizations employing Australian and Vietnamese workers. Two leadership approaches, *transactional* and *transformational*, were tested for their relationship to subordinate job satisfaction. The results indicate that neither transactional nor transformational

leadership behaviour alone is sufficient when working with
multicultural workforces such as the Australians and the
Vietnamese. Rather a mix of certain elements of each is deemed
necessary. In addition, the different ethnic work groups required
leaders to display certain behaviour attributes to differing degrees.
The authors point out that while the findings are exploratory, they
should be useful for designing supervisory leadership training for
organizations and leaders who wish to develop diversity skills for
managing the increasing multicultural workforce of the new
millennium.

One important aspect of globalization is the increasing use of
expatriates by organizations, both in the public and private sectors.
In the international human resource management literature, the
predominant research focus has, however, been the use of
expatriates by multinational corporations. But, as Richardson
indicates, increased internationalization and expatriation are not
confined to business organizations alone. With the advances in
information technology, education and education systems are
becoming increasingly international. The internet makes it possible
for educational services to be provided globally. Educational
institutions in the developed world now compete fiercely for
international students and the prestige of a university is boosted by
the number of its international staff. Consequently, academics are
also experiencing growing levels of international mobility and
globalization is impacting on academic careers.

In spite of the long history of the use of expatriate academics in
many countries, Richardson rightly points out that very little
research has been done on the experiences of expatriate academics
and the development of careers. Richardson has clearly identified
an important gap in the literature and her contribution attempts to
fill that gap. She argues that, if we are to develop an understanding
of expatriation and expatriate management issues, expatriate
academics, as an increasingly large group, can no longer be ignored.
This contribution, based on expatriate academics in Singapore and
New Zealand, attempts to illuminate our understanding of
expatriates in a more general sense by reflecting on the experiences
of expatriate academics. The essay contributes to the literature as it
evaluates the extent to which existing literature on expatriation can
be applied to expatriate academics. In so doing, it highlights some
of the differences between the experiences of expatriate academics

and those of expatriate managers as portrayed in the current literature. The author points to the limitations of using the current literature on expatriate managers as a framework for understanding expatriate academics.

The impact of globalization is being felt in both the private and public sectors in almost every country. In this respect, New Zealand is no exception. Just as in the transition economies of Eastern and Central Europe, Africa and Latin America, the New Zealand Government has been keen to subject the public sector to private sector efficiency measures. Hence, attempts have been made to expose the public sector to market forces. This has been ongoing since the 1980s when the New Zealand government began liberalizing the economy. In this respect, it adopted measures to reduce income tax and initiated the commercialization, corporatization and privatization of enterprises. The government has also used various means to reduce the power of trade unions and has encouraged flexibility in employment practices. In essence, the government initiatives are aimed at introducing private sector discipline to the public sector to ensure the effective and efficient provision of services.

Steve McKenna's contribution analyses the impact that the new public management has had on the organization and management of human resources in scientific research in New Zealand. In a sense, it focuses on how a public sector organization has been responding to the forces of globalization. Drawing on a case study of a government scientific research body in New Zealand, McKenna shows convincingly how the commercialization of the organization brings to the fore the effects of the various aspects of economic globalization on human resources.

Focusing on a domestic company, Budhwar and Fadzil examine the employment system developed by a large financial institution in Malaysia to achieve survival and competitiveness in the midst of globalization and economic crisis. As the authors point out, the rapid economic development in East Asia took the world by storm and contributed a great deal to the globalization of business. The recent economic crisis in East Asia abruptly disrupted their remarkable economic run, however, and organizations suddenly found themselves engulfed in crisis. Organizational responses to the economic downturn took many forms, including restructuring, mergers and/or acquisitions. The authors assert that such changes directly or indirectly influence an organization's employment systems, practices and employee relations. Hence, firms are searching for more efficient ways to manage their human resources, improve employee relations, enhance firms' performance and achieve both firm and national competitiveness. From the authors' perspective, this can be achieved with the help of Islamic principles. They point to the recent emergence in the literature of the role of Islamic principles in the successful management of organizations. They also draw on evidence from the literature to show that some organizations which run on Islamic principles function successfully and out-perform others, not only during normal conditions but even in turbulent times. To the authors, the explanations for this successful management practice lie in the organizations' HRM/employment policies and practices and their organizational cultures. It is argued that, if these policies are rooted in Islamic principles, and in a predominantly Muslim country like Malaysia, they will strongly reflect the Islamic values held by the people and can then enhance organizational performance. Arguably, this is because the policies help to create social cohesion.

Based on a case study, this contribution examines: (a) the globalization of business and its role in the emergence of the recent Asian crisis; (b) the impacts of globalization and the economic crisis on firms operating in East Asia, particularly in Malaysia; (c) *how* and *why* a large Malaysian financial institution, run on Islamic and Malaysian work principles, is prospering, even in the present crisis; (d) the key role of both external (Malaysian work culture and Islamic principles) and internal factors and variables (such as ILMs, organizational culture and HRM) in enabling the firm under study to continuously improve and sustain its high levels of performance; and (e) the main implications of the growth of Islam to the globalization of business.

Yoko Sano's contribution is a plea for the deregulation of labour markets in Japan as she believes this would have a positive impact on new business development and the creation of employment. The contribution deals with the recent or emerging changes in employment in Japan. In her view, changes in the Japanese economic environment have resulted in rising unemployment and a shift to non-traditional employment systems. Economic data indicate that the Japanese unemployment rate exceeded that of the US in March, 1999, and it is continuing to rise. She highlights the declining employment levels in manufacturing and distribution and the increase in employment in the service sector. Following this, she argues that deregulation would increase employment levels in almost all sectors in Japan. In her view it is essential to deregulate the labour market as globalization and competitive pressures are forcing Japanese companies to restructure their employment systems. This can seriously undermine the life-time employment system leading to significant job losses.

The contribution argues forcefully that even the service sector has problems as it contends with the effects of globalization. It is asserted that global competitors will attack inefficient organizations, particularly in the Japanese public sector as it is inefficient and lacks cost competitiveness. These factors would slow down the growth of employment levels in Japan. Thus, it is argued that, in order to balance the level of employment, Japan needs to focus on economic recovery, the introduction of new technology, and deregulation of markets, including labour markets.

Using a questionnaire survey of small enterprises, this study attempts to predict what would happen to business firms if the present labour market legislation is deregulated. The focus of the research was labour standard regulation: deregulation of layoffs, work hours, child labour, employment contract and regulation of age discrimination. It examined the consequences of deregulation on employers' labour costs, productivity, employees' loyalty to company, human relations and team work, employees' morale and probability of business chances. A number of interesting findings are highlighted. In particular, the study shows that, in general, the deregulation of the Japanese labour market would increase labour market flexibility and make small and new business activities more competitive, especially in the global market.

In recent years, the economic reforms in China have opened up opportunities for foreign investment in the country. Consequently, the Chinese economy is responding to the forces of economic globalization as more multinational firms set up subsidiaries in China. This has created new jobs in the public sector but at the same time the economic reforms have led to a decrease in state jobs. The decline in state jobs has made it difficult for universities to perform their traditional role of arranging placements for their graduates. In an increasingly competitive labour market with shrinking public sector jobs and opportunities created by foreign companies for Chinese to work overseas, universities students are increasingly relying on their own initiatives to find jobs. Cheng's contribution looks at the attempts by young university students to find jobs upon graduation. In this regard, Cheng examines the use, by the students, of *guanxi* (connection or relationship) as a networking mechanism to find jobs. With the extensive family ties of the Chinese across Asia, Chinese students see opportunities to work abroad and *guanxi* is a means to realize such ambitions. In the HRM literature, Min Chen (1995) has pointed out that Chinese people attach great importance to cultivating, maintaining and developing *guanxi*. It is maintained that *la* (pulling) *guanxi* is the most commonly used strategy by Chinese in network construction. Pulling *guanxi* means the efforts to establish and build up relationships with others where no previous relationship existed, or where an existing relationship is not close enough to be useful. Although *guanxi*, as a form of relationship networking to foster wealth creation among Chinese is well documented in the literature, Cheng's study is novel in its analysis of *guanxi* as a job search strategy. The contribution discusses how the opportunities created by globalization have spurred new ways of finding jobs.

The concluding essay contains a summary of the key points which emerge from the various contributions. The overall lack of 'alignment' between the forces of globalization and the local response at national level is revealed as a major element of the many themes requiring further useful research. The search for consequences of advantage to the many interested parties touched by globalization may prove unending, yet the need for it appears repeatedly in these contributions. The number of such 'parties' is vast and varied from Chief Executives to trade union officials, from corporate headquarters to national governments, including both groups and individuals. The task for research is daunting but the studies in this volume attempt to provide a clear indication of what globalization means for employment, work and management.

REFERENCES

Alexander, G. (1999) 'Japanese Industry in a Spin Over Nissan's U-turn', *The Sunday Times*, Business Section, 24 October 1999, p.8.
Debrah, Y.A., McGovern, I. and Budhwar, P. (2000) 'Complementarity or Competition: the Development of Human Resources in a South-East Asian Growth Triangle: Indonesia, Malaysia and Singapore', *International Journal of Human Resource Management*, Vol.11, No.2, pp.314–35.

Donahue, T.R. (1994) *International Labour Standards and Global Economic Integration: Proceedings of a Symposium*. Washington, D.C.: US Department of Labour, July.

Frenkel, S.J. and Peetz, D. (1998) 'Globalisation and Industrial Relations in East Asia: The Three Country Comparison', *Industrial Relations*, Vol.37, No.3, pp.282–310.

Frenkel. S.J. and Royal, C. (1998) 'Corporate–Subsidiary Relations, Local Contexts and Workplace Change in Global Corporations', *Relations Industrielles/Industrial Relations*, Vol.53, No.1, pp.154–83.

Graham, F. (1998) 'Traditional Employment Systems are Fragmenting', *Financial Times* Survey: Japan, Tuesday 14 July, p.5.

Harney, A. (2000) 'Young Japanese Losing Interest in Life-Long Relationship with one Employer', *Financial Times*, 8 April, 2000, p.5.

Harukiyo, H. and Hook, G. (1998) *Japanese Business Management: Restructuring for Low Growth and Globalisation*, London: Routledge.

Horton, R.J. (1998) *Globalisation and the Nation-State*, London: MacMillan.

Islam, I. and Chowdhury, A. (1997) *Asia-Pacific Economies: A Survey*. London: Routledge.

Kamoche, K. (2000) 'From Boom to Bust: The Challenges of Managing People in Thailand', *International Journal of Human Resource Management*, Vol.11, No.2, pp.452–68.

Kelly, P.F. and Olds, K. (1999) 'Questions in a Crisis: The Contested Meanings of Globalisation in the Asia-Pacific', in Olds, K., Dickens, P., Kelly, P.F., Kong, L. and Yeung, H.W. (1999) *Globalisation and the Asia Pacific: Contested Territories*, London: Routledge, pp.1–15.

Knight, R. (1998) 'Global Finance – The Great Equaliser in Mastering Global Business: Navigating the Tides of Global Finance', *Financial Times* Survey, 2 February, pp.5–6.

Lasserre, P. and Schutte, H. (1995) *Strategies for Asia Pacific*, London: Macmillan.

Lee, E. (1996) 'Globalisation and Employment: Is Anxiety Justified?' *International Labour Review*, Vol.135, No.5, pp.485–97.

Low, L., Ramstetter, E.D. and Yeung, H.W. (1998) 'Accounting for Outward Direct Investment from Hong Kong and Singapore: Who Controls What?' in Baldwin, R.E, Lipsey, R.E. and Richardson, D.J. (eds.) *Geography and Ownership as Bases for Economic Accounting*, Chicago: University of Chicago Press, pp.139–68.

Min Chen (1995) *Asia Management Systems: Chinese, Japanese and Korean Styles of Business*, London: Routledge.

Montagnon, P. (1999) 'Asia-Governments Breathe More Easily', *Financial Times*, World Economy and Finance 13, 24 September, pp.XIII.

Pyke, D. (1998.) 'Strategies for Global Sourcing in Mastering Global Business: Creating the Global Organisation'. *Financial Times* Survey, January, pp.2–4.

Wagstyl, S. (1998) 'Asia Shockwaves Still Spreading', Financial Times Survey – Global Business Outlook, 13 January 1998, pp.1–2.

Wiseman, J. (1998) *Global Nation? Australia and the Politics of Globalisation*, Cambridge: Cambridge University Press.

Yeung, H.W. (1999a) 'Introduction: Competing in the Global Economy: The Globalisation of Business Firms from Emerging Economies', in Yeung, H.W. (ed.) *The Globalisation of Business Firms from Emerging Economies*, Vol.1. Cheltenham: Elgar, pp.XII–XLVI.

Yeung, H.W. (1999b) 'Regulating Investment Abroad? The Political Economy of Regionalism of Singaporean Firms', *Antipode* 31, No.3, pp.245–73.

2

Globalization and Confrontation: The Transformation of the Australian Coal Industry

PETER WARING, DUNCAN MACDONALD
and JOHN BURGESS

The Australian coal industry is a largely export-focused industry which has a long history of industrial disputation and militant unionism. In recent years a range of extreme pressures have generated significant changes to labour process strategies at the workplace level. These pressures include: the shift towards export sector production; the removal of export price controls; increasing foreign ownership; a reduction in the number of producers through acquisitions and industry exits; the shift towards workplace based enterprise bargaining; changes to the institutional arrangements governing employment relations; the shift away from underground to open cut production; shifts in both domestic and international product market conditions.

This essay is organized into five sections. The initial section provides an orientation to the coal industry, outlining in macro-terms, the principal features of the Australian coal industry. The second section describes those forces (that we collectively label as globalization) which we contend are impacting upon employment relations in the Australian coal industry. The third section characterizes both state and employer responses to these forces, arguing that market structures and the monopsonistic power of buyers, ensure that simple cost-cutting is a self defeating strategy in the coal industry. Section four considers the strategies of the Construction, Forestry, Mining and Energy Union (CFMEU) (the miners' union) to counter state and employer initiatives in the coal industry. In particular, it evaluates the CFMEU's global campaign against Rio Tinto. Finally, it concludes by arguing that the experience of the Australian coal industry can assist in improving aspects of contemporary globalization debates.

DESCRIPTION OF THE INDUSTRY

The coal industry is Australia's largest commodity export industry. A small number of very large multinational minerals companies and a large number of smaller producers dominate the coal industry. Australia exports the majority of its coal. Exports have grown to such an extent that Australia is the world's largest exporter of coal; and nearly half of the exported coal goes to Japan. Despite this increase in production, employment in the coal industry has declined gradually and substantially since the early 1980s. Recent changes in the market for coal have been used as a rationale for the reform of coal industry industrial relations, but the primary reason is due to the effects of globalization.

The Australian coal industry is Australia's largest commodity export industry earning export income of around $AUS 9.5 billion in 1997–98[1] (Waring and Graham, 1999: 4). There are approximately 118 coalmines producing 217 million tonnes of coal in Australia with the vast majority of production located in central Queensland and Northern New South Wales (NSW). Coal produced, includes high quality thermal (steaming), semi-soft and hard coking coals.

A small number of very large multinational minerals companies and a large number of smaller producers dominate the coal industry. The four largest producers are BHP Ltd, Rio Tinto Ltd, Shell and Oakbridge Pty Ltd (wholly owned by the American mining company, Cyprus Amax). Their respective productive capacity can be seen from Table 1.

Output has grown substantially since the post-war mechanization of the coal industry and the move to open-cut production. An important stimulus to Australian coal production was provided by the oil price shocks of the 1970s that encouraged energy consumers to switch to coal consumption.

Table 2 shows the growth in Australian saleable coal production. In line with the growth in coal production there has been a steady increase in Australia's coal exports. Indeed since the 1960s, exports have grown at an average rate of 13 per cent per annum while domestic consumption has increased by only 3 per cent per annum (Waring and Graham, 1999: 2). Exports have grown to such an extent that Australia is the world's largest exporter of coal, accounting for approximately 32 per cent of world coal trade in 1997 (Waring and

TABLE 1

LEADING AUSTRALIAN BLACK COAL PRODUCERS, 1997

Company	Saleable Production (Mt)	Percentage of total
BHP	54.6	25.2
Rio Tinto	30.3	13.9
Shell	18.2	8.4
Oakbridge	14.9	6.8
MIM	10.7	4.9
Peabody Resources	10.1	4.7
Powercoal	8.8	4.0
Other	69.6	32.1
Total	216.9	100.0

Source: Industry Commission (1999: C5)

TABLE 2

SALEABLE COAL PRODUCTION BY STATE AND MINE TYPE (MT)

Year	Underground Production			Open-cut Production			Total Aust.
	NSW	QLD	Totala	NSW	QLD	Total	
1970	Na	Na	33	Na	Na	12	45
1975	Na	Na	30	Na	Na	31	61
1980	31	3	35	12	26	42	77
1985	39	4	44	23	57	85	129
1986	41	4	46	25	62	93	139
1987	44	4	49	26	65	96	145
1988	39	4	44	27	65	97	141
1989	43	4	49	30	70	106	155
1990	46	6	53	33	71	110	163
1991	46	7	54	35	72	114	168
1992	44	9	54	41	78	126	180
1993	43	9	54	42	77	126	180
1994	42	11	54	44	78	130	184
1995	45	12	57	45	82	136	194
1996	47	11	59	47	84	140	199
1997	49	14	63	56	89	154	217

a Includes other states' production

Source: Industry Commission (1999: C2)

Graham, 1999: 2). Australia exports the majority of its coal (75 per cent), and 46 per cent of its exports are sold to Japan.

As can be seen from Table 3, the combined exports of thermal and coking coals have increased from just 18 million tonnes in 1970 to over 157 million tonnes in 1997. Of Australia's thermal coal exports, 53.9 per cent is sold to Japanese utilities and trading companies and 16.8 per cent is exported to the Republic of Korea. Significant tonnages are also exported to Taiwan and other parts of Asia. Thermal or steaming coal as it is sometimes referred, is primarily used in power generation.

TABLE 3
COAL EXPORTS BY TYPE AND BY STATE (MT)

Year	Coking Coal Exports			Thermal Coal Exports			Total Coal Exports		
	NSW	QLD	Total	NSW	QLD	Total	NSW	QLD	Aus
1970	Na	Na	17	Na	Na	1	12	6	18
1975	Na	Na	26	Na	Na	3	14	15	30
1980	Na	Na	34	Na	Na	10	23	20	43
1985	Na	Na	50	Na	Na	38	41	47	88
1986	15	34	49	26	18	43	40	52	92
1987	16	39	55	27	20	47	43	59	102
1988	17	39	56	25	19	44	42	58	100
1989	17	39	56	23	20	43	40	58	99
1990	17	40	57	28	21	49	46	61	107
1991	21	44	66	32	22	54	54	67	120
1992	22	46	68	34	24	58	56	70	126
1993	24	50	74	35	23	58	59	73	132
1994	23	49	72	35	24	59	58	73	131
1995	22	52	75	38	24	62	60	77	137
1996	24	53	77	40	24	64	64	76	141
1997	25	59	84	49	25	74	74	84	157

Source: Industry Commission (1999:C5)

TABLE 4
EMPLOYMENT BY STATE AND MINE TYPE[a] ('000 PERSONS)

Year	Underground Employment			Open Cut Employment			Total Empl. Aust.
	NSW	QLD	Total[b]	NSW	QLD	Total	
1980	16.3	2.3	19.7	1.5	5.4	7.9	27.6
1981	18.4	2.4	21.4	2.3	6.0	9.4	30.8
1982	17.7	2.4	20.6	3.0	6.4	10.7	31.3
1983	15.8	2.0	18.4	3.3	7.3	11.9	30.3
1984	15.0	1.9	17.7	3.6	8.0	12.9	30.5
1985	15.3	2.0	17.9	4.1	8.6	14.0	31.9
1986	15.7	1.9	18.2	4.4	8.6	14.3	32.7
1987	13.4	1.4	15.4	4.1	8.4	13.8	29.1
1988	12.4	1.4	14.4	4.2	8.1	13.6	28.0
1989	12.3	1.6	14.5	5.0	8.6	14.8	29.3
1990	12.0	1.7	14.3	5.0	9.0	15.3	29.6
1991	11.1	2.0	13.5	5.1	8.9	15.1	28.6
1992	9.9	1.8	12.2	5.1	8.9	15.2	27.4
1993	9.1	2.0	11.4	5.1	8.7	15.1	26.4
1994	9.1	2.0	11.1	4.8	8.3	14.4	25.5
1995	8.8	2.3	11.2	5.0	8.5	14.6	25.8
1996	9.0	2.3	11.4	5.3	8.4	14.8	26.2
1997	8.0	2.1	10.2	5.1	7.5	13.6	23.8

a   Employment working in or about a coal mine or coal preparation plant, including administrative, technical; and clerical staff. Also includes employees from both the mine operators and outside and outside contractors. Employment as at December of stated year.

b   Includes other States' employment.

Source: Productivity Commission (1999:C8)

Employment in the coal industry has declined gradually and substantially since the early 1980s (see Table 4). NSW Joint Coal Board and Queensland Coal Board statistics demonstrates that from 1980–96, employment in the industry has fallen by 27 per cent while black coal production has increased by 160 per cent in the same period. This clearly reflects massive increases in labour productivity as a result of a switch to more capital intensive mining methods (such as open cut mining and longwall mining) together with changes to work practices.

GLOBALIZATION AND INSTITUTIONAL CHANGE IN THE AUSTRALIAN COAL INDUSTRY

Recent changes in the market for coal have been used as a rationale for the reform of coal industry industrial relations. In this section, the peculiar coal market characteristics are discussed and juxtaposed on the reforms to industrial relations arrangements.

There are three basic means of selling coal in the international market: long term contracts; by tender; and by selling coal on the spot market. Since Australia began to export coal to Japan in the 1960s, the predominant means of selling coal was through long term contracts of 10 to 15 years (Industry Commission, 1999: D12). These provided Japanese buyers with security of supply and tended to stabilize prices. However, due to a variety of different pressures including the oil price shocks of the 1970s and the effect of new contracted prices, the system of long term contracts broke down and was replaced with annual negotiations for volumes and prices. These negotiations were struck over such a large proportion of the world seaborne coal trade that they generally established international market rates for coal otherwise known as Japanese benchmark prices (JBP).

Some commentators (CFMEU, 1994; Asia-Pacific Strategies, 1997) have argued that Japanese buyers of coal operate as a collective or cartel in order to maximize their bargaining power in benchmark price negotiations. Asia-Pacific Strategies (1997) have argued that econometric studies indicate that Japanese buyers paid different prices for coal supplied by different countries (Industry Commission, 1999: 31). This they argue indicates willingness on behalf of Japanese buyers to sustain excess supply even if this means paying more for coal in the shorter term. In 1999 however, the

Japanese Power Utilities (JPU) 'discontinued collective negotiations in favour of individual bargaining' (Industry Commission, 1999: D13). This effectively meant that they would conduct individual negotiations with suppliers. Waring and Graham (1998) argue that this is a result of the spot market eroding the benchmark pricing system as buyers replace emphasis on security of supply for lower prices.

In its submission to the Industry Commission (1999), Asia Pacific strategies rejected the notion that Japanese buyers in practice are now negotiating individually. They claimed:

> I'm very sceptical that the abandonment of benchmarking is going to cause any real change to this behavioural characteristic (forming buying cartels), its almost a national characteristic in as far as the Japanese negotiators are concerned. They compete in their home markets but when they're dealing with a foreign supplier, they seem to naturally create a monopsony or an oligopsony (Industry Commission (1999: D14)

It is clear, that the 'spot' market has increasingly become a favoured way for large utilities to fulfil between 20 and 30 per cent of their coal requirements while paying a discounted rate. The spot market operates when buyers advertise a spot tender (usually for relatively small tonnages) and suppliers contract to fill the tender using surplus coal. While this increases supply risks it also enables buyers to purchase coal at a substantially discounted rate.

The other increasingly popular sales mechanism is through the letting of significant tenders. These tenders are to supply reasonably long-term contracts for coal of up to seven years. These contracts are competed for and, in times of excess supply, producers will offer a 'buy-in' rate that for the first 12 or 18 months of the contract offers coal at a discounted rate, which is sometimes lower than spot market prices.

A further factor, which some commentators have argued has led to the intensification of intra-national competition, has been the removal of export price controls on coal. These controls were an initiative of the Labor government in 1973 and gave the Federal government the power to block sales of exported coal where it believed that the price was too low and therefore not in the national interest. The Australian Senate in a 36–34 vote, decided to remove these price controls in 1997. The then Minister for Resources and Energy, Warwick Parer argued that these controls drove 'investment and orders to other countries' and that their abolition would remove a 'major hurdle to investment and jobs in Australia' (Parer, 29.5.97). The CFMEU however, disagreed with this contention and in the October 1998 issue of the union's journal *Common Cause*, claimed that the abolition of the controls had facilitated the crisis in the industry.

The crisis in the industry was precipitated by a dramatic fall in coal prices which was accompanied by massive reductions in employment. Chronic oversupply of both thermal and hard coking coals in 1997–98 led to a price war among producers which, in turn, saw spot coal prices drop as low as $22 dollar a tonne or around 40 per cent less than the Japanese benchmark price (Hextall, 31.7.98). The oversupply situation was a result of optimistic forecasts of demand scenarios in Asia and uncoordinated investment decisions to build new mines to meet forecasted demand. In response, many Australian producers offered loss making 'buy-in' prices to offload their coal to ensure at least positive cash-flow. An example of such an arrangement occurred in mid 1998, when Macquarie Coal was reported to have won a-term contract with Taiwan's Taipower of approximately 500,000 tonnes per annum, where the first year buy-in price was just $US 15 a tonne, or about $US 7 a tonne lower than the already depressed coal spot market price (Kirkwood, 1998).

Such a loss-making contract caused the miners' union, the CFMEU, to call for a moratorium on the development of new coal mines and a more united approach on coal marketing. However, this call was rejected by the NSW Minerals Council as they argued that 'competition not managed trade would resolve any problems facing the industry' and that 'the decision to proceed with a particular mine was up to the owner' (Kirkwood, 1998). Yet this was not the view taken by all observers. For example, a special report on the Australian coal industry by the *Australian Financial Review* argued that:

> No-one doubts that the coal producers are doing it tough. Bosses grumble that 20 per cent of the industry should be shut down, then the rest would do all right. The problem is, no-one agrees on which 20 per cent (Hextall, 29.9.98).

The above figure of 20 per cent accords with the assessment by Waring and Graham (1998: 4) who argued that 'capacity in 1997 represented excess capacity of over 20 per cent in 1997'.

In the late 1990s, Australian coal producers responded to the depressed coal market by retrenching employees, closing marginal operations and, in all cases, advocating workplace reform to increase productivity. According to a study by Australian Mineral Economics, employment in NSW coal mines in the financial year 1997–98, fell from 14,351 to 11,625 or by 2726 workers – nearly 19 per cent (Kirkwood, 26.10.98) while annual output of saleable coal per employee rose to 8110 tonnes in 1997–98 from 6,920 tonnes the year before. These statistics generally accord with those of the Joint Coal Board in Table 5.

TABLE 5

EMPLOYMENT AND PRODUCTIVITY IN THE NSW COAL INDUSTRY,
1996/7–97/8

	1996–97	1997–98	Net Change
Employment	14351	11695	–2656
Saleable output per employee, tonnes	6920	8110	+1190

Source: Joint Coal Board (1999), 'Summary of NSW Black Coal Statistics'

These statistics indicate that between the financial year periods of 1996–97 and 1997–98, employment declined in the NSW black coal by 2656 jobs while saleable output per employee rose dramatically by 1190 tonnes (or over 17 per cent) in the same period. However, despite this massive increase in productivity, the NSW Minerals Council recorded an overall loss for the NSW coal industry of $186 million in 1997–98. This was the first overall loss in 11 years and came with a 91 per cent increase in producer debt.

While most industry analysts agreed with the CFMEU assessment that the downturn in the coal industry was due to over-capacity, they also argued that coking coal demand was affected by a reduction in steel making in Asia, principally caused by the Asian financial crisis and the recession that followed. However, strong demand for thermal coal led to the almost paradoxical situation of record Australian export volumes but reduced export revenue as a result of lower contract and spot prices. This strong demand for thermal coal was interpreted as the result of Asian industry switching to relatively cheaper energy sources such as coal as they attempted to export their way out of the Asian economic downturn (Hextall, 29.9.98). It is universally accepted, though, that if the Australian dollar had not depreciated relative to the US dollar (coal contracts are written in US dollars) the downturn in the Australian coal industry would have been much worse. Some producers however, who had engaged in currency hedging at $US70/$Aus dollar for example, were unable to secure the full benefit of the Australian dollar slide to just below US 60 cents in late 1998.

Structural changes in the market have been accompanied by persistent calls from coal producers to reform industrial relations arrangements. This advocacy has led to radical institutional change that has taken place in just a ten-year period. For instance, prior to 1988, coal industrial relations arrangements were highly centralized and disputes were determined by a specialist industrial tribunal – the Coal Industry Tribunal. Coal miners enjoyed a three week shut down over Christmas; a similar but shorter shutdown over Easter; seven-hour shifts; five-day production only; seniority arrangements and preference to unionists. By 1999, the Coal Industry Tribunal had been abolished and industrial relations arrangements had shifted to the jurisdiction of the Australian Industrial Relations Commission. Highly centralized industrial relations were made highly decentralized, with most individual mines covered by a second or third generation enterprise agreements. At some mines, non-union collective agreements and individual contracts underpin workplace industrial relations. Seniority arrangements have been abolished from the coal industry award and only persist in some enterprise agreements. Preference to unionists clauses have been made void and it is illegal to maintain closed shops. Almost all enterprise agreements provide for flexible working arrangements including year-round continuous production, and many provide for extended shift arrangements including the working of 12-hour shifts.

This transformation, justified by changes to market structures, has been pursued by governments of both political persuasions and is indicative of the lobbying success of employer representatives such as the NSW Minerals Council. For employers and their representatives, these changes are an important first step in removing the 'special' status afforded to the coal industry. It meant that their often advocated 'normalization' reforms for coal could proceed. Normalization referred to the process of bringing coal industry wages and conditions as well as work practices in line with Australian industry averages. For the coal unions though, 'normalization' was simply a euphemism for reducing wages and conditions.

STATE AND EMPLOYER RESPONSES

Changes to industrial relations in the coal industry were not simply driven by employers using the Workplace Relations Act 1996. Actions and counter actions, claims and counter-claims were justified through an increasing mountain of research reports. These reports, sponsored by both the federal government and some large producers were consistent in their attempt at highlighting the need for changes in work practices and industrial relations arrangements to ensure the profitability and productivity of the industry. For example, Rio Tinto sponsored at least five studies during 1996–97.

The recurring theme in the majority of this research is the need to radically reform industrial relations arrangements in the coal industry to change work culture and hence become more internationally competitive. A useful summation of the research outcomes and conclusions of the above research is contained in the arguments of Rio Tinto's submission to the Industry Commission's report into the Australian Black Coal (Rio Tinto, 1997). It argues that the Australian coal mining industry suffers from a high cost structure when compared to Australian metalliferous mines or coal mining operations in Indonesia or parts of the Americas. According to Rio Tinto, this is because of: poor work practices leading to low labour productivity; over-manning of mines, high employee benefits in terms of wages and leave entitlements and the absence of competition in rail and port services. In particular it points to the industry's high strike frequency, the operation of seniority systems; the operation of the preference to unionists clause and reasons for low labour productivity which they claim requires an '80 per cent improvement...to match comparable hard rock mining' (Rio Tinto, 1997: 2). The submission argues that change is required to work practices because of international competition and the pressure placed on coal prices due to 'electricity deregulation in Australia and overseas' (Rio Tinto, 1997: 3).

TABLE 6

ENTERPRISE AGREEMENTS IN COAL MINING AND METALLIFEROUS MINING

Coal Mining Industry	Metalliferous Mining Industry
92% of agreements remain at least partially dependant on the parent award.	84% of agreements totally replace the award.
No coal agreements included a provision for employment of part-time production or engineering personnel.	44% of agreements allowed for part-time employment.
22% of agreements allowed casual labour to be used on site, typically from a pool of retrenched coal miners.	79% of agreements allowed casual labour to be used on site without specification of labour source.
95% of agreements adopted a 35-hour ordinary time week	93% of agreements adopted a 38-hour or 40-hour ordinary time week.
74% of coal mining agreements place significant restrictions on the use of contractors.	11% of metalliferous agreements place significant restrictions on the use of contractors.
100% of agreements set annual leave entitlements at five weeks (or six weeks for continuous shift workers).	81% of agreements set annual leave entitlements at four weeks (or five weeks for continuous shift workers).
46% of agreements have a 'no forced retrenchments policy'	No agreements have a 'No forced retrenchments policy'.
There are no known agreements which relinquish the Production and Engineering award clause requiring forced redundancies by seniority (last in, first out).	Only about 14% of metalliferous agreements require forced redundancies by seniority (last in, first out).

Source: Wooden, M.; Robertson, F. and Cernaz, R., 'Coal Industry Awards and Agreements and the Implications for Work Practices and Working Conditions', Working Paper Series 141, National Institute of Labour Studies, November 1996 in Rio Tinto (1997:34).

One of the submission's key claims is that enterprise bargaining has failed to achieve significant workplace reform in the coal industry because in their view it has, 'resulted in high wages for employees, without significant benefits to employers' (Rio Tinto, 1997: 35). To support this claim, Rio Tinto draw on research commissioned from the National Institute of Labour Studies which compared conditions within coal enterprise agreements with conditions in metalliferous mines (see Table 6).

However, the Rio Tinto submission also criticizes the Australian Industrial Relations framework and its system of industrial tribunals which, they claim, 'have emphasised compromise in dispute settlement even when rights under awards and agreements to make change are at stake' (Rio Tinto, 1997: 44). Moreover they argue that competitive pressures mean that:

> There is no longer time to go through the convoluted dispute settlement processes that have made custom and practice so hard to change in the Australian coal industry and which consume so much of management's time... Work practices need to be able to change continuously if necessary. This requires management to have greater discretion to make change; and to make change without having to pay a (more than) offsetting price (Rio Tinto, 1997: 45).

Rio Tinto's 'Killing the Goose' submission appears to have made a substantial impression on the authors of the Productivity Commission's report into the Australian Black Coal Mining Industry. The ills of the industry, according to this report, lie in the restrictive work practices resulting in turn from excessive union power and an overly accommodative tribunal system.

One of the most fundamental changes to industrial relations in the coal industry came with the election of the Howard government in March 1996. The Coalition's industrial relations policy, while proposing radical reforms to industrial relations allayed worker concerns by claiming that 'no worker would be worse off' (Bray and Waring, 1998). However, for unions, the future under the Coalition seemed bleak. Freedom of association was stressed but it was apparent from the outset that freedom to disassociate was the primary concern of the government (see Bray and Waring, 1998).

While all unions were to be adversely affected by the legislative provisions, the CFMEU along with the Maritime Union of Australia (MUA) were to be especially targeted; (a) because of their long-standing records of industrial militancy, and (b) the industries they covered were considered to be of critical importance to the economic prosperity of the country. Various instances concerning the waterfront culminating in the Patricks/MUA confrontation clearly revealed the Government's agenda in respect to the MUA but there is ample evidence in the Hunter Valley No 1 dispute that the miners' union was to be the subject of special attention (Waring and Lynch, 1998).

On 1 January 1997 the substantive parts of the Workplace Relations and Other Amendment Legislation Act came into operation, excluding the provisions relating to Australian Workplace Agreements which came into effect in March 1997. Almost immediately after the new laws came into effect, the CFMEU leadership was said to have received reports from numerous delegates at mining operations throughout NSW and Queensland indicating a new resolve by management to use the Workplace Relations Act 1996 (WRA) to drive change. In particular, mine management in some cases, stated to delegates that they were no longer required to: provide an automatic payroll deduction system for union dues; stop production for union meetings; recognize the preference to unionists clause or seek the agreement of union delegates to bring contractors onto the minesite. This new resolve came mostly from those larger producers who had not committed to framework agreements (see below). Resistance to these issues frequently led to disputes, some of which flared into serious stoppages.

The combination of new opportunities to weaken union power and the dramatic fall in coal prices led some of the larger producers, the so called 'uglies' (see below) to attempt to displace the miners' union and individualize the employment relationship. This essay will draw on perhaps the two most serious examples of this strategy. The first and most significant of these attempts began soon after the Australian Workplace Agreement provisions came into effect in March 1997. Management at the Rio Tinto owned Hunter Valley open-cut mine began offering individual contracts to members of the workforce. Initially, seven accepted which led to over 12 weeks of industrial action and involved state and federal governments, the AIRC, the federal court and various community groups.

At the Gordonstone underground mine in central Queensland, a picket line has been in place for the last 20 months, making it the longest serving picket line in Australia's history. The picket began when the miners employed at the mine were locked in an enterprise bargaining dispute with the owner, American resources company, Arco Ltd. When it became clear that the existing workforce would not accept the terms and conditions offered by Arco, management sacked the entire unionized workforce of 312 and started running the mine with non-unionists. However, the miners' union took Arco to the Australian Industrial Relations Commission in what was Australia's biggest unfair dismissal case. The commission found that Arco had unfairly terminated the employment of the miners and ordered the company to reinstate and compensate the dismissed miners. Reinstatement though was thwarted when Arco sold its Australian coal assets to Rio Tinto who immediately established a labour hire company which employed non-unionists to work the mine. In the face of continued protest at the entrance of the mine, Rio Tinto even went as far as flying in the non-unionists to avoid passing through the protests on the picket line.

Ironically, only a few months prior to Arco dismissing its workforce, mine management had erected a two-metre placard which read 'Home of the World's Best Miners' after they had broken a number of international production records for an underground mine. Recent media reports indicate that Rio Tinto management have since buried the placard on the mine site.

It should be appreciated however that not all producers chose to adopt the aggressive confrontational approach used by Rio Tinto in response to the crisis situation in the industry. Some large producers, such as BHP, preferred a more cooperative strategy that, as detailed below, involved the signing of framework agreements with the CFMEU. This partnership approach provided the producers with certain guarantees of industrial peace and commitments in regard to improved efficiencies in return for the preservation of various traditional industrial entitlements including the use of seniority in hiring and firing. There is some discussion of the respective 'success' of these alternative approaches in the following section.

Looking beyond industrial relations, there is some evidence to suggest that large producers such as Rio Tinto are using the cyclical downturn in the global coal market to force marginal producers out of the market. For example, Rio Tinto, at the height of the price decline in mid 1998, bought Arco's Australian coal interests. Moreover, it was widely rumoured that Rio Tinto was positioning to purchase Cyprus Amax's Australian coal interests (Askew, 1999). Such a purchase would increase Rio Tinto's exposure by over one quarter, somewhat ironic given the company's past lambasting (criticism) of the industry's inefficiencies.

This strategy of increasing market share is facilitated by fierce intra-national competition in the face of falling coal prices. Large producers such as Rio Tinto are able to compete more effectively with smaller producers by cutting costs, including labour costs and achieving functional and numerical flexibilities. Smaller producers however, are often unable and/or unwilling to confront the CFMEU to achieve similar cost advantages and improvements to managerial prerogative. Yet this strategy of forcing out smaller producers in order to gain increased market share may be self-defeating. The history of the international coal market indicates that large buyers are willing to fund unprofitable new entrants into the industry to ensure that no single producer obtains too much market power (Colley, 1998). In this way, the drive to increase market share through intensifying the labour process may be thwarted by buyers' attempts to stimulate competition among suppliers. Moreover, this strategy may be self-defeating as the market price is likely to follow any reduction in producers' costs, ensuring that projected earnings fall along with asset values.

TRADE UNION RESPONSES

During 1996 when the new Howard government was attempting to pass its controversial Workplace Relations and Other Amendment Bill 1996 through the Senate, the CFMEU began a campaign to ensure its survival through a period of Conservative government. Firstly, they moved to negotiate and certify as many certified agreements as possible under the Industrial Relations Act 1988 (as amended). Second, they actively sought the agreement of so called 'friendly' companies to sign framework agreements. These agreements were an initiative of the ACTU but were modified for the coal industry. Essentially, they committed employers to recognizing existing award rights and the union's role in collective bargaining. In return, the union offered its cooperation and claimed that those organizations who had signed framework agreements would be less likely to be caught up in national or district wide disputes. The largest producers to sign framework agreements were BHP Coal Pty Ltd and Oakbridge Pty Ltd, while a number of smaller producers also sought framework agreements.

The results of these framework agreements have been mixed. In the case of BHP Coal (the largest producer) the agreement has been relatively successful, in terms of providing a consultative framework where workplace reforms have been negotiated in good faith. However, in the case of Oakbridge Pty Ltd, local issues have eroded the utility of the agreement for both parties, such that while the parties have not withdrawn from the agreement, it is no longer being exclusively relied upon. The agreements have also served the union's wider strategy of publicly separating the 'uglies' from the 'friendlies' although this has not prevented the 'friendlies' from seeking workplace reforms similar to that sought by the 'uglies', in response to poor market conditions.

In an interview with Tony Maher, the national president of the miners' union, he explained corporate responses to the market crisis in the following terms:

> They want the same things, I mean really I have said it before, all bosses are bastards. And in a depressed market situation they all want the world. And it doesn't matter whether they're Rio Tinto or BHP, they all want the same thing. It's just that they differ on the means of getting it. And that's what's annoying about Rio's propaganda. They would have the share market believe that they're the only ones making yards. And they all want heaps of productivity and they're getting it. BHP reduced its workforce by 25–30 per cent without a day's lost time – contrast that in terms of lost production at Rio Tinto, contrast that in terms of days and resources in litigation. And their agreements provide for continuous improvement programs, I mean what you can't get through that is not worth having. They're getting more flexibility in terms of streams. And they're getting that through consultation with the workforce. It doesn't mean that we love the fact that we're giving them a better deal. I mean they're just doing it suit to their commercial ends to have it done the easy way. It's not that they're made of different stuff, they're still major multinationals who have business goals, and they are determined to get them as any other bastard. That's my experience and I have no hesitation in condemning them when they step over the line. It's quite an antagonistic relationship despite the fact that we talk to them a bit more. But so what, I mean they are all bastards, they tell you that they need this to stay in business and then they give away a bit more price-wise and then they're back to rip up the last agreement and wanting more the next day. Now that makes them bastards in my view.

Aside from local and regional campaigns against the efforts of transnationals to take advantage of state support and the decline in the product market to press for change, the CFMEU has also worked to draw attention to the problems of the industry. In particular, it has used the coal crisis to argue that the industry's problems stem from Australian producers' individualistic investment and marketing decisions. For the CFMEU, there was no doubt about the origins of the crisis in the coal industry. In a press release they claimed:

> The coal industry is, however, currently dominated by multinational corporations who are competing against each other to drive down the price of coal on the international market. The Australian community is paying the price for this cut-throat policy, with the coal companies showing more commitment to increasing profits than ensuring a fair return to the Australian people. The coal industry has retrenched 4,000 workers in the last 2 years. For each job lost in the coal industry three are lost in the wider workforce (CFMEU, 21.9.98).

The CFMEU's response to the coal crisis was to rail against the federal government's inaction and rejection of the CFMEU's call to establish export price controls. They argued:

> The Government's response to the strike has been to say it is powerless to intervene in the price setting for a commodity whose value is set internationally. Such a view ignores the fact that it is coal producers in Australia, responding to pressure from the cartel of the Japanese steel mills, that set the global benchmark for coal prices. The price of coal is not determined by the market, but has been engineered to suit overseas companies. It is scandalous that the Federal Government is standing idly by while an important national resource is sold off to the lowest bidder. That there have been thousands of job losses, and many more to come, because of this flagrant price fixing makes their lack of action all the more unforgivable.

An indication of the CFMEU's frustration over coal prices occurred on the 13th of December 1998. In what was described by media as a 'lightening strike' (Hughes, 14.12.98) 22,000 members of the mining division of the CFMEU went on a 48 hour strike in response to reports that major coal producers had accepted unprecedented cuts in contract prices for premium hard coking coal. The Queensland producers (Shell Coal, MIM and North Goonyella) had reportedly agreed to an 18 per cent reduction in the benchmark price for coking coal in addition to a 30 per cent reduction in volume. The coal miners' union was acting on a resolution endorsed by the union's membership in August 1998 which provided the national leadership with a mandate to call industrial action in protest over coal prices. Tony Maher (the miners' union president) described the strike as a 'political protest over the Federal government's refusal to intervene in an over-supplied coal market by imposing controls on mine numbers while companies undercut each other on prices' (Norrington and Askew, 14.12.98).

An 18 per cent reduction in coking coal prices in late 1998 was followed by a 13 per cent reduction in thermal coal contract prices in February 1999, establishing a new benchmark price of $US29.95 a tonne. Threatening to take industrial action over the cuts, the CFMEU leadership met in early March 1999 to consider their reaction. Rather than taking industrial action, the unions' leadership decided to launch a community awareness campaign on what they described as the devastating effects of the price cuts.

Smith (1994) in an economic analysis of the coal industry, has argued that cooperative industrial relations outcomes will emerge where employers and unions can agree on the state of the market for coal. While there is some conjecture about the accuracy of this contention, historical, statistical and contemporary evidence does suggest that industrial relations in the coal industry are inextricably linked and dependant (to some extent) on the state of the international market for coal.

In the face of what it perceived to be continual attacks on its members, the CFMEU in 1998 launched its global campaign against Rio Tinto. This campaign was designed to place pressure on the company's leadership to change its employment relations practices by drawing international attention to what the union argues is unethical and immoral corporate behaviour. So far the campaign has resulted in a number of questions being raised concerning the company in parliaments throughout Europe and the

United Kingdom. These questions have centred on Rio Tinto's environmental, industrial and human rights records. For instance in Rio Tinto's home base London, a group of 29 British MPs have sponsored a motion in the House of Commons condemning the company's record. The motion describes Rio Tinto as 'probably the most uncaring and ruthless company in the world judged by its appalling record of human and trade union rights violations, community destruction, environmental damage and disregard for the lives of indigenous people in many of the 40 countries where it operates' (*Common Cause*, May 1998). Moreover, a recent British Select Committee on Foreign Affairs questioned Rio Tinto's Andrew Vickerman[2] on the Hunter Valley dispute. Mr Vickerman replied by stating:

> The specific dispute you referred to, the one in the Hunter Valley of New South Wales is not a dispute about union recognition or collective bargaining, it is a dispute about the removal of outdated, restrictive work practices to introduce flexibility to ensure the long term viability of that coalmine.

The CFMEU has also used the International Federation of Chemical, Energy, Mine and General Workers Union (ICEM) and other international unions with which it has fraternal relations to place pressure on the company. This pressure has included the distribution of a highly critical 'stakeholders report' (ICEM, 1998, 1999) to Rio Tinto shareholders at the company's Annual General Meeting in 1998 and 1999. There are some signs that the global campaign is having an effect on the company. For example, on 13 May 1998 the company's chairman, Robert Wilson issued a statement saying, 'Rio Tinto has not embarked on an anti-union crusade. That is nonsense. There are several countries around the world where we have been the first mining company to sign union recognition agreements.' Moreover, it has recently released a statement of business practice which claims that 'employees will have the right to choose whether or not they wish to be represented collectively'. This statement has recently been criticized by ICTFU, which claimed that 'the vague wording of the statement, along with the lack of commitment to a comprehensive list of appropriate international treaties, gives rise to the impression that the statement is no more than a public relations exercise' (ICEM, 1999: 2).

In an interview, the CFMEU's national industrial research officer argued that the campaign had had most impact in countries with social-democratic governments. He claimed that the impact of the campaign had been:

> Surprisingly significant. We find that in the Australian context under a Conservative government, Rio Tinto is not worried about its image in Australia and basically rely on the media which is always anti-union and the government which it has had a close working relationship with. But in Europe, it's a whole different ball game. They have a Labour government, in Britain; social-democrats and the left have basically the majority in the European Parliament; there's various European laws that bind Rio Tinto – we find them much more sensitive to criticism in Europe, so therefore we've found that things that we've done in Europe have galvanized the company into action to fight us over in Europe. We find that when we have a question raised in the British Parliament about them, their senior management visits every MP seeking to combat everything we've said. They are talking to the ICEM and it's early days yet, but the campaign is causing them heartburn at the international level, and most people who are researchers, who are decision makers are aware that there is controversy surrounding Rio Tinto. And that impacts upon their ability to start negotiations over new mines with governments. There is a stink around Rio Tinto, and they would like to present themselves as being a very clean company, being very ethical as efficient producers, but the controversy surrounding Rio Tinto...impacts upon their ability to move easily around the world. So we think the international campaign's actually been quite successful. It hasn't been successful in terms of there being a conclusion, but it's certainly been worth our while and shows that it's not enough to fight the battle on the ground – you can have a strong workplace structure and a good national union, but if you try and fight a multinational in Australia you're often not getting them where it hurts.

For the union, this experience has demonstrated that it is not enough to simply implement wage campaigns against transnationals at the local level without a complementary and effective global strategy. To date though, there is little evidence to suggest that the global campaign has stifled Rio Tinto's strategy for the Hunter Valley mine or indeed the rest of the coal industry.

CONCLUDING COMMENTS

Two potential flaws in the contemporary globalization debate have emerged from the analysis in this study. First, the forces of globalization are often presented as homogenous across industries and nation states. Clearly, while the global seaborne coal trade has grown considerably in the last few decades most pressures on Australian producers have emanated from intensified intra-national, not international competition. Moreover, these pressures have been exacerbated by buyers using their bargaining power and a range of market tactics to drive down prices. The Australian coal industry has suffered considerably in the period 1997–99 from over-supply caused in the main by speculative over-investment in productive capacity. These investment decisions were in response to optimistic forecasts in the mid-1990s of Asian energy needs into the next century. Nevertheless some of the excess investment has come from companies with interests in operations whose future viability is dependent on a guaranteed supply of coal at competitive prices. While vertical integration has long been a profit-maximizing strategy, the role of the same commercial interests as both supplier and customer in the global energy market adds a further complexity to the globalization phenomenon. Moreover, despite this period of crisis in the coal industry, both government agencies and industry analysts are forecasting demand/supply scenarios that clearly favour the Australian coal industry and its array of multinational investors over the longer term (see Table 7).

Waring and Graham (1998) argue that Australia will continue to take advantage of its abundant reserves of high quality coal in addition to its proximity to developing Asian economies to increase its coal exports into the next century, although they caution that 'current price trends and pressures on the Australian coal supply have created significant uncertainty regarding the outlook for Australian coal supply'. A more detailed and optimistic assessment

TABLE 7

WORLD SEABORNE STEAM COAL SUPPLY TO 2010

	1998	2000	2005	2010
Australia	87	103	141	165
Colombia	28	33	53	54
South Africa	65	69	76	77
Indonesia	43	52	61	69
China	27	30	35	43
Venezula	6	8	18	23
Canada/CIS/Poland	31	30	28	23
Total	287	325	412	454

Source: Glencore International (1999: 6).

of the future of the international coal market is given by the large Swiss trading company, Glencore International, who argue:

We will note that Australia is by far the world's largest coal exporter of steaming coal and in order to meet the demand scenarios expected in the future, Australia will have to grow to fulfill these demand capacities. It is clear that the growth demand in Asia is dependent upon Australia's ability to increase its supplies. Australia should easily be able to meet this demand from identified greenfield and brownfield developments. As will be explained in the outlook for future prices, Australia will act as supplier into Asia and the swing supplier into Europe as well as setting the price caps for the world steam coal prices. We firmly believe by the year 2000, Australia will export in excess of 100 million tonnes of coal and in excess of 150 million tonnes by the year 2005 (Glencore International, 1999).

Glencore International claim that Australia's main competitors, Indonesia and South Africa, will be prevented from taking advantage of future growth in the Asian market because of quality and infrastructure problems. In the case of Indonesia and China, exports will also be limited by planned expansion in electricity generation capacity. The majority of South African coal is likely to be supplied to European markets as Germany reduces high levels of subsidies to its domestic coal industry.

Based on world demand/supply scenarios, Glencore International's analysts claim that 'the dominant supplier being

Australia will dictate future coal prices' (p.4). Moreover they state that, 'As Australia is the dominant supplier with around 35–37 per cent of the world seaborne steam coal supply during the years 2000, 2005 and 2010, the cost parameters in Australia during these years will dictate the international world steam coal market' (p.4).

However, for labour and its collective representation, such an international domination of the world market will be of little benefit while ever intra-national competitive pressures remain so intense. Government policy that continues to support such a competitive environment in combination with anti-collectivist industrial legislation will see workers face ongoing reductions in earnings, intensification of work effort and job insecurity regardless of the extent to which Australia as a whole may predominate in the market. Variations in employer responses to the current crisis situation were observed indicating, once again, the falsehood of TINA. However, with the continuing demise of BHP, the ranks of the 'friendlies' are being diminished and reduced membership and, consequently, dwindling resources are limiting the effectiveness of the union. Globalization may be the rhetoric, but worker exploitation in the face of unbridled domestic competition and an individualistic legal environment is the reality.

Somewhat in opposition to this pessimistic scenario, the second apparent flaw in the globalization debate relates to the rather negative perceptions concerning the ability of labour to organize on an international basis. While some may argue that the global campaign has not yet delivered for the CFMEU, there is some evidence that it has placed substantial pressure on Rio Tinto in countries where the state is dominated by social democratic parties. Perhaps sufficient international pressure, particularly in the form of reduced cooperation on the part of governments in countries seen as important for the future investment plans of corporations, may lead them to place less emphasis on marginalizing trade unions and reducing worker entitlements.

Our analysis of the Australian coal industry reminds us of the importance of studying 'globalization' not simply as a set of pre-determined, ahistorical and homogenous forces affecting nation states, but from an industry perspective which is historically grounded. While certain structural features new to the international economy in the last three decades may have impinged somewhat on the choices of key actors, this analysis demonstrates that the decisions of employers, unions and the state can be at least as significant for employment and industrial relations as the forces of the new globalized environment.

NOTES

1. This is expected to fall to around $AUS 8.7 billion in 1998-99 due to lower coal prices.
2. Andrew Vickerman is head of Rio Tinto's external affairs department. It must also be said that representatives from Shell, Rio Tinto, BP and Unilever were asked to appear before the select committee on transnational corporate behaviour on the 21st of May 1998.

REFERENCES

Askew, K. (15.12.98) 'Coal Strike "Small" Burden', *Sydney Morning Herald.*
Askew, K. (16.12.98) 'BHP Price for Coking Coal Down by 15 Per Cent', *Sydney Morning Herald.*
Askew, K. and Cleary, P. (12.2.99) 'Black Coal Dulled by Work Practices, Freight Charges', *Sydney Morning Herald.*
Bagwell, S. (21.12.98) 'Price Falls May Force Industry Shake-up: Rio Tinto Head', *Australian Financial Review.*
Bray, M. and Waring, P. (1998) 'The Rhetoric and Reality of Bargaining Structures Under the Howard Government', *Labour & Industry* Vol.9, No.2, December.
British Parliament (1998) *Select Committee on Foreign Affairs Minutes of Evidence*, 21 May.
CFMEU (1998) 'Crisis in Coal: Crisis for Australia' CFMEU Media Release, 21 September.
CFMEU (1998) 'Federal Government's Simplistic Approach Wrecking Coal Industry', CFMEU Media Release, 15 December.
CFMEU (1998) 'National Coal Strike an Overwhelming Success', CFMEU Media Release, 14 December.
CFMEU (1998) 'National Coal Strike to End at 11pm Tonight – Union Campaign against Price Cuts to Continue', CFMEU Media Release, 15 December.
CFMEU (1998) 'National Coal Strike: 20,000 Miners Walk off the Job', CFMEU Media Release, 13 December.
CFMEU (1998a) – 'Industry Commission Attacks Job Security and Safety Standards in Coal', CFMEU Media Release, 2 April 1998.
Colley, P. (1998) 'Industry Policy and the Australia–Japan Coal Trade', *Journal of Australian Political Economy*, No.41, June.
Common Cause (1998) 'Jobs at Coal Summit', CFMEU.
Field, N. (18.1.99) 'BHP on Coal: It's a Seven-year Hitch', *Australian Financial Review.*
Glencore International (1999) 'World Coal Outlook 1999', Unpublished report.
Graham, P. and Waring, T. (1998) 'The Economics of Australian Coal Supply, ABARE Conference Paper 98.24, ABARE.
Hextall, B. (31.7.98) 'Coal Producers Locked into Price War', *Australian Financial Review*, September 29.
Hextall, B. (29.9.98) 'Coals to Newcastle our $9bn Export Dilemma', *Australian Financial Review.*
Hextall, B. (20.1.99) 'NSW Defies Coal Industry Gloom', *Australian Financial Review.*
Hextall, B. (4.1.99) 'Best Practice Could Keep Mines Going', *Australian Financial Review.*
Hextall, B. (14.4.99) 'Coal and Allied Sees Glimmer of Hope for Industry', *Australian Financial Review.*
Howarth, I. (16.12.98) 'BHP Takes Heavy Cut in Coking Coal Price', *Australian Financial Review.*
Howarth, I. and Hextall, B. (16.3.99) 'Resources Crisis: Mines Close', *Australian Financial Review.*

Hughes, J. (14.12.98) 'Lightening Strike Threatens Coal Talks', *The Australian*.
ICEM (1998) *Rio Tinto-Tainted Titan: The Stakeholders Report 1997*, International Federation of Chemical, Energy, Mine and General Workers Union.
ICEM (1999) *Rio Tinto – Behind the Façade: The Stakeholders Report 1998*, International Federation of Chemical, Energy, Mine and General Workers Union.
Kirkwood, I. (20.6.98) 'Coal Union Wants Brake on New Mines', *Newcastle Herald*.
Kirkwood, I. (16.1.99) 'Miners Fear Cuts: New Japan Coal Talks', *Newcastle Herald*.
Maguire, P. (26.5.99) 'Another 75 Coal Jobs May End Soon', *Newcastle Herald*.
Newcastle Herald (18.5.99) 'Fierce Japanese Coal Price Cuts Force Rio Tinto Hand'
Newcastle Herald (29.10.98) '72 Jobs Lost in Mine Shutdown'.
Newcastle Herald (26.10.98) 'Grim for Coal Jobs'.
Newcastle Herald (19.3.99) 'Hunter Coal "Sold Out"'.
Newcastle Herald (28.4.99) 'Overreaction to Coal Price Cuts'.
Norrington, B. and Askew, K. (14.12.98) 'Miners Risk Penalties in Protest Strike', *Sydney Morning Herald*.
Norrington, B. (15.12.98) 'Jail Threat Ends Strike at Three Mines', *Sydney Morning Herald*.
Norrington, B. (16.12.98) 'Coal Crisis Forecast', *Sydney Morning Herald*.
Parer, Senator W. (29.5.97) 'Senate Vote Ends Export Controls on Resource Commodities', Ministerial Press Release.
Productivity Commission, (1999) *The Australian Black Coal Industry Inquiry Report*, Australian Government Publishing Service.
Rio Tinto (1998) 'Killing the Goose: The Urgent Need for Reform in Australia's Black Coal Industry' *Submission to the Industry Commission*, Rio Tinto Energy.
Waring, P. and Lynch, C. (1998) 'The Case of the Hunter Valley Open Cut Mine Dispute: Coalfields Collectivism versus Corporate Individualism' in Harbridge, R., Gadd, C. and Crawford, A. (eds.) *Current Research in Industrial Relations, Proceedings of the 12th AIRAANZ Conference*, AIRAANZ, Wellington.
Washington, S. (14.12.98) 'Miners Strike Over Cut in Coal Price', *Australian Financial Review*.
Watson, M. (23.4.99) 'Mines are Bleeding', *Newcastle Herald*.
West, G. (16.1.99) 'Rio Tinto Defers $500 Million Coal Mine', *Australian Financial Review*.
West, G. (30.9.98) 'BHP Shuts Coking-coal Mine', *Australian Financial Review*.
Wyatt, S. (12.12.98) 'Coal Price Cuts May Shut Mines', *Australian Financial Review*.
Wyatt, S. (14.12.98) 'Commodities Crash to New Lows', *Australian Financial Review*.
Wyatt, S. (19.3.99) 'Lower Coal Prices Flag Higher Sales', *Australian Financial Review*.

3

Australian Trade Unions' Responses to Human Resource Management Initiatives in a Globalized Era

PETER HOLLAND, LINDSAY NELSON
and CATHY FISHER

The replacement of the personnel tradition with the more pro-active Human Resource Management (HRM) approach has created considerable interest and debate in recent years. Within the development of the HRM philosophy, it has been elevated to take an active role in the business strategic planning processes (Tichy *et al.*, 1982; Beer *et al.*, 1984; Dyer and Holder, 1988). With respect to Human Resource (HR) policy areas, it is assumed that sophisticated policies will be coordinated and integrated to support the strategic notion of human resources as a source of competitive advantage (Kamoche, 1986; Lado and Wilson, 1994; Barney and Wright, 1998). It is expected that these changes will be accompanied by greater involvement in HRM matters by all managers and employees as part of their everyday work. If this goal of a unified workforce committed to common goals is to be realized, it is critical that industrial relations reflect this philosophy. The most appropriate approach draws from the unitarist understanding of the employer/employee relationship where it is assumed that the relationship is a partnership (Farnham and Pimlott, 1986). Employee commitment becomes a pivotal precondition for success. In short, the quality of the employer/employee relationship may ultimately determine the success of HRM. This view raises questions about whether dual commitment to both the organization and union is possible, or indeed whether such an approach precludes the need for unions (Guest, 1989; 1995). Accordingly, this essay focuses on the role of trade unions and their strategies in maintaining a pro-active position within workplaces that embrace an HR framework. For the research we have selected greenfield sites, which are relatively free from past cultural influences and negative stereotypes, because they offer an untarnished opportunity for the practice of effective HR principles and the observation of union responses.

HUMAN RESOURCE MANAGEMENT PERSPECTIVE

Fundamentally the transition from an old-style personnel approach to the more pro-active HR stance is characterized by a number of key features. First, the transition from the personnel model to a strategic HRM model demands that HR matters be given priority in the design of business strategy. For those involved in the HR function this focus implies major re-positioning within the organization. HR must be moved away from an administrative, 'housekeeping' role to one that makes a major contribution to the strategic planning and design of the organization (Dowling and Schuler, 1990). Many have welcomed this move away from what Tyson and Fell (1986) had called 'clerks of the works' to the role of 'architect', where the former was largely involved in routine administration and record keeping and the latter would be involved in policy formulation and management matters (Sisson, 1995). Structurally, the role for HR involves an HR representative on the senior management planning committee and effective access of senior HR personnel to the CEO. Direct access to the CEO through a formal reporting relationship can reflect the degree to which senior management acknowledges and draws from HR for strategic input (Tichy et al., 1982; Beer et al., 1984; Dyer and Holder, 1988; Boxall and Dowling, 1990; Nininger, 1980; Golden and Ramanujam, 1985; Lawler, 1995).

Second, not only would there be recognition of the importance of HR input within the top level planning processes, there would also be the expectation that the various HR policy areas should be tightly integrated. This is different from the fragmented approach taken within the old personnel model where 'many of these personnel and labour relations activities and systems seem to have a life of their own, isolated from and independent of other personnel and labour relations activities and systems' (Beer et al., 1984: 2).

In general, discussions of strategic human resource management have the notion of integration between human resource policy areas at their core. Specifically this means that the policy areas of recruitment and selection, training, appraisal and rewards would be clearly coordinated (Miller and Burack, 1981; Lengnick-Hall and Lengnick-Hall, 1988; Baird and Meshoulam, 1988; Wright and McMahan, 1992; Buller and Napier, 1993; Purcell and Ahlstrand, 1995; Lawler, 1995; Torrington and Hall, 1998). The focus on the resource-based view of the firm within the HR literature has reinforced the importance of this synergy. It is argued that the horizontal integration of HR policy areas coupled with the vertical linkage with business strategy enables an organization to achieve competitive advantage from building and defending human resources that add unique value which cannot be readily copied (Kamoche, 1996; Lado and Wilson, 1994; Barney and Wright, 1998; Boxall, 1994).

A third feature of the HR approach is that HR matters should become everyone's responsibility. Ideally HR should be accepted and used by all managers and employees as part of their everyday work. HR is seen to be an organization-wide attitude, not a functional specialty. If organizations are to move away from a disconnected set of policies to a united focus on productive employee/management relationships, HRM, so the argument goes, must become everyone's concern and it must be supported and be part of general management.

Line managers are expected to take a much more pro-active role within the HR approach. It could be argued that line managers have always been important and, within the older personnel model, were often relied upon to carry out personnel tasks. There is a difference, however, in the way that line managers are involved in the HR approach. Traditionally the role of line manager is reactive and responsive to outside direction. Within the HRM approach, however, the line manager is considered to be much more pro-active. There is an expectation that they will initiate ways of enhancing the effective use of human resources in order to facilitate business strategy. There is a focus on the bottom line and quality of product and service (Legge, 1995).

Overall then, the features addressed so far include a much more active role for the HR function in senior level strategic planning processes, tighter integration of basic policy areas and stronger involvement of line managers in HR processes. The final important area within the HR approach relates to changes needed to industrial relations.

HRM AND INDUSTRIAL RELATIONS

One of the dominant characteristics of industrial relations (IR) has been the development of a formalized system which Dunlop (1958) termed a web of rules. IR legislation in the USA is rooted in the belief that there was an unequal and adversarial employment relationship resulting in arbitrary treatment of workers and employer opposition to attempts by employees to organize (Dulebohn *et al.*, 1995). The same could be said to have been the case in Australia, where collective bargaining was encouraged under the protective mantle of legislation fostering conciliation and arbitration (Deery *et al.*, 1997). In the UK the liberal collectivist style prevailed. IR was seen as processes of control over the employment relationship, organization of work and relations between employee and employer (Gospel and Palmer, 1993). These approaches are clearly based upon what is commonly termed the pluralistic assumptions, in which the various different interests need to be 'managed'.

These pluralist assumptions underlying older style personnel management no longer need apply, as HR philosophy ideally appeals to management and employees alike. Everyone would share the same goals and there need be little conflict of interest. This 'unitarist' approach reinforces the need for a high level of integrated commitment that characterizes the psychological contract within an HR framework. This is in stark contrast to compliance which was seen to be a feature of personnel management and a regulated approach to industrial relations.

With a decline in unionism, a move to decentralized bargaining and the emergence of HRM, the ground has shifted dramatically from a pluralist to a unitarist perspective within the employment relationship. Legge (1995) and Guest (1995) refer to these changes as the 'new realism' in IR, while Mabey and Salaman (1995), citing Millward et al (1992) and Clark and Winchester (1994) speak of the 'new industrial relations'. It could be argued, however, that the unitarist ideal is an incorrect portrayal of reality, rarely describing what actually occurs. Nevertheless, it is a view that is not to be dismissed as it still forms the basis for the industrial relations approach encapsulated within the term 'human resource management' (Blyton and Turnbull, 1998). This HRM approach, usually represented by Beer *et al.*'s (1984) mapping of the term, supports union avoidance/marginalization and as such represents a fundamental difference between HRM and IR. This latter point is manifested in discussions attempting to reconcile HRM with IR which centre on a basic contradiction: that where IR is concerned with collectivism, especially in bargaining, HRM emphasizes commitment to the organization and individualism.

From this contradiction flow several issues. First, whether IR and HRM can successfully co-exist. Although Storey (1992) says that both IR and HRM systems can co-exist, remaining relatively compartmentalized, this does little to resolve the underlying tension, since they spring from different philosophical positions. Second, given the vision of employee commitment to the organization, whether they can also and at the same time be committed to the union (Guest, 1995; Gordon and Ladd, 1990). Third, the extent to which organizational flexibility and managerial prerogative are compatible with employee needs (Deery *et al.*, 1997). These and similar issues focus interest on how unions might respond to such workplace changes. Some time ago, Legge (1988) felt that there was no empirical support for concluding that IR had collapsed in the face of 'macho' management. However, the fact remains that then, as now, the level of unionism has significantly declined (Guest, 1995; Deery *et al.*, 1997), and of growing interest is the strategic response of trade unions to unitarist styles of management and a shrinking membership base.

Lucio and Weston (1992) suggest trade unions have three alternatives as a response:

1. Conciliatory/concessionary, when confronted with a hostile environment.

2. Extending the role and scope of collective bargaining to embrace other matters such as training, skill development, and career development.

3. Acting with a greater degree of independence at the workplace: in essence taking a contingency approach to localized issues.

Others, such as Guest (1995) and Bacon and Storey (1996) take the view that unions should embrace the ideals of HRM. This holds for the 'soft' version of HRM (Storey, 1987) which champions such things as fairness in selection, training, and open communications, all of which emphasize mutuality of interests. But it should be remembered that unions will always seek to maximize outcomes for members, in which case at differing times and circumstances each of the Lucio and Weston (1992) responses may be appropriate. At the interface between management and unions, therefore, is the research interest of this study: whether unions have entered into the spirit of HRM by giving their support and seeking greater involvement, or have responded in a more traditional, adversarial way. An interesting question is the extent to which unions are adapting to their changed environment. On the obverse side are the attitudes and actions of management insofar as these set the climate for unions. The following sections of this study explore these issues from an Australian perspective, in the context of significant change in the landscape of industrial relations over the past two decades.

THE CHANGING LANDSCAPE OF AUSTRALIAN
INDUSTRIAL RELATIONS

The Australian industrial relations system, its formal institutions and legal structures have undergone significant change over the past two decades as the pressures of globalization including increased competition, deregulation and the emergence of newly industrializing countries have forced Australia to restructure to compete more effectively in the developing global economy. The deterioration in Australia's competitiveness during the 1980s became the catalyst for the systematic dismantling of the centralized framework of industrial regulation during this period (Rimmer and Zappala, 1988; Morris, 1996). The evolving system has seen Australia move through a variety of stages of 'managed decentralisation' (McDonald and Rimmer, 1989) to coordinated and then fragment flexibility (Davis and Lansbury, 1998). These changes have substantially affected the industrial relations landscape and the players both in terms of procedural changes and the way they have had to adjust to remain relevant in this new dynamic system.

The reform of the highly rigid and centralized labour market was seen by many as the key to increasing competitiveness (Rimmer and Zappala, 1988; Quiggin, 1996). In this context, the Hawke federal Labor government embarked on a micro-economic reform agenda focusing specifically on labour market reform. In March

1987 centralized wage-fixation was dropped in favour of policies which encompassed industrial efficiency in the determination of wages (Fox *et al.*, 1995).

The initial focus of the micro-economic reform was the removal of excessive costs and restrictive work and management practices, while introducing elements of multi-skilling (Quiggin, 1996). The development of this framework was envisaged to be the catalyst for enhanced industrial efficiency. For the workforce the opportunity for increased remuneration through skill enhancement incentives and improved career prospects completed the 'win–win' scenario. Further workplace reform followed with a new wage system linked to the reform of the industrial award system. Wage increases were to be paid in accordance with a new principle – Structural Efficiency, which came to be known as 'award restructuring'[1] (Macken, 1989; Fox *et al.*, 1995).

Award restructuring facilitated the process of limited or 'managed decentralised' productivity bargaining between the parties to awards (MacDonald and Rimmer, 1989), providing the platform for further workplace reforms through enterprise-based agreements (Still and Mortimer, 1993; Curtain *et al.*, 1992). It also provided the foundation for the further decentralization of workplace reform to the enterprise (Rimmer, 1994), allowing more flexibility and innovative processes and agreements (Mathews, 1990).

The National Wage Case of October 1991 established the next stage in micro-economic or workplace reform – The Enterprise Bargaining Principle[2] – which provided for enterprise specific agreements to become the main vehicle in the determination of working conditions and rates of pay (Charlesworth, 1997: 101). A key procedural reform undertaken by the Australian Industrial Relations Commission (AIRC) under this principle was reduction of its role as arbitrator over total wage outcomes, preferring the role of conciliation between the parties, to ensure minimal safety net provisions (Morris, 1996). This development thus placed the responsibility for enterprise bargaining firmly in the hands of the negotiating parties (Fox *et al.*, 1995; Keenoy and Kelly, 1998).

Further reforms followed the establishment of the Enterprise Bargaining Principle. This was primarily driven by the Keating federal Labor government which considered that the pace of reform needed to be increased (Kramar *et al.*, 1997). The legislation which followed included Certified Workplace Agreements in 1992, the Enterprise Awards Principle in October 1993[3] and the Industrial Relations Reform Act 1993, which consolidated these changes. The thrust of these changes was the progressive shift of responsibility for the substance of agreements firmly into the workplace, while further reducing the role of third parties (trade unions) to the negotiations (Fox *et al.*, 1995).

The election of the Howard federal Coalition (Conservative) government in 1996 provided further impetus to the decentralizing of labour regulation and workplace reform. As Kramar *et al.* (1997) note, the objectives of the Workplace Relations Act 1996 were to 'reflect the Coalition's wish to entrench the workplace as the focus for industrial relations and provide employers and employees with a choice over the form of agreement to rule in the workplace' (p.115).

The key objectives of the Act include:

- a more direct relationship between employers and employees, with a much reduced role for third-party intervention;

- a simplified system for all participants, without the heavy regulatory burden;

- encouraging international competitiveness through higher productivity and a flexible labour market;

- ensuring the primary responsibility for determining matters affecting the relationship between employers and employees rests with the employers and employees at the workplace or enterprise level;

- providing that the means for wages and conditions of employment are as far as possible by agreement of employers and employees at the workplace or enterprise level, upon a foundation of minimum standards.
(Workplace Relations Act: cited in Clark, 1997: 31–2).

The Act also provides for the development of 'enterprise unions' and an end to compulsory unionism. This continued de-regulation has created a substantial change in the regulatory environment of the labour market. These changes have been predicated on the philosophy that a more dynamic and competitive economic environment can best be enhanced by decentralizing responsibility to the workplace, as management and the workforce best understand the needs and constraints within the enterprise (Fox *et al.*, 1995; Clark, 1997; Keenoy and Kelly, 1998).

AUSTRALIAN TRADE UNIONS IN A DYNAMIC ENVIRONMENT

Since the mid-1980s the Australian trade union movement has, as Davis and Lansbury (1998: 116) describe, 'been in the midst of an extraordinary period of change'. The objective of this change, or more accurately internal restructuring, has been to reform the union movement to ensure its continuing relevance. The initial changes focused on streamlining the actual structure of the union movement from its historical craft/trade foundations to one based on 20 industrial or occupational sectors (Davis and Lansbury, 1998). The systematic rationalization and consolidation of trade unions through a process of mergers and amalgamations was seen as developing a more efficient and effective union movement (ACTU/TDC, 1987). The proposed benefits of this industrially-based union structure were expected to include less conflictual labour relations and more efficient and effective organizational units, minimal duplication and larger pools of resources to target communication, recruitment and retention (ACTU/TDC, 1987).

The process of amalgamation was facilitated by federal Labor government legislation. The Industrial Relations Act 1988, and the Industrial Relations Amendment Act 1990 allowed for the easing of restrictions on union amalgamations (Fox *et al.*, 1995). The process of merger and amalgamation has resulted in a systematic reduction of trade unions by more than 50 per cent since 1987 (See Table 1).

TABLE 1
THE TOTAL NUMBER OF TRADE UNIONS IN AUSTRALIA

Date	Number of Trade Unions
1987	326
1988	308
1989	299
1990	295
1991	275
1992	227
1993	188
1994	157
1995	142
1996[4]	132

Source: ABS No.6323.0 Trade Union Statistics

This process of mergers and amalgamations has resulted in membership of the top 20 unions accounting for 86 per cent of the membership, and the average number of unions per workplace during the period 1990–95 decreasing from 2 to 1.5 (AWIRS, 1995).[5] Despite the problems of factional rivalry (Peetz, 1998) the process of rationalization has proceeded in a systematic and relatively smooth manner. The result of these extensive mergers is a trade union structure which is seen as more relevant and able to operate efficiently in the new industrial environment. It is worth noting that these changes were taking place under the umbrella of a federal Labor government whose close ties with the trade union movement are reflected in the Prices and Incomes Accord (1983–96) agreement. In this context, the election of the federal Coalition with an overtly anti-union philosophy would see the trade union movement in a good position to cope with this more hostile environment.

RESEARCHING GREENFIELD SITES

The term greenfield site has entered the general usage in the management literature to describe a location where no previous commercial activity has taken place. However, Preece (1993: 103) takes this definition a stage further by identifying three (ideal) types of greenfield site:

- *Company greenfield*, where a new company is established and begins operations for the first time on the site;

- *Replacement greenfield*, where an existing company builds and opens a new plant, and one or more of the company's older plants are closed, with the work and maybe some of the employees transferring to the new site;

- *Expansion greenfield*, where a new plant is built and opened by an existing company with other plants. These continue in operation, at least in the short term.

While there are variations on these ideal types, the consistent feature all these sites provide is the opportunity to break with past practices. The key aspect in researching greenfield sites is that organizations are presented with an occasion to advance new policy initiatives, as management is unencumbered by a pre-existing culture (Storey, 1989; Guest, 1991, 1995; Legge, 1995). In the context of human resource management, greenfield sites provide the opportunity to develop initiatives as well as sophisticated and integrative policies and practices across a range of human resource areas (Kocken *et al.*, 1986; Sisson, 1994).

Of particular importance is the opportunity to develop the type of workforce and employment relationships that management desires (Guest, 1991). In the development of employee relations, management has the opportunity to develop a framework for the relationship it considers most appropriate (Lucio and Weston, 1992). In describing industrial relations at greenfield sites, Guest (1991) outlines a number of central concepts or themes associated with these organizations. One is the idea that good HRM will obviate the need for unions. By contrast incompetent management will only serve to encourage unionism. As noted earlier, integral with the unitarist positioning of HRM is employee commitment, which in respect of industrial relations, raises questions over whether dual commitment to both organization and union is possible (Legge, 1995). However, as Guest (1991) and Legge (1995) both acknowledge, many factors will influence this choice, not least the traditional policies of the country or region in which the greenfield site is located.

METHODOLOGY

A qualitative approach was taken for this research. Semi-structured interviews were undertaken with trade union representatives and human resource managers in 15 organizations across a variety of sectors including light and heavy manufacturing, service and high technology, specifically call centres (see Table 2). These research sites represent a cross-section of the three types of greenfield sites identified by Preece (1993). Human resource managers were selected because of their involvement in the development of human resource and employee relations policies and their linkage to senior management (Boxall and Dowling, 1990; Dowling and Fisher, 1997). Trade union representatives provided an alternative perspective in terms of the development and impact of HRM policies at the respective greenfield sites. They were also central to the issue of how the trade union movement has dealt with the development of the new policies and patterns of work. The nature of the questions allowed the managers and employee representatives to discuss issues relating to human resources management and employee relations at the greenfield sites within the context of the organizational setting. Anonymity was requested because of the high profile of several of the organizations. Accordingly, the analysis focuses on themes emerging from the study as opposed to an analysis of particular cases in the research.

TABLE 2

ORGANIZATIONS BY INDUSTRY SECTOR

Industry	Number of Firms
High Technology (call centres)	5
Service and Transport	4
Manufacturing (light)	4
Manufacturing (heavy)	2
Total	15

RESULTS AND DISCUSSION

As outlined earlier, the key features of an HR approach include a more active role for HR in senior level strategic planning processes, tighter integration of basic HR policy areas, stronger involvement of line managers in HR processes and a new style of industrial relations that supports the unitarist perspective. In this section evidence from greenfield sites will be reviewed to determine whether an HR approach is indeed in place in these newly-formed organizations.

One of the fundamental characteristics of an HR approach is that HR is taken seriously at the senior decision making level and that there is an HR representative in the central decision making group (Tichy *et al.*, 1982; Beer *et al.*, 1984; Dyer and Holder, 1988). The results of the research show that this is largely the case in the greenfield sites that were under investigation. In all but one of the organizations studied there was an HR representative in the central decision making group who was given substantial recognition in the decisions about the new site. Indeed those involved in the HR area were seen to provide invaluable expertise. For example, site managers made the following comments:

> *They [HR] would make policy decisions on where we should cut and slash, where we need to grow, how to realign the business, what happens to people if we close.*

> *HR were fully involved in the set up of the site – we were in constant communication.*

> *He [HR manager] was part of the initial group of people that made all the central decisions.*

HR managers made the following comments:

> *Yeah I was involved in the whole damn lot. High involvement... Certainly knowing the financial consequences and taking the final decision.*

> *Basically I am part of the central team. Initially there was just me and the general manager and the operations guy... We just all pitched in and got on with it, I didn't think of myself as being anything other than part of the team.*

A second feature of an HR approach is a serious attempt to create well-developed and integrated HR policies and practices (Lengnick-Hall and Lengnick-Hall, 1988; Baird and Meshoulam, 1988; Wright and McMahan, 1992; Buller and Napier, 1993; Lawler, 1995, Torrington and Hall, 1998). Again in all but one of the case study organizations there was a very clear commitment to thorough recruitment and selection processes, training and development and performance appraisal. Further, these areas were clearly connected and reinforced each other.

Recruitment and selection processes, for example, were stringent with two organizations using a three-level screening process. Another organization demanded that applicants, who were selected on the basis of relevant technical ability, complete what was called a 'long interview' where trainees were not considered to be employed until they had completed and passed an intensive six-week course concluding with an exam. Only 50 per cent of these recruits made it to full-time employment. A replacement greenfield site organization introduced the expectation of totally flexible work patterns and minimum restriction in terms of demarcations as central to the selection process. These terms and conditions had not previously been part of the traditional ethos of this manufacturing organization. Despite minor industrial action by a group refusing these terms and conditions, after negotiation they were accepted by employees and trade union representatives.

With respect to training, most of the companies had designed their own processes and took considerable pride in the quality of the course. Indeed most had their training courses accredited, and work closely with the local education providers. A representative within one company for example explained that: '*The training is our own design, it has been recognised and it is nationally accepted but it is specifically tailored to what we want*'. Another organization had set up a partnership agreement with an external provider (TAFE College[6]) with follow-up sessions on site in an accredited skill centre. They are now seen as a regional development centre for engineering. Their HR manager made the comment that the training was '*seen as an investment*'. Within the call centres the focus was 'on-the-job' training. In general there is a set course that needs to be completed and then careful monitoring of the employee's progress with a 'buddy' system in place in most sites.

Performance appraisal was particularly well developed in the call centres. The system was characterized by ongoing feedback focusing on behavioural aspects and on-the-job performance or hard targets, a well-developed coaching system, team meetings and quality listening. In one of the organizations, performance appraisal and training were considered to be strongly interconnected, with training closely attuned to performance problems. While this is linked to the contentious issue of (excessive) monitoring, organizations in general emphasized the team-building aspects of this approach to managing and developing employees.

Another key feature of HRM is the devolution of HR practice to line managers and the more general willingness of all employees to take responsibility for HR matters. This was well supported in the organizations that were studied. In the call centres for example, there was not an HR person on site as these centres were part of larger organizational structures. The sites drew heavily from the advice provided by the central HR function but these managers were also extremely keen to make sure that the traditional HR areas were effectively carried out. Indeed, the role of the team leader in training and performance feedback was generally seen as critical to the success of the operation. In some of the organizations, line manager responsibility was well developed. As two HR managers note:

> *They have involvement with counselling and the general supervision of their people – they handle them completely – day to day, time cards and all that sort of thing. With*

respect to other HR areas, their involvement in human resource planning has increased, performance appraisal certainly increased, training and development certainly increased, labour increased, health and safety increased.

Yes, they do most of it... Basically they identify recruitment needs etc. ...we [the HR area] are basically a support area.

The general consensus across the research sites was support for, and evidence of, the development of the key HR characteristics. The important area of industrial relations was investigated. The following section reviews union recognition and conditions of employment within the sites investigated.

Trade Union Recognition on Greenfield Sites

Against the background of falling levels of unionism, increasing decentralized bargaining, and legislation that provides for union exclusion from the negotiating process, it could be expected that increasingly greenfield sites would exclude unions. It came as a surprise therefore that this was not generally the case and we have no evidence of overt tactics against union recognition in greenfield sites.

This, we suggest, is because the majority of these sites are subsidiaries of existing companies. Call centres, for example, are established and ultimately controlled by the parent organization notwithstanding that they have a large degree of operational autonomy. Thus in greenfield companies HRM policies, including employee relations, decentralized bargaining and the extent of union recognition, are influenced by the parent company. There is, however, a concerted effort to hold the number of recognized unions to a minimum. This is openly admitted by all organizations included in the study who, although preferring to deal with just one union, often accept two or three unions. Holding the number of unions to a minimum is made easier in certain areas by the process of trade union mergers and amalgamations (see Table 1), and in sectors such as banking, which traditionally has only one recognized union.

However, in greenfield sites where the parent company is located overseas, the approach to unions appears to favour excluding them if at all possible. Unions report great difficulty in gaining access to these sites: requests for meetings are ignored and company officials are said to be 'unavailable' for contact by telephone. Where possible, these greenfield site organizations do not want to deal with third parties such as unions, preferring (where possible) to deal directly with employees, and they are said by unions to hold the view: *'If we must have a union it has got to be compliant.'* From these examples it can be tentatively suggested that whatever the variation of greenfield site encountered, the objective is to recognize only one or two unions at most. This strategy inevitably causes tension and friction between competing unions. The winning union accepts occupations outside its main areas of interest and expertise, with the result that some workers receive less than adequate coverage and representation. Somewhat surprisingly it was discovered that greenfield managers, although holding a desire to be union-free, are not pursuing strategies aimed towards this end. On the contrary, they report largely satisfactory relations with unions and in some instances see them as a useful vehicle for achieving company goals. Indeed this may well support the apprehension that some in the union movement have with this form of selection, where the most compliant union is chosen.

The New Employment Relationship

Despite the maintenance of trade union presences, the subtleties of the changing employment relationship can be identified through the changing attitude of management towards the relationship, rather than the handling of conflict and negotiations. The main theme emerging from the analysis is management attempts to contain conflict within the work groups (team-leader) and then the organization (HR department). Only when this breaks down does there appear an opportunity for third party intervention, and even then this is not assured. As one manager notes in this context:

> There are no union issues unless they first come across the manager's desk. This is not necessarily in the agreement (with unions)... it is how we operate... we have an open door policy – any staff member can come and see management.

Many of the organizations, particularly those in the service industry, focused on the role of the team leaders as central to the development of good employee–employer relations through communication and conflict handing. As one manager put it: *'We do have grievances but we negotiate with the employee.'* The changing nature of the relationship also reflects the development of the unitarist philosophy where employees are expected to align their views with management. As a senior manager commented: *'There is an understanding that you work together to survive.'* Where problems are identified they are seen by management in the context of a breakdown in communication between management and employees and not because of differing perspectives or agendas. This was exemplified by one manager who noted: *'Most union-management problems turn out to be a case of poor communication with employees.'* The inference is that with improved management–employee communication, relations will improve and areas of potential conflict will be overcome. This was further illustrated by one HR manager who stated with regard to the role of the union:

> *I have got a business to run, I can't wait every five minutes to consult with someone to get things happening – it doesn't work... they want us to tie everything to scale and ask permission.*

This developing 'wall' around the employee–employer relationship has also been identified by union officials. In the context of dealing with what have often been considered 'bread and butter' union issues (such as scales of pay and conditions), a union official explains:

> *We had a safety issue during construction when a crane jib hit power lines, there was a near electrocution. The employer and the federal government legislation have made it difficult to gain access to the site unless employees are prepared to walk off the job or impose bans.*

At a call centre similar sentiments were voiced by union officials with regard to the issues of new organizations moving into Australia. As one union official put it:

> *Companies from outside Australia do not have a history of dealing with unions or collective bargaining. Employees are 'shit-scared'... they don't want to be identified as union members so they are exploited. If they put their head up it will get chopped-off and they will be out the door.*

One union member illustrated this point with a company the union is currently dealing with. The organization is a Canadian-owned subsidiary with a history of anti-union strategies. The union had cause to deal with the organization when it was reported to them that: *'At the time of recruitment potential employees were asked – Are they prepared to join a union? If the person says yes it appears they are not taken on.'* Those that did take employment were required to sign a contract that reflected Canadian terms and conditions including flat rates of pay (which was 20 per cent below the Australian standard minimum wage level), no shift allowances or penalty rates. As the senior unionist noted:

> *We were fortunate in that we were able to get called into the industrial negotiations and turn that around to bring them in line with Australian standards (the appropriate award). However, they (the employees) are not paid to that agreement and that was the position of the employer – they're on individual contracts...the (individual) contract system is supposed to have some consultation, but I think it is fair to say that it is one-sided.*

Other issues identified by union officers include the changing of terms and conditions by the employers if the employee is not prepared to follow company policies or is seen as a 'trouble-maker'. As one unionist notes: *'Employers can make work-life untenable for workers without actually sacking them by reducing their hours, changing their roster.'* one unionist illustrates this point with a case where an employee was reduced from 30 to 5 hours per week. This so-called 'flexibility' was built into the contractual arrangements.

These problems continue to highlight a growing concern by union officials and the need to develop strategies to combat aggressive and anti-union employers. An increasingly common tactic is the outsourcing of the recruitment and selection process. An example which highlights this is of a major UK company's call centre setting up in Tasmania. As the union official responsible for call centres explains:

> *We are trying to contact the management of [company name] but we are finding it difficult. A national training company has been engaged to employ people on their*

behalf. However, the local agent for them is refusing to give us the name of the HR manager till they get clearance from their client. So we are now trying other means.

To contend with these issues and problems the ACTU is developing a policy platform. A key strategy one senior union officer notes is: *'We believe one way to counter their tactics is to go global, enlisting the aid of unions in other countries.'* However, the way this will be undertaken has yet to be formulated.

Conditions of Employment

As already indicated, greenfield sites are influenced by parent organizations, most noticeably in respect of conditions of employment. At one site for example, which is jointly owned by local business interests and a national company, conditions and processes of decentralized bargaining closely follow those of the parent company. As the general manager comments: *'There is no point in reinventing the wheel.'* It needs to be made clear, however, that although there is a common model for bargaining agreements, the new site is free to set pay rates and other details of employment conditions that are appropriate to the location.

Unions draw attention to the problem of organizations, typically call centres, owned by international companies which have poor working conditions, but feel frustrated in being unable to gain access. In spite of attempts to make contact, management refuses entry for unions (where possible), who therefore draw on informal sources – usually employees – for their information. A similar lack of cooperation was experienced during the course of this study. These unofficial sources report rates of pay lower than the relevant award, which in Australia constitutes the legal minimum, and to working conditions at a lower standard than under award standards. Under Australian Workplace Agreements (individual agreements) employees may nominate a bargaining agent, but unions hold out little hope that workers will nominate a union because of fear of management reprisals. Unions consulted for this study were unaware of any union input in respect of terms and conditions at these call centres anywhere in Australia.

Globalization

The impact of globalization is apparent as a driving force behind the continuous deregulation of the labour market and the need to drive down cost to maintain competitive advantage. Union concerns are principally focused on the effects of the global market on working conditions, especially in call centres. It is here that contrasts are readily made with longer standing Australian-based companies and the 'international' greenfield sites. A sharp diminution in working conditions, including pay, and oppressive management techniques, which contribute to stressful work and a high turnover rate, characterize several of the 'international' organizations. Unions clearly perceive this as international companies seeking to impose poorer working conditions from overseas on Australian workers.

Another issue is the ease with which international companies are able to move. Newspapers report that governments often grant taxation concessions and other payments, sometimes in kind, to attract greenfield site enterprises. Although some companies invest in heavy and complex machinery at these sites, which indicates a level of commitment to the site, call centres are especially vulnerable to closing and re-locating elsewhere. This is because of their use of computers, which require little other than a building to house the technology. This factor adds to the transient nature of the industry and gives unions little in the way of leverage over recalcitrant employers. To combat the worst effects of this situation, unions are currently seeking alliances with the international union movement to improve and maintain reasonable working conditions.

The issue of globalization illustrates another option many of these greenfield organizations have, particularly in regionally depressed areas – the threat of leaving if conditions are not to their liking. An example of this is a European airline call centre which had complaints about the accents of some of its staff. Their response was to close that call centre in Europe and set up a new one in Melbourne. A precursor to this tactic is the process of driving down terms and conditions to ensure the best deal for the organization (and consolidating their position as an employer in that region). One example which illustrates this issue is a call centre set up in regionally depressed area. The key reason for setting up in these areas is the expectation of a stable workforce which needs employment. However, because of the working conditions – the stressful nature of the work, the monitoring of calls, an eight-minute meal break, the indignity of operatives being required to put their hand up if they wish to go to the toilet or get a drink – turnover has been high. To counter this trend the 'core' organization has begun to set-up its employees in firms outside the organization as a new company. It then outsources the work they formerly did, but each of the firms must bid against the other to win the contract. The effect of this is to drive terms and conditions down even further in order to win contracts.

Another strategy is to play states (particularly state governments) off against each other. An example of this is where the New South Wales (NSW) government offered a UK-owned call centre $2.3 million to remain in NSW; however, this company was lost to Tasmania when the state government reportedly offered a bid for $7.3 million, including a greenfield site and tax concessions. One senior unionist notes that with increased mergers and alliances this sort of thing is likely to become a global issue. The unionist points particularly to one airline which is about to set up a call centre in Tasmania. This airline is in the process of joining the Star Alliance of Airlines, which will ultimately have one call centre for the world. In this context, the mobility of capital is fundamentally reconstructing the employer–employee relationship in favour of the employer, further subjugating the bargaining capacity of individual trade unions.

CONCLUSION

This study found little evidence to support the Lucio and Weston (1991; 1992) model of union response patterns among greenfield site organizations. Although there were examples of each of the three categories, there was no consistency in the responses that was helpful to confirming or formulating theory.

It is clear that trade union strategies are missing, and this is highlighted by their collective inability to develop a strong presence in low-level and non-union workplaces, particularly when faced with sophisticated human resource management techniques. Unions, in this period of turbulence, are trying to adapt as rapidly as they can to a hostile environment. While accepting globalization and the need for organizations to be competitive, this places them at a tactical disadvantage in their dealings with employers. It is imperative therefore that trade unions develop policies and strategies which focus on contemporary employment issues, such as wages and conditions of employment, for campaigning, organizing and recruiting in these workplaces. The fact that the sectors of high technology and light manufacturing (which dominate greenfield site development in Australia) are the fastest growing employment sectors is important. However, the fact that the workforce in these sectors is characterized by young and predominantly female employees – the groups which have the lowest representation within the trade union movement – identifies these industries as vital to organize for union survival, growth and future.

Evidence of strategies and policies to organize and recruit in these areas are emerging in the UK, USA and Canada (ACTU, 1999), ironically the use of call centres and internet web-sites are being used to provide a contact point for employees in these sectors. When contact is made with the unions, off-site meeting are initiated to develop targeted campaigns and pressure tactics within these workplaces. Evidence from Canada has identified this as an effective tool in developing trade union presence in these workplaces (ACTU, 1999). On an international level, staff exchanges have been identified as an important process in disseminating information, tactics, knowledge and experience. The International Confederation of Free trade Unions is also developing a website for affiliate trade unions to access and distribute information regarding strategies, campaigns and rogue employers.

It could be that in Australia the union movement lags behind developments in the UK, US, Canada and Europe and that domestic strategies will emerge eventually. At present, however, Australian unions appear to be on the defensive, struggling to be relevant in a changing world and faced with falling membership which shows no sign of recovery. This has reduced them to a position where they are forced to adopt a reactive approach and have yet to seize the initiative along the lines suggested by either Lucio and Weston (1991, 1992) or trade unions under similar pressures in other countries. While the trade unions have put in place a process of internal reform which is seeing them move from a traditional service model to a recruitment and retention model (Stuart, 1995), this still remains a low-priority area within many trade unions (Holland, 1999). It is clear therefore that investing in the development of organizing, recruitment and campaign strategies must become a high priority if trade unions in the short term are to make advances in these new and emerging employment sectors, and in the long term if they are to maintain a relevant role in the workplace.

NOTES

1. Award Restructuring involves a number of measures to alleviate problems such as the removal of obsolete job classifications the broad-banding of several narrow classifications, the establishment and defining of links between training, skills and wages and ensuring that work arrangements enhance flexibility and efficiency.
2. The term 'enterprise bargaining' refers to a particular process, bargaining, conducted at a particular level, the enterprise. It could operate with any substantive issue, agenda, relate to collective and/or individual bargaining and could either co-exist with, or be completely independent of, the process of conciliation or arbitration. The workplace rules arising from enterprise bargaining could supplant, complement or replace those arising from other processes including conciliation and arbitration (Fox *et al.*, 1995, p.615).
3. Introduced by the Australian Industrial Relations Commission in June 1993 to replace the Enterprise Bargaining Principle. Its essential difference was the incorporation of technical features associated with the traditional award system (Fox *et al.*, 1995, p.621).
4. This was the last year official records were maintained on trade union numbers.
5. AWIRS – Australian Workplace Industrial Relations Survey.
6. TAFE stands for Technical and Further Education.

REFERENCES

ABS No.6323.0, Trade Union Statistics.
ACTU/TDC (1987) *Australia Reconstructed*, Canberra: AGPS.
ACTU (1999) *Unions@Work: The Challenge for Unions to Create a Just and Fair Society*, Melbourne: ACTU.
Bacon, N. and Storey, J. (1996) 'Individualism and Collectivism and the Changing Role of Trade Unions' in P. Ackers, C. Smith and P. Smith (eds.), *The New Workplace and Industrial Relations*, London: Routledge.
Baird, L. and Meshoulam, I. (1988) 'Managing Two Fits of Strategic Human Resource Management', *Academy of Management Review*, Vol.13, pp.116–28.
Barney, J and Wright, P. (1998). 'On Becoming a Strategic Partner: The Role of Human Resources in Gaining Competitive Advantage', *Human Resource Management*, Vol.37, No.1, pp.31–46.
Beaumont, P.B. (1991) 'Trade unions and HRM', *Industrial Relations Journal*, Vol.23, No.4, pp.300–308.
Beer, M., Spector, B., Lawrence, P.R., Mills, Q.N. and Walton, R.E. (1984) *Managing Human Assets*, New York: Free Press.
Blyton, P. and Turnbull, P. (1998) *The Dynamics of Employee Relations* (2nd ed.), London: Macmillan Press.
Boxall, P. (1994) 'Placing HR Strategy at the Heart of Business Success', *Personnel Management*, Vol.26, No.7, pp.32–5.
Boxall, P.F. and Dowling, P.J. (1990) 'Human Resource Management and the Industrial Relations Tradition', *Labour & Industry*, Vol.3, pp.195–214.
Buller, P.F. and Napier, N.K. (1993) 'Strategy and Human Resource Management Integration in Fast Growth Versus Other Mid-sized Firms', *British Journal of Management*, Vol.4, pp.77–90.
Charlesworth, S. (1997) Enterprise Bargaining and Women Workers: The Seven Perils of Flexibility, *Labour & Industry*, Vol., No.2, pp.101–16.
Clark, D. (1997) *Student Economic Brief*. Victoria : AFR Books.
Clark, J. and Winchester, D. (1994) 'Management and Trade Unions' in K. Sisson (eds.), *Personnel Management: A Comprehensive Guide to Theory and Practice in Britain*. London: Blackwell, pp.694–723.

Davis, E. and Lansbury, R. (1998) 'Employment Relations in Australia' in G. Bamber, and R. Lansbury. (eds), *International and Comparative Employment Relations*. Sydney: Allen & Unwin, pp.110–43.

Deery, S., Plowman, D. and Walsh, J. (1997) *Industrial Relations: A Contemporary Analysis*, Sydney: McGraw-Hill.

Dowling, P.J. and Fisher, C. (1997) 'The Australian HR Professional: A 1995 Profile', *Asia Pacific Journal of Human Resources*, Vol.35, pp.1–20.

Dowling, P.J. and Schuler, R. (1990) 'Human Resource Management' in R. Blanpain (eds.) *Comparative Labour Law and Industrial Relations in Industrialised Market Economies*. Deventer, The Netherlands: Kluwer, pp.125–49.

Dulebohn, J. H., Ferris, G. R. and Stodd, J. T. (1995) The History and Evolution of Human Resource Management in G.R. Ferris, S.D. Rosen and D.T. Barnham (eds.), *Handbook of Human Resource Management*. Cambridge, Mass: Blackwell, pp.18–41.

Dunlop, J. (1958) *Industrial Relations Systems*, New York: Holt, Rinehart & Winston.

Dyer, L and Holder, G. (1988) 'A Strategic Perspective of Human Resource Management' in L. Dyer and G. Holder (eds.), *Human Resource Management: Evolving Roles and Responsibilities*. Washington: The Bureau of National Affairs, pp.1–46.

Farnham, D. and Pimlott, J. (1986) *Understanding Industrial Relations*. London: Holt, Rinehart & Winston.

Fox, C., Howard, W., and Pittard, M. (1995) *Industrial Relations in Australia: Development, Law and Operation*. Melbourne: Longman.

Golden, K.A. and Ramanujam, V., (1985) 'Between a Dream and a Nightmare: On the Integration of the HRM and Strategic Business Planning Process', *Human Resource Management*, Vol.24, No.4, pp.429–52.

Gordon, D. and Ladd, R. (1990) 'Dual Allegiance: Renewal, Reconsideration and Recantation', *Personnel Psychology*, Vol.43, pp.37–69.

Gospel, H. F. and Palmer, G. (1993) *British Industrial Relations* (2nd ed.). London: Routledge.

Guest, D. E. (1991) 'Human Resource Management: Its Implications for Industrial Relations and Trade Unions' in J. Storey (eds.) *New Perspectives on Human Resource Management*. London: Routledge, pp.41–55.

Guest, D. (1995) 'Human Resource Management, Trade Unions and Industrial Relations' in J. Storey (eds.) *Human Resource Management: A Critical Text*. London: Routledge, pp.110–41.

Holland, P. (1999) 'Organising Works: Meeting the Challenge of Declining Trade Union Membership', *International Employment Relations Review*, Vol.5, pp.63–74.

Kocken, T.A., Katz, H. and McKersie, R. (1986) *The Transformation of American Industrial Relations*. New York: Basic Books.

Kamoche, K. (1986) 'Strategic Human Resource Management within a Resource-Capability View of the Firm', *Journal of Management*, Vol.33, pp.213–33.

Keennoy, T. and Kelly, D. (1998) *The Employment Relationship in Australia* (2nd ed.). Sydney: Harcourt-Brace.

Kramar, R., McGraw, P. and Schuler, R. (1997) *Human Resource Management in Australia* (3rd ed.). Sydney: Longman.

Lado, A and Wilson, M. (1994) 'Human Resource Systems and Sustainable Competitive Advantage: A Competency Based Perspective', *Academy of Management Review*, Vol.19, No.4, pp.699–727.

Lawler, E. (1995) 'Strategic Human Resource Management: An Idea Whose Time has come' in B. Downie and M. Coates (eds.), *Managing Human Resources in the 1990s and Beyond: Is the Workplace Being Transformed?* Ontario: Queen's University Press, pp.46–70.

Legge K. (1988) 'Personnel Management in Recession and Recovery', *Personnel Review*, Vol.17, pp.3–69.

Legge, K. (1995) *Human Resource Management: Rhetoric and Realities*. London: Macmillan.

Lengnick-Hall, C.A. and Lengnick-Hall, M.L. (1988) 'Strategic Human Resource Management: A Review of the Literature and a Proposed Typology', *Academy of Management Review*, Vol.13, pp.454–70.

Lucio, M.M. and Weston, S. (1991) Worker Representation and Worker Rights in the

Context of New Management Strategies. Paper presented at the British Universities Industrial Relations Association Annual Conference, University of Manchester.

Lucio, M.M. and Weston, S. (1992) 'Human Resource Management and Trade Union Responses: Bringing the Politics of the Workplace Back into the Debate', in P. Blyton and P. Turnbull (eds.), *Reassessing Human Resource Management*. London: Sage, pp.215–32.

Macken, J.J. (1989) *Award Restructuring*, Armadale, NSW: Federation Press.

Marchington, M. (1995) 'Fairy Tales and Magic Wands: New Employment Practices in Perspective', *Employee Relations*, Vol.15, No.1, pp.51–66.

McDonald, T. and Rimmer, M. (1989) 'Award Structure and the Second Tier', *Australian Bulletin of Labour*, Vol.14, No.3, pp.469–91.

Matthews, J. (1989) *Tools of Change – New Technology and the Democratisation of Work*. Sydney: Pluto Press.

Mabey, C. and Salaman, G. (1995) *Strategic Human Resource Management*. London: Blackwell.

Miller, E.L., and Burack, E.H., (1981) 'A status report of HR planning from the perspective of HR planners', *Human Resource Planning*, Vol.4, No.2, pp.33–40.

Millward, N., Stevens, M., Smart, D. and Hawes, W. (1992) *Workplace Industrial Relations in Transition*. Aldershot: Gower.

Morris, R. (1996) 'The Age of Workplace Reform in Australia' in P. Mortimer, P. Leece and R. Morris (eds.) *Workplace Reform and Enterprise Bargaining*. Sydney: Harcourt-Brace, pp.11–24.

Nininger, J.R. (1980) 'Human Resources and Strategic Planning: A Vital Link', *Optimum*, Vol.11, No.4, pp.33–46.

Peetz, D. (1998) *Unions in a Contrary World: The Future of the Australian Trade Union Movement*. Cambridge: University Press.

Purcell, J. and Ahlstrand, B. (1995) *Human Resource Management in the Multi-Divisional Company*. New York: Oxford University Press.

Preece, D. (1993) 'Human Resource Specialist and Technical Change at Greenfield Sites' in J. Clark (eds.), *Human Resource Management & Technical Change*. London. Sage, pp.101–15.

Quiggin, J. (1996) *Great Expectations: Microeconomic Reform and Australia*. Sydney: Allen & Unwin.

Rimmer, M. and Zappala, G. (1988) 'Labour Market Flexibility and the Second Tier', *Australian Bulletin of Labour*, Vol.14, No.4, pp.564–91.

Rimmer, S. (1994) *Australian Labour Market and Microeconomic Reform*. Melbourne: La Trobe University Press.

Sisson, K. (1994) *Personnel Management: A Comprehensive Guide to Theory and Practice*, Oxford: Blackwell.

Sisson, K. (1995) 'Human Resource Management and the Personnel Function' in J. Storey (eds.) *Human Resource Management: A Critical Text*. London: Routledge, pp.87–109.

Stills, L. and Mortimer, D. (1996) 'The Effectiveness of Award Restructuring and the Training Levy in Providing a More Educated Workforce' in D. Mortimer, P. Leece and R. Morris (eds.), *Workplace Reform and Enterprise Bargaining*. Sydney: Harcourt-Brace, pp.37–54.

Storey, J. (1987) *Developments in the Management of Human Resources: An Interim Report*, Warwick Papers in Industrial relations, No.17, IRRU, School of Industrial and Business Studies, University of Warwick, November.

Storey, J. (1989) *New Perspectives in Human Resource Management*, London: Routledge.

Storey, J. (1992) *Developments in the Management of Human Resources*, Oxford: Blackwell.

Stuart, M. (1995) *Organising Works – Report to ACTU Executive and Council*, Melbourne: ACTU.

Tichy, N.M., Fombrun, C.J., and Devanna, M. (1982) 'Strategic Human Resources Management', *Sloan Management Review*, Winter, pp.47–60.

Torrington, D. and Hall, L. (1998) *Human Resource Management*, London: Prentice Hall.

Tyson, S. and Fell, A. (1986) *Evaluating the Personnel Function*, London: Hutchinson.

Wright, P.M. and McMahan, G. (1992) 'Theoretical Perspectives for Strategic Human Resource Management', *Journal of Management*, Vol.18, No.2, pp.295–320.

4

Labour Responses to Globalization: The Australian Experience

BERNARD McKENNA

This essay challenges the triumphalist claims made by the proponents of globalization by considering its effect on Australia while Labor governments held office from 1983 to 1996, using a discursive approach. As a discourse, globalization is related to neo-liberal and technocratic discourses (see Waterman, 1998). Under a neo-liberal, technocratic hegemony, the Australian Labor governments of 1983–96 increased social inequity and drove Australia towards a possible Brazilian or Asian economic crisis. The essay is in six parts: a short description of Australian political economy from 1983 to the present; a short description of technocratic discourse; a consideration of labour's role within a globalized hypercapitalism; a description of neo-classical globalist discourse during Labor's rule; an explanation of why globalization was bad for Australian workers; and a review of the implications for labour of this phenomenon.

AUSTRALIAN ECONOMY UNDER LABOR: 1983-96

From March 1983 to March 1996, Labor governments led by Bob Hawke and Paul Keating[1] won five elections to govern Australia in the longest stretch of Labor rule in the nation's history. Profound changes were wrought in the nation's economy. Although a large segment of the trade union movement, especially the metal trade unions, advocated the Swedish corporatist model (ACTU/TDC, 1987), the Labor government embraced free trade externally, and deregulation and privatization domestically. Crucial to gaining trade union support for this ideological backflip were the claims made about Australia becoming a 'value-added' economy rather than relying on resource exports. However, Australia continues to run up massive trade deficits with monthly current account deficits of around $1.5 billion. In April 1999, for example, the monthly deficit was $1.9 billion. The trade deficit represents nearly 6 per cent of GDP. Net foreign debt by March 1999 was $241.6 billion, 41 per cent of GDP, and the servicing ratio is 9.6 per cent (Aylmer, 1999b: 1).

The then Labor Opposition and the Australian Council of Trade Unions (or ACTU, the peak union council) signed an 'Accord' in February 1983, which was instrumental not only in winning the March 1983 election for Labor, but also in providing a public perception of industrial harmony between the government and the union movement for the whole period of Labor rule until 1996 during which there were seven 'Accords'.

Once in office, the Labor government quickly assembled an extra-parliamentary 'summit' of delegates drawn mostly from (big) business, the trade union movement, state and local governments, and some social stakeholders (such as those representing social services). The communiqué of this National Economic Summit signed by all at the end of the Summit drew the labour movement (government and unions) into a capitalist orthodoxy characterized by neo-classical economics and technocratic control. Ironically the Hawke-Keating Labor governments introduced a radical neo-liberal policy agenda that deeply wounded Australian trade unionism, possibly mortally. Indeed, such was Labor's conversion that one of its most trenchant right-wing critics said:

> The staggering thing about the degree of change in the industrial debate is that I can't recall an instance of a democratic government moving with the swiftness that this government has moved... The Government has reacted to our policy agenda to an incredible degree (Randall and Williams, 1986: 16).[2]

By the time of Accord Mark II in 1985 the Australian union movement had committed itself to accepting responsibility for strengthening the economy. The Accord identifies the 'trade union movement's strong record of compliance...establish[ing] a basis for the continuation of low industrial disputation, international competitiveness, strong economic growth and moderating inflation'.[3] The ACTU leadership capitulated easily, accepting that their restraint would 'lock in' the presumed benefits of a rapid devaluation in 1985 which had been caused by the market response to the underlying balance of payments problem that had been occurring for some time, as a result of declining terms of trade and an eroded manufacturing base. Yet when the currency markets finally realized this and sold off Australian dollars, the conservative response was to blame the workers' lack of productivity or excessively high wages. The Labor movement provided no dialectical challenge at all to the neo-classical economic orthodoxy.

The Hawke-Keating governments vigorously implemented economic rationalist policies (privatization, deregulation, enterprise bargaining). Rees (1995) claims that economic rationalists 'captured' the Labor governments, and Tomlinson (1996: 7) asserts that Keating became 'a captive of economic fundamentalism' in Treasury. However, economic rationalist advocates argue that the Australian economy was in such dire straits that these measures prevented terminal economic decline for Australia and restored living standards (although there is little interest shown in distributive justice).[4] James, Jones, and Norton (1993) claim that 'most economic rationalists believe that Australia was at a critical turning point in its history and that the serious and immediate economic problems we faced reflected a long-term decline in our economic performance' (p.xxiv; see Blandy, 1993: 35; Norton, 1995: 230).

These Labor governments set up an ideological framework that facilitated neo-liberal policies in their own time and allowed the conservative Howard government that replaced it to simply elaborate these policy directions when Labor lost office. Crucial to this ideological framework, I argue, was the formation of a technocratic discourse which incorporated neo-liberal principles including neo-classical economic theory. Labor policy was 'marked progressively by the development and implementation of a technocratic rationality' (Luke, Nakata, Singh, and Smith, 1993: 140) which, according to Stewart (1990: 140), ignored and silenced the distributional implications.

FEATURES OF TECHNOCRATIC DISCOURSE

Using a critical discourse method (Fairclough, 1992; Halliday, 1994; Halliday and Martin, 1993) to characterize the technocratic discourse used by the Labor governments, I will show that globalist claims are inextricably linked with neo-liberal ideology and technophilic hyperbole to produce questionable 'mantras'.

Technocratic Discourse

Contemporary technocratic discourse draws interdiscursively from scientific, technological, and neo-classical economic discourses. Its ideological and hegemonic effect is to eliminate dialectical political encounter (Saul, 1997; Bewes, 1997). I will briefly elaborate the discursive features of technocratic discourse.[5] The term 'technocracy' is used here in the sense suggested by Meynaud (1968) to indicate that modern state power is shared by the government in power, but also increasingly by a bureaucracy, and a technocracy comprising economic planners, strategic thinkers, and scientific and social scientific experts.[6] Technocrats transform 'discourses of expert knowledge into discourses of social policy' (Lemke, 1995: 58). Marcuse identifies them as 'makers of politics and purveyors of mass information' (1968: 28). Rifkin claims that the technocracy are the 'catalysts of the Third Industrial Revolution and the ones responsible for keeping the high-tech economy running' (1995: 175).

Apparent objectivity: What most characterizes technocratic discourse is that, although it has a hegemonic function, it often consciously represents itself as a supplier of neutral and objective 'facts', free of all interests and values except truth, used to decide policy (Lemke, 1995: 70). It does so by appearing to be scientific and by presenting its epistemic claims as objective knowledge (Lemke, 1995: 69). The technocratic elite claims a right to rule on the grounds of its ability to use its expert knowledge to solve social problems (70–71). When realized in government policies, however, they produce or reproduce structural equality or inequality.

This apparent objectivity disingenuously depoliticizes the discourse (Marcuse, 1968: 79), and limits effective participation to those who speak and understand technocratic language (see Bewes, 1997: 10). Paradoxically, however, although an exclusionary discourse, its textual traces must be widespread if it is to be hegemonically effective. It links itself to 'everyday' life (see Bewes, 1997: 10; Saul, 1997: ch.2; Marcuse, 1968: ch.4), becoming 'the jargon of authenticity' (Adorno, 1973). Like scientific discourse, technocratic discourse takes the familiar and reconstrues this into abstract and hypothetical notions (McKenna, 1997; see Marcuse, 1968: 81); unlike scientific discourse, these abstract notions are repeated as 'mantras' within public discourse.

The word *globalization* is a typical linguistic condensation with mantric effect. In tandem with certain others words such as *communication technology* and *trade liberalization* (see Bauman, 1998; Graham, 1998; Saul, 1997), the underlying claims go unchallenged. At the same time, in the workplace, unions repeated mantras of *enterprise*, *flexibility*, and *empowerment*. Such mantras normalize ideological abstractions by construing the hypothesized ideology as fact, enclosing the ideology 'within the circle of conditions prescribed by the formula' (Marcuse, 1968: 79). The ACTU played a vital role in disseminating the neo-classical and technocratic mantras of the Labor government.

As nouns, technocratic mantric words are crucial to the success of the discourse (Adorno, 1973: 6–10; Bewes, 1997: 10; Lemke, 1995: 59–66; Marcuse, 1968: 79–83; Saul, 1997: 64) because they turn sentences into declarations to be accepted: the noun 'repels demonstration, qualification, negation of its codified and declared meaning' (Marcuse, 1968: 79). As Halliday and Martin (1993: 39) contend, these nouns are 'less negotiable, since you can argue with a clause but you can't argue with a nominal group' and so help close debate.

The more they are used, the more meaningless mantric nostrums become. Nevertheless, they hegemonically infuse everyday language, reinforcing and naturalizing the overarching rationality of a neo-classical political-economic system. Such mantric notions include *enterprise, efficiency, globalization, productivity, international competitiveness, trade liberalization, the information economy*, and so on. This condensation into mantric words allows technocratic discourse 'to tailor the apparent scientific "facts"' to the needs of its policy arguments (Lemke, 1995: 75). Juxtaposed with other public policy words, they form a 'Holy Trinity' of words): *trade liberalization, financial markets*, and *communication technology* (Saul, 1997: 20–21).

Even apparently innocuous words like flexibility entered the political lexicon when the Labor government used it to justify increased centralization of the wage fixation process. Industrial Relations Minister Ralph Willis, defended this process arguing that the wage system was sufficiently flexible to adapt to changing circumstances. Keating asserted that centralized wage fixing would provide for downward flexibility of wages and that flexibility was the very essence of the Prices and Incomes Accord. Keating described floating the exchange rate as a *flexible* policy option, and deregulating the financial markets as providing the maximum *flexibility* in financial markets. However, the conservatives used *flexibility* repeatedly, linking it with downward projection of wages and conditions. John Howard, for example, demanded that the Treasurer 'has to provide a wages system which is flexible enough to accommodate the different levels of affordability of Australian industry'. By the 1990s, Labor was using the notion of flexibility to mean the same thing as the Conservatives. In 1993, Industrial Relations Minister Laurie Brereton, introducing the new Industrial Relations Reform Bill, stressed that the bill is designed to produce a more flexible award system:

> The more widespread insertion of enterprise flexibility clauses into awards will be encouraged. This will allow agreements to be reached at individual enterprises or workplaces to vary award provisions in line with their particular needs, subject to the employees not being disadvantaged.

Thus, by linking *flexibility* with *enterprise*, a neo-liberal term, Labor shifted flexibility into an opposing discourse. This was common in Labor's rule.

Technocratic discourse assumes unproblematically the efficacy and desirability of new technology (Graham, 1998; Saul, 1995). Its presence and trajectory are never questioned: it is inexorable, and manifests immutable and self-evident market economic laws (Graham, 1998; Saul, 1997). According to Pusey, technocratic proponents see the operations of market and technology overcoming the 'stubbornly resisting sludge' of civil society (1996: 69–70). Linguistically, people are removed from sentences, in the same way that they are removed from the technological and political-economic models that technocrats use to formulate policies. In keeping with such a rationale, technocratic texts are characterized often by 'agentless passive clause structures' (Lemke, 1995: 60) excluding human activity. For example, the Australian Department of Foreign Affairs and Trade document, *In the National Interest,* states that globalization:

is driven by many factors, of which technology, the related mobility of people, goods and ideas, and a liberal trading environment are perhaps the most important (DFAT, 1997: 1).

Although there is a reference to humans in this sentence, *mobility of people*, it is as an economic concept. Globalization is represented as an inevitable outcome of a set of neo-liberal phenomena which are implied in both the premise and conclusion.

Furthermore, technocratic discourse tends to be tautologous in two ways. First, the pseudo-scientific basis on which a statement is based rests upon categorizations where the definition determines the categorization of the phenomenon: that is, the definition contains, at least in part, the phenomenon being described. The following extract from the Hilmer Report (Hilmer, 1993) upon which both the Labor and Conservative governments based their microeconomic reforms provides a good instance of such tautology:

> As the Prime Minister has observed, 'the engine which drives efficiency is free and open competition.'[7] Competition is also a positive force that assists economic growth and job creation. It has triggered initiative and discovery in fields ranging from the invention of the telephone to the opening of new retail store and small manufacturing operations. In fact, it is these developments in smaller firms, prompted by the belief of these firms in their ability to compete, that are the main source of both new jobs and value-added exports.

Hilmer presents here a tortured form of syllogism that rests on shaky, but clearly ideological, premises. In short, Hilmer proposes the following logic:

1. Competition leads to efficiency.
2. Competition leads to growth and job creation.
3. Competition (renamed as positive force) triggers initiative and discovery.
4. Initiative and discovery (like Bell's) creates smaller firms.
5. Smaller firms are competitive.
6. Smaller firms create new jobs and more competition (return to 1).

The optimistic claims made by Hilmer about the effect of such reforms are simply not borne out by the results to date (see Quiggin, 1997d).

LABOUR, GLOBALIZATION, AND HYPERCAPITALISM

Globalization occurs within the context of contemporary hypercapitalism (Graham, forthcoming; Kennedy, 1998; Agger, 1989; Horkheimer and Adorno, 1944/1998), which is characterized as the time of capitalism's ostensible triumph, but also a time when it responds to such contradictions as the monopolizing tendency, the massive levels of unemployment, and its commodification of increasingly abstract 'products' (see Bonefeld and Holloway, 1995). The most significant feature of hypercapitalism is the increasingly abstract nature of the commodities it produces, particularly the 'information' economy and speculative capital flows. Under hypercapitalist conditions, economic growth is increasingly 'alchemic' and 'illusory' (Graham, 1998), and its abstract financial markets are 'parasitic' (Kennedy, 1998). Globalist protagonists speak fervently of an *information* or *knowledge economy* (see Agger, 1993; Fukuyama, 1995; Kellner, 1989: 212; Kennedy, 1998). The four characteristics of this globalized hypercapitalism (what some call postmodernity) are:

- Capital movement has been globalized and its velocity logarithmically increased (Rifkin, 1995).

- How goods and services are produced has changed significantly.

- Labour processes have been remodelled in various ways in an attempt to maximize output.

- Consumers and consumption have been consciously manipulated in an attempt to significantly alter demand size and type.

Capital movements: Because capital is now mobile and speculative (Sherden, 1998; Saul, 1997: ch.4), globalization has changed the power relations between nation-state and corporation; and markets have been freed of many government regulations (Thurow, 1996; Brown, 1997). Although niche production has increased, there is little evidence of transnationals losing their enormous significance in global production (see Sklair, 1995). Consequently, owners and managers of capital in advanced industrial countries can determine the type and size of production within smaller and less-developed countries like Australia to such an extent that many nation-states compete to entice capital (Reich, 1992). This clearly affects employment and working patterns within nation-states (Bryan,1995; Rifkin, 1995; Waterman, 1998).

This mobility also obviously weakens the bargaining capacity of workers and nations, as the choice may often be a low-paying job or no job at all. Western corporations for at least 20 years now have been 'retreating from off-shore manufacturing in developing countries' to 'sites in metropolitan countries where market access is optimal and ever increasing pools of immigrants and refugees supply the cheap labour' (Ong, 1991: 304). The effect of this can be seen most obviously in Australia's textile, clothing, and footwear industry which relies strongly on low-wage workers (mostly immigrant women) in the legitimate sector and a large black market of outsourcing, again of mostly recent immigrant women. The Textile, Clothing, and Footwear Union's 1994 national research project concluded that there were around 300,000 clothing industry outworkers typically working '12 to 18 hour days, 7 days a week for about a third of the award rate of pay, and with no access to even the minimum conditions enjoyed by factory workers' (TCFUA, 1995: 4).

As well, globalized speculative financial markets now affect domestic exchange rates, stock prices, commodity prices, and interest rates by factoring in global rather than national factors. The 1998 'Asian crisis' shows how brutally this works. Often the impact on a nation's share prices or currency is unrelated to factors over which governments have little or no control. Because speculative shifts occur in nano-seconds, and are often triggered by computer programs making human involvement even more disembodied, they produce an economic climate that is perhaps more complicated and unpredictable than it ever was.

Few nations could have matched the vigour with which the Hawke government, under the strong guidance of Treasurer Keating, deregulated the banking and international finance markets within Australia in 1983 and 1984. With these 'free-market' forces unleashed, and with the technological advances facilitating international trade in stocks and commodities, the national boundaries of control have been severely compromised. The outcomes remain highly questionable.[8] Foreign direct investment in Australia, the type most likely to set up new plant, fell dramatically from 50 per cent of foreign investment in 1979–80 to 15 per cent five years later. However, increased indirect lending increased the debt-servicing costs (Stretton, 1987: 44). As nation-states try to make themselves attractive to global capital they have been sucked into a bidding competition for capital flows. In Australia, states bid against each other to provide incentives for transnational capital. Federally, the Labor government criticized the previous conservative administration for 'the biggest post-war blowout in wages'. By contrast, wage control and fiscal rectitude (labelled the 'trilogy') were to be part of Labor's attempt to make Australia more competitive (McKenna, 1999).

A consequence of these changes, says Allen (1992 in DuGay, 1996: 2), is that the identity of a modern national economy has become problematic (see Kennedy, 1998; Graham, 1998; Thurow, 1996; Reich, 1992). The global scale of many economic activities has reduced the agency and integrity of national economies which have become 'sites across which international forces move at varying rates' (DuGay, 1996: 2). For example, France's attempt to ban encryption technology is sneered at by globalist advocate, Thomas Friedman (1999), who says that if France were a stock he'd sell it, presumably because it refuses to acquiesce to all the requirements of a so-called globalized economy.

Production of goods and services: There has been a prodigious shift in productive output from manufacturing to services. Failure to acknowledge this, says Bagguley (1991: 166), may well lead us to a 'narrow and possibly misleading basis for a general account of the changing experience of employment'. Nevertheless, although production has been shifting to information technologies from the traditional manufacturing base (Ikeda, 1996; Strange, 1994; Hall, 1996: 224), changes within manufacturing are still significant.

Labour processes: These changes in the applications of technology and capital impact heavily on the deployment and mode of labour, on employer–employee relations, and on employee disposition. Corporations select different labour pools according to varying needs and circumstances, thereby producing different labour relations within and between countries (Lipietz, 1986). Invariably, national wages and labour conditions are affected by the degree to which the labour sector is related to international conditions. Thus the more integrated to international conditions is the employing enterprise, the more variability is likely to occur within labour markets according to changing needs and conditions. This imposes a flexibility 'imperative' on not only the internationally linked enterprises, but also those less obviously linked; for example, to provide an 'adaptable' and 'efficient' infrastructure attractive to international capital, employers and governments might apply these flexibility principles to railways, telecommunications, and finance industries and its workers.

This 'direct confrontation with the rigidities of Fordism', or flexible accumulation (Harvey, 1989: 147) affected the Australian labour force in Australia during the 1980s in three significant ways. First, flexible employment patterns increased part-time, fixed-contract and short-term working, where employees have even less involvement in workplace decisions (Boreham, 1992; see McRobbie, 1996; Murray, 1989). Australian employment patterns from 1983 to 1996 displayed a consistent rise in the proportion of the labour force employed in part-time work and a continual decline in the proportion in full-time work. In 1993, 17.5 per cent of the labour force was employed part-time and 82.5 per cent full-time. Part-time workers accounted for 20.1 per cent in 1988, 23.9 per cent in 1993, and 24.8 per cent in March 1996 (ABS 6203.0, *Labour Force, Australia*, March 1993 and May 1996). As well, private firms, the public service, and local governments continue to contract out functions which are not just ancillary (such as cleaning, mowing parks), but which are staple functions (for example, use of accountancy and legal professionals by Tax Office and Attorney-General's Department).

Second, labour processes have become more flexible. In Australia, this was achieved through productivity trade-offs between unions and employers that reduced job demarcations and encouraged 'multi-skilling' (see Buggy, 1992). From 1991, even more demands were placed on the unions to provide greater flexibility through 'enterprise bargaining' rounds which could be struck at the enterprise level. Among the core objectives of this new award-setting mechanism was the demonstrable improvement of productivity, flexibility and profitability for the firm or organization (Blain, 1993). Ironically, a number of studies have indicated that poor management, not the trade unions, hampered the implementation and outcomes of flexibility arrangements in the Australian work force (Boreham, Hall, and Harley, 1996; Harley, 1995; Rimmer and Watts, 1994; Fells, 1993; Pearson, 1993; Green and McDonald, 1991; Bramble, 1988). Bramble (1988) concludes that 'intensified management control and employment losses' have characterized the Australian workplace in the 1980s. Green and MacDonald (1991: 583), using the Australian Workplace Industrial Relations Survey (AWIRS) of 2300 establishments, found that 'the majority of Australian companies, left to themselves, would make little progress' in getting efficiency gains through flexibility arrangements and that, paradoxically, 'such gains would be more likely under a system of compulsory arbitration'.

Third, in a broader sense, flexibility arrangements could be seen as an aspect of global fragmentation. That is, traditional work forces are fragmented by changed patterns of behaviour (for example, increased numbers of women; part-time work; multi-skilling) and by multiple locations.

Consumption patterns and worker identity: Capitalism's growth imperative has led to serious attempts to manipulate the patterns and amount of consumption (Coyle, 1998). Because individual consumption is regarded within a liberal capitalist framework as an act of choice within a free enterprise market, those who promote consumption do so by 'instrumentalizing' the autonomy of the consumer (Rose, 1992: 155). Ideologically this is construed as actors maximizing quality of life through choosing goods and services that determine a lifestyle. Each good or service has both utility and cultural-capital, or signifying value in Bourdieuian (1984) terms (see Jameson, 1981; Featherstone, 1991).

Bauman (1987) argues that the hegemonizing discourse of the market has become so replete that the privileged position of the producer has given way to the 'sovereignty of the consumer' and that 'civic culture' has given way to 'consumer culture'. The implication of this for Bauman (1987) and for Heelas (1991) is that the 'individualistic self-ethic is likely to undermine the psychological valiancy of the relational, "other directed" moral fabric' that is implied in active citizenship (Heelas, 1991: 85). Thus, even identity as a worker, or solidarity as part of union collectivity is supplanted by the self-orientation of consumption. According to DuGay (1996), in our current enterprise culture, 'freedom and independence emanate not from civil rights but from individual choices exercised in the market' (p.77). This enterprise discourse creates a market-based universe at the centre of which is the 'active "enterprising" consumer', construed as 'a self-regulating, individual actor seeking to maximize the worth of his or her existence to him/herself through personalized acts of choice' (p.80). What is good or virtuous in this universe 'is determined by the apparent needs, desires and projected preferences of the "sovereign consumer"' (p.77), not by a more public or collective oriented ethic.

When, in 1988, the Labor government scrapped the Conciliation and Arbitration Commission, with its power to arbitrate awards on a national basis for craft-based unions, and replaced it with the Industrial Relations Commission empowered only to ratify enterprise-based awards, an entirely new set of practices and relations of power was set in place. Whereas the previous body maintained basic wages and conditions, ensured relativities, and determined wages on the reasonable needs and desires of the worker, the new body does little more than ratify agreements at the level of the enterprise in a fragmented labour market.

In summary, the impact of the global economy was:

- Australia, as a smaller nation must entice capital flows to it. Fundamental to this is a demonstrable commitment to neo-classical economics.

- The parameters of monetary and fiscal policy are set largely extraneously.

- Capital inflow is hotter and less committed than at any time this century.

- 'Flexible' workers have less security than ever.

- Collectivist ideals of civic culture have been supplanted by an individualist ethic.

GLOBALIST DISCOURSE IN AUSTRALIAN POLITICS 1983-96

Labor's abandonment of labourist discourse and its replacement by neo-liberalism can be understood largely through its response to the external sector of the economy: globalization and international competitiveness. The discourse of Labor's response to the global market works displayed four characteristics:

- It gave the market anthropomorphic features.
- Globalization seemed to reveal serious economic flaws.
- The market mechanism was conflated with globalization.
- The new globalist circumstances, it was claimed, required new national attributes, renamed as *opportunity*, due to factors no longer in control of the nation.

Anthropomorphic features: Discursively, the most important anthropomorphic feature of the global market is that it makes judgements. For example, the then Opposition Leader, Andrew Peacock berated Treasurer Keating for calling into question the market's *judgement*. We respect the decision that was taken. Australia has been, he said, 'constantly under the spotlight of the international markets as they made their decisions'. Because market judgements are considered infallible, to question them borders on impertinence. For example, Howard scoffed at Prime Minister Hawke for having 'the nerve and the gall to say that financial markets in Australia had been behaving in an irrational way'. This infallible crypto-human entity also has the power to punish. If the market does not like a performance, its judgement is backed with punitive powers, according to a Conservative frontbencher, who said that the market has passed judgement on the government's wages policy by 'selling Australian dollars hand over fist'.

The human element of market decisions is occluded ironically by anthropomorphizing the abstract notion of the market. These human features include judgement and sentiment; but the market also has the attributes of scientific principle (infallibility, replicability). Thus, the abstracted phenomenon eliminates people, but paradoxically has human attributes itself.

Revealing flaws: Like technocratic discourse, globalist discourse presents an ontological reality that cannot be resisted: a grim 'reality'. For example, Trade Minister John Dawkins, when floating the Australian dollar, asserted that we were going to 'live in the harsher reality of the real world'. Images such as the 'spotlight'; 'having to live in the real world'; and 'the harsh light of international competition' abound. What this light revealed, according to the Labor government, was an inward looking manufacturing industry, shielded from international competition.

Globalism and the market conflation provide a new 'challenge': By adopting the market mechanism as a feature of the international, rather than the national, economy and therefore something that was inevitable and unavoidable, the Labor government represented itself as being forced by the international community to accept market economics. Trade Minister Dawkins, for example, claimed that 'We are trying to establish the circumstances in which Australia can benefit from the new improved international competitiveness which now exists in the economy.' Thus competitiveness became an imperative acknowledged by both sides.

In Australia, this new competitiveness was to be achieved primarily through lower labour costs and the devalued dollar; not through more enterprising and innovative management; or enhanced infrastructure; or research and development for these were discursively precluded. It is as though the government simply followed a formula that transcended government volition.

New national attributes: The new set of circumstances and the performance measures they brought required specific national attributes. This is renamed as an *opportunity*. The most important of these is the level of wages. Trade Minister Dawkins explains the new circumstances: 'Australia needs to take advantage of this new opportunity to ensure that it can begin to reverse its international performance and to strengthen its performance in every way that it can.'

The conservatives automatically equated international competitiveness with lower wages for workers. Deputy Opposition Leader, John Howard saw it quite clearly: 'If the gains to our import competing industries and our export industries are to be retained, it is imperative that those industries not pay the additional burden of full indexation of their employee's [sic] wages.' Drawing on the now bipartisan Profit-Investment-Job (can't have jobs if there's insufficient profit to re-invest) rationale, Howard argued that 'if we have a future increase in wages on the basis of past productivity...we will erode the present level of company profitability and, therefore, interfere with employment levels.'

The crude simplicity of neo-classical economic discourse focused on the micro-economics of the factory, particularly wages. Profit share was excluded from debate by the Profit-Investment-Jobs doxa. However, Stretton (1987: 12) reminds us that 'Competition may extinguish inefficiency but it does not create efficiency.' He argues that, to revive manufacturing industry, a government needs to support it with adequate public infrastructure and services, research and education, technological transfer services and, where appropriate, public manufacture. However, Labor never challenged this neo-liberal orthodoxy. At the time of the 1985 currency crisis, Industrial Relations Minister, Willis, stated:

> the devaluation provides an opportunity for this country...which should be seized. This government had in place a wages policy which can ensure that we can seize that opportunity... Devaluation certainly means a reduction of the real income of a country, but...if we handle the matter correctly that can become a basis for considerable growth in the future. We will handle it appropriately through the wages policy.

In the 1985–86 Budget Treasurer, Keating rejected an agreed inflation adjusted wage increase so that Australia could be more internationally competitive.

WHY GLOBALIZATION WAS BAD FOR AUSTRALIAN WORKERS

The Accord was claimed as a considerable economic success by the Labor government. Morris (1989: 364–5), the Industrial Relations minister, in an address to the 1989 ACTU conference identified the achievements as:

- 1.5 million new jobs between 1983 and 1989
- inflation significantly reduced to below world levels
- a 'social justice' strategy for those outside the workforce
- compulsory superannuation coverage for the whole workforce
- extensive (re)training for the workforce
- greater employment opportunities for women

- improved occupational health and safety standards
- termination and redundancy benefit improvements
- lower industrial disputation.

On the other hand, the reform agenda of both the Labor and Conservative governments could be seen as a failure. Green (1998) identifies the inherent contradiction of the current stop–go policies based on market economics as the cause of this failure. That is, each time that demand expands in Australia, unsustainable increases in the current account deficit also occur. This forces the government to attract larger capital inflows with higher interest rates, which also slow expansion. Battin (1996: 112) agrees, saying that this stop–go policy binds Australia into a continual cycle of inconsistent policy measures. Every time there is a good economic indicator (GDP rising or unemployment falling), there are calls for anti-inflationary brakes, particularly reduced government expenditure and increased interest rates. Yet, as Green (1998: 2) says, 'we have become so accustomed to the danger of excessive demand that we no longer appreciate the danger of its opposite: inadequate demand.' Of course, Treasurer Keating relentlessly pursued such policies throughout the latter half of the 1980s causing Australian interest rates to rocket above 20 per cent. At no stage did he consider government intervention to promote import replacement of those items most often imported, like capital items and electronic consumer goods.

Instead the Hawke and Keating Labor governments adopted a 'small government' withdrawing from welfare assistance, public utilities, and government enterprises. Despite the success of the Car Plan and the Steel Plan, the Labor government did not extend this mild socialist planning to other sectors. Instead, it depoliticized this issue by technocratizing its discourse and practice. Deregulation, privatization, and small government were justified as coming to terms with the 'real world' of globalization and competition.

Trade unions short-changed in trade-off: The most significant loss for the trade union movement was Labor's abandonment of full employment as a commitment, replaced by a vaguer commitment to 'jobs' or 'job creation'. Full employment was not identified once in the 1990s by the Labor government, except in the December 1993 Green Paper, *Restoring Full Employment*, which had insufficient time to be implemented in any case (Quiggin, 1997a). Another important loss was 'security', which was supplanted by the discourses of 'flexibility' and 'enterprise', terms that were combined to form 'enterprise flexibility' introduced by the government in 1994. By allowing the employer to negotiate directly with the employees, with or without union involvement (*Research Manual of Industrial Law*, 1997: 27, 574), this new system no longer quasi-judicially incorporated trade unions into the social and legal fabric of the nation. This ended a significant democratizing feature of Australian society.

Withdrawal from planning: Labor's withdrawal from planning in the high value-added domain of manufacturing is especially puzzling, given that employer and employee organizations in the metals industries understood and accepted the importance of government intervention in directing industry policy. The MTIA, the employers body, called for investment in such industries, while the Amalgamated Metal Workers Union had urged a National Economic Development strategy to 'strengthen our tradeables sector, particularly our manufacturing industry' (Green, 1998: 3). The Australian Manufacturing Council countered the Garnaut Report, recommending greater deregulation, with the Pappas, Carter and Evans Report, arguing for more intervention. The Pappas Report advocated 'government intervention at a firm or industry level – through tax breaks, incentives, research and development, trade deal, partnerships – to help build a series of major export-orientated firms' (Kelly, 1994: 676). Clearly, significant sections of Australian management and ownership would have welcomed more government intervention. Yet the Labor government failed to take up the challenge of identifying and assisting the development of these high value-adding industries.

Manufacturing decline: The Australian trade union movement entrusted the Hawke Labor government with the task of transforming the production and industrial relations culture of Australia. Crucial to the initial agreement, Accord Mark I, was a tripartite socialist strategy intended to achieve full employment through government planning and intervention. Unions would act responsibly by not pursuing sectional claims, and by accommodating change and restraint. Such an agreement assumed that owners of capital would commit themselves to resolving the 'crisis' by relinquishing some of their power as the union movement had done by foregoing wage increases and accepting compulsory contributions to superannuation.

Unions supported workplace change. The major impediments to change, according to an AWIRS survey conducted between October 1989 and May 1990, were, in order, lack of money or resources (29 per cent), management or organization policy (20 per cent), unions (14 per cent), government rules and regulations (12 per cent), and awards (7 per cent) with 20 per cent in the 'other' category (Dabscheck, 1995: 92). Even when resisted by unions, change was rarely precluded (91), a conclusion supported by Rimmer and Watts (1994: 76). However, change did not always bring benefits. Despite Australian auto workers providing the biggest falls in net hourly earnings between 1981 and 1988 (along with Sweden), the post-Fordist benefits did not ensue for them (Bramble, 1993). While Australian productivity had improved, the relative international gap in car manufacture time was still considerable in 1989 (Australia 36 hours; Europe 22.7; US 19.6; Japan 13.2).

The fundamental flaw in the Accord approach appears to be the assumption that capitalism would be prepared to make the same civic-minded sacrifices as the union movement. In general, the union movement adopted post-Fordist policies which claimed that economic recovery would come about by enhancing productivity 'through increased skill levels, autonomy and responsibility for workers, achieved in an environment of worker-management co-operation' (Harley, 1995: 117). The 1987 ACTU/TDC document, *Australia Reconstructed*, shows that the union movement was concerned not just with distribution of production as it offered to work within progressive new management and production techniques. The labour movement believed in the predicted prosperity that would come as capitalist production was re-organized and labour was empowered (Harley, 1995: 118). During the 1980s Australian interventionist advocates (including Dow, Clegg, Boreham, Ewer, Mathews) proposed a manufacturing strategy that socialized investment decisions through tripartism at the macro level, and promoted post-Fordist production methods at the micro level (see Flew, 1989). Thus Mathews (1988, 1989), one of the more optimistic advocates, claimed that it was possible to have a 'post-socialist paradigm' centred on democratized social institutions (1988: 54). By reducing or dismantling 'rigidities' in the productive process, these progressive industrial optimists claimed that Australia could enter the 'emergent post-Fordist technocratic paradigm' (Mathews, 1990: 34; see Badham and Mathews, 1989).

The Structural Efficiency Principle set down in the August 1988 National Wage Case was intended to give effect to this post-Fordist workplace. It advocated career paths, multiskilling, new wage relativities, increased flexibility, and new classification structures in awards. However, management, it now appears, used this principle to reassert a narrow managerialism to minimize labour costs, while the unions were looking to enhance Australian industry by boosting productivity (Curtain and Mathews, 1992).

New management techniques were used by some more successful firms to enhance their productivity by upgrading the skills and capacities of their workforce, and by restructuring management processes and the organization of work (Mathews, 1990; Skinner, 1988). Although real productivity improvements came from changes in management policies using 'incorporation strategies rather than award changes' (Fells, 1993: 273), Australian management practices in the 1980s were primarily outdated, directed mostly to cutting labour costs 'rather than…long-term strategic planning or development of human resources' (Mathews, 1990: 31). Because award restructuring 'left management goals, organisation and processes untouched' (Fells, 1993: 268), there was a strong perception among workers that 'award restructuring was a process of enabling the company to "take away" conditions for very little in return' (p.269).

Even within the logic of capitalism, Australian capital performed badly during the Hawke and Keating years. The Karpin Report, *Enterprising Nation*, shows that Australian management is less well educated, less skilful and less knowledgeable than their overseas counterparts (Karpin, 1995: 35). Furthermore, it points out that in 1992 Australia had the least significant manufacturing sector of ten industrialized nations including Canada, Sweden and the Netherlands: Australia's manufacturing contributed 16 per cent to GDP, while the ten-nation average was 26 per cent (highest, 38 per cent in Germany). Although Australia's GDP grew an average 2.7 per cent per annum in the 1980s, manufacturing growth was 1.7

per cent and its sectoral share dropped by 1.7 per cent to 16.7 per cent of GDP in 1990–91 (Anthony, 1993: 49). Because, in capitalist production, power and resources are deployed, and investments made, by the owners/managers, the forces that determine the limit of productive work are quite often 'outside the control of the individual worker' (Fells, 1993: 264). Consequently, capital must shoulder much of the blame for Australia's continuing poor manufacturing performance. Although both the Labor government and the trade union movement accommodated the interests of capitalism, especially increased profit share, Conservative criticism did not abate, suggesting that capitalism's profit imperative is insatiable and unrelenting.

Union membership: Union membership fell in absolute and relative terms during the course of the Labor government (Singleton, 1990: 187). In 1992, only 39.6 per cent of the workforce was unionized (Dabscheck, 1995: 121). Some industrial relations analysts such as Kenyon and Lewis (1997) argue that the centralized wage-fixing system distanced members and produced limited returns for them. Furthermore, unions were unable to adapt quickly to the decentralized system because their structure and culture had been built around a strong centralism (especially in the most recent times).

Clearly, if unionism is to be, and appear to be, beneficial to the average worker, its legitimacy needs to be bound into the plurality of sectional interest and the communality of nationhood. By this I mean that the right of trade unions to advance working-class interests, especially in times of considerable change, must be strongly defended. A 1997 OECD report shows that highly unionized areas were associated with less downgrading of work and employment in the UK and the USA during the times of greatest restructuring (Harcourt, 1998: 5).

Inequality: Inequality increased during Labor's reign. Nevile (1995: 13) asserts that there 'is no doubt that income distribution became more unequal in the 1980s than it had been for several decades. Distribution of disposable income (allowing for social security payments and tax) moved modestly to greater inequality between 1981–82 and 1989–90. The worst conclusion is that the slide was 13 per cent (using equivalent private income as the measure), and the best conclusion is that the slide was 6 per cent (using equivalent disposable income with no exclusions as the measure) (Nevile, 1995: 16). Importantly, Nevile concludes that the 'major forces causing increases in inequality occurred in the market-place, not in the tax and social security system which moderated the increase in inequality' (p.17). As an indication of the growing inequality, the average income of couples with children in the top 20 per cent of that cohort rose 14 per cent, while that for the bottom 20 per cent rose by 3 per cent, less than the inflation rate. Saunders (1993), too, argues strongly that neo-classical economics has increased inequality in Australia. These findings are consistent with overseas evidence about the effect of market forces on inequality (see Karoly, 1993, for the effect of the Reagan years on inequality).

At a national level, globalization can impact adversely on workers in three ways, according to an OECD (1997) report on global employment: by substituting capital for labour in industrialized countries; by outsourcing to cheap labour countries; and by relocating firms from high to low wage countries (see Harcourt, 1998). In Mexico the costs of globalization fell most heavily on low-income families (Argy, 1998a; Thurow, 1996: 1). Combined with economic rationalist doctrine, globalization has forced governments to adopt market-friendly policies that disadvantage the most marginalized and low-paid in our society, says Hamilton (1997).

Postmodernity, therefore, does not alter the relationship of capital and labour, it simply shifts it into a new mode: 'Postmodernity does not end conflict between capital and labour, it simply redirects power in favour of multinational capital and against the peripheral workforce, which is the predominant feature of a international division of labour' (O'Brien, 1992: 328).

Chronic balance of trade problems: Because Australia's manufacturing base did not mature to the extent necessary to provide extensive skilled employment opportunities, or to alter its trade mix, the country remains heavily dependent on the volatile resources sector to keep its Balance of Trade from becoming a complete disaster. Fortuitously, tourism, a predominantly low-skill industry, provides another major source of import revenue. This makes the country vulnerable to protectionist agriculture policies and to world production levels. For example, the Asian economic crisis caused Australian miners to cut back production levels. In 1999–2000, Australian miners will slash their investment level by 42 per cent, driving the Australian business investment climate to its lowest ebb in 15 years (Aylmer, 1999a).

In the light of the 1996 OECD Report *Technology and Industrial Performance* which says that 'competitiveness in high-technology industries is driven mainly by technology factors and much less by wage and exchange rate movements, while the reverse is true in low-technology industries' (Green, 1998: p.4), it would seem that Australia's wage fixation was inappropriate. Consequently, Australia now relies more heavily than before on speculative capital flows into such areas as property and foreign takeovers of indigenous companies to achieve appropriate balance of payments levels.

Loss of integrity of the state: At an international level, economic globalization fragments the state. Bauman (1993: 232) claims that nation-states

> police orderly conditions in localities that increasingly become little more than transit stations in the world-wide travel of goods and money administered by the multinational (more correctly: non-national) companies.

Luke (1996) asserts that the impact of globalized information technology is to produce shifts that 'split cultures, economies, and societies between the demands of nominal nationality and actual transnationality' (p.127).

REVIEW OF IMPLICATIONS

Reconstructing the Worker-Subject
The modern worker in this new order is now 'understood and targeted as an active participant in the activity of work, not merely as an instrument of production but as a human being realizing his or her self through work, or as a democratic citizen with certain capacities and rights' (Miller and Rose, 1995: 430). The Business Council of Australia's (BCA) 1987 document, *Towards an Enterprise Based Industrial Relations System*, sought 'a fundamental re-orientation of the system' (in Dabscheck, 1990: 3). In particular,

it wanted the industrial relations system to move away from one largely focused outside the enterprise, and adversarial in nature, to one which was centred on the enterprise. Such a move, they argued, would develop mutual trust and interest, strengthening the relationship between employers and employees. A spate of new wave management books in the 1980s, such as Dertouzos, Lester and Solow's (1989) *Made in America: Regaining the Productive Edge*; Kanter's (1989) *When Giants Learn to Dance*; Peters and Waterman's (1982) *In Search of Excellence;* and Hickmann and Silva's (1985) *Creating Excellence: Managing Corporate Culture, Strategy and Change in the New Age* similarly advocated a new entrepreneurialism that was to be instilled in the workers, not just management. Such a world view eliminates notions of class interest by assuming the mutuality of employer and employee interest.

Managers who instil an appropriate 'culture' into workers (DuGay, 1996) use an 'ensemble of norms and techniques of conduct that enables the self-actualizing capacities of individuals to become aligned with the goals and objectives of the organization for which they work' (p.41). By linking the individual worker to the enterprise, the interests of capitalism are better served because workers align personal goals with ideals of individualism rather than those of group solidarity as workers (Miller and Rose, 1995: 453). These combined discourses of globalism, market economics, and enterprise achieved a link between the global economy and the national interest, and aligned the national interest with individualism and enterprise. Through individualism and enterprise, the individual would, putatively, achieve self-fulfilment. (see DuGay, 1996: 56–7; Wood, 1989). Maintaining class solidarity would be highly improbable within this culture. Miller and Rose (1995) argue that we should treat very cautiously this vision of the new worker identity that is constructed in a global production context which prioritizes 'responsiveness to customer needs'. It is possible, even probable, that such a reorganization of production regimes 'could well rebound harshly on those who are called upon to give so much more of themselves in their work' (p.459). By aligning with the goals of the workplace through 'enterprise', other forms of alignment through class, gender or ethical disposition are occluded.

The BCA saw enterprise and unionism as antithetical. Their 1989 industrial relations policy document, *Enterprise Based Bargaining Units: A Better Way of Working* (1989), claimed that the 'biggest single industrial relations impediment to more efficient competitive Australian workplaces is the antiquated structure of our trade union movement... Ideally what is needed is one bargaining unit at each workplace' (Dabscheck, 1990: 2). The BCA proposed to 'jettison' the current industrial relations approach because it rested on 'the outmoded assumption of conflict', and to replace it with 'employee relations' (Dabscheck, 1990 3). Although the likely purpose was 'to undermine the collectives that workers have traditionally used to defend and advance their rights and interests at the workplace – namely, trade unions' (Dabscheck (1990: 4), the Labor government assisted this process by replacing centralized setting of wages and conditions with enterprise bargaining at the individual workplace. Forcing unions to abandon almost a century of strong centralized wage fixing and to move to a 'voluntarist tradition of collective bargaining' (Littler, Quinlan and Kitay, 1989: 510), the government allowed employers to take advantage of the 'comparatively under-developed industrial relations structures and processes at the workplace' (Littler, Quinlan and Kitay, 1989: 510). By the time of Accord Mark VII (1991) award setting had moved almost entirely to the workplace, or enterprise. The Textile Clothing and Footwear, the Liquor and Hospitality, and the Miscellaneous Workers unions complained to the ACTU that they had difficulty negotiating with employers (Dabscheck, 1995: 107). Evidence from OECD countries supports the claim that women workers are more advantaged by 'strong institutionalised regulation of the labour market' (*Directions in Government*, June 1993 32). Perhaps the most damaging aspect of enterprise level bargaining is that wage levels could now be determined by the very poorest or the most venal small business. Finally, as Battin (1996) points out, whereas centralized wage fixing allowed the social wage to be implemented by governments, under enterprise bargaining this is less possible.

The 'enterprise focus' produces three major negative impacts, according to O'Brien (1992). First, it induces award-free and union-free industries and workplaces using company unions or staff associations as bargaining units. Second, at the enterprise level, individual employees or groups of workers would be more vulnerable to a determined employer assault than is possible with awards and union surveillance. This prediction seems to be borne out in a survey of Industrial Commission findings in 1997

('Enterprise Flexibility Agreements' in 1997 Research Manual of Industrial Law CCH Australia: 27, 754; 27, 811; 28, 001; 28, 003) which identified instances of inadequately consulting employees; presenting agreements on a take-it-or-leave-it basis; lack of informed consent; inadequate notification; coercion; and refusing union entry. Third, unions would be left to defend members as individuals, and not as part of wider collectivities (O'Brien, 1992: 327-332).

Who's Flexible Now?

While workplaces may work more effectively if they are flexible, as Harley (1995) believes to be so, it appears that the whole weight of flexibility during these years fell almost exclusively on the labour force. However, as Stegman (1993) points out, there is an enormous structural inflexibility in the Australian economy which seems to be accepted as a given in orthodox conservative analyses. The high interest rate policy used by Keating as Treasurer in the 1980s and culminating in 1990 was an 'appropriate' contractionary monetary policy to deal with the rising current account and balance of payments deficits because of the 'inability of a national economy, with an inflexible propensity to import, to sustain high domestic growth without commensurate growth in the value of its exports' (Stegman, 1993: 53). Such is the case in Australia. It is unable to produce large capital items, and Australian consumers in more prosperous times often produce import increases above the level of GDP growth. For example, in the nine months to March 1999, Australian goods imports rose by 9.3 per cent while the economy grew by less than 5 per cent (Aylmer, 1999c).

The crucial element here is why this inflexibility occurs. One important reason is that when producers do increase investment, it invariably raises imports, because Australia is a poor producer of capital equipment, thereby damaging the balance of payments. It might be argued, then, that a way to reduce this major structural form of inflexibility would be for the government to intervene in the economy, as it did successfully with the Steel Plan and the Car Plan, to produce capital equipment in Australia, thereby reducing its dependency on imports. Yet such a possibility seems to be ideologically excluded.

Within the workplace, labour flexibility 'is not the sole precondition for improved performance'; other factors such as adequate levels of capital investment, new production techniques, and a properly resourced strategic and participative management role are also required (Green and Macdonald, 1991: 566; see Bramble, 1988). Of the seven types of flexibility identified in the nationwide AWIRS survey (Harley, 1995: 31–76), Australian management generally adopted the least sophisticated form of flexibility (Harley, 1995; Green and Macdonald, 1991). Pay flexibility, which allows the level of pay to be varied to reflect supply and demand in the external labour market, is one such form. Two other forms of unsophisticated flexibility used by Australian management include working time flexibility (altering start/stop time; limiting overtime; early/late retirement; flexible annual leave), and numerical flexibility (allowing management to employ people as conditions dictate). More effectively, functional flexibility, which allows management to redeploy employees quickly between various activities, was used extensively and accepted by the trade union movement. However, there was little evidence of widespread use of more sophisticated flexibility devices such as product innovation; technical organizational flexibility which considers the workplace as an integrated productive unit utilizing flexible systems of purchase and inventory (for example, JIT); and procedural flexibility (decision making procedures; mechanisms for introducing change).

In other words, Australian management in general took advantage of the changed power relationship between labour and capital, as Kalecki (1943) has suggested is the norm, to force labour costs down through contracts and casual/temporary employment. Australian management showed little propensity for the cooperative, sharing strategy advocated in the BCA documents. By 1991, it was evident that managers had the degree of flexibility that they needed under the currently operating award system. Only 6 per cent of managers identified the award system as a barrier to change, while 57 per cent saw no barriers to change at the workplace. In fact, the greatest single barrier (19 per cent) to change is identified as technology or resources (Green and Macdonald, 1991: 579). We have to ask then why the demand for greater labour flexibility monopolized political discussion at this time given its low priority by workplace managers. Furthermore there is inconclusive evidence to support the proposition that 'workplaces facing overseas competition...and workplaces with lower union density were more likely, other things being equal, to carry out the reforms in question' (Nunes, Crockett, and Dawkins, 1993: 86).

Increased flexibility, as a rule, negatively affects workers' lives. For example, flexible working hours cause difficulties for parents faced with inflexible child care and school hours. As a result, women are more likely to be negatively affected in many cases. As well, higher levels of peripheral employment are 'overwhelmingly associated with negative outcomes for labour': low pay levels, lack of security; low skill formation and worker autonomy (Harley, 1995: 73). Thus, as Harley (1995: 72) points out, making a workplace more flexible will involve issues about the relative power of capital and labour. Positive outcomes for labour are those that involve training, autonomy, worker input to decisions, presence of trade unions, and consultative procedural flexibility, little of which manifested during this time.

Challenging the Orthodoxy

Although neo-liberal policy makers assume that globalized market mechanisms are self-evidently good for the economy, there is a growing number of economists who are expressing considerable reservation about its global impact. Paul Krugman of MIT, for example, is advocating that Asian economies place restraints on capital movements and that the world markets – assumed to be infallible by Australian political parties in the 1990s – simply got it wrong (see Krugman, 1998). In Australia, Argy (1998a, 1998b), Quiggin (1996; 1997a, b, c, d; 1998) and Green (1998) are three notable economists who are expressing not just reserve, but in some cases outright opposition to the market-based, deregulated operation of global markets. According to Argy (1998a; 1998b), the Asian crisis was caused by 'an orgy of imprudent, exuberant lending...investment fund managers...[who] were driven by herd instinct, greed, and stupidity...and a complete somersault' by international credit rating agencies (1998a: 1). Korea's lack of government regulation of the banking sector exacerbated the problem induced by globalized capitalism, whereas countries with more pro-active industry policies involving government intervention such as Taiwan, Singapore, India, and China have survived better than those economies that do not have such policies. Stewart (1990: 120–21) shows how the level playing field in a TNC-dominated information sector greatly disadvantages Australia.

The phenomenon of globalization was discursively construed through technocratic discourse and neo-classical economics to render opposition passive and ineffectual. Technocratic discourse, I argue, is the most effective discursive means of maintaining hegemonic control because it seeks to obtain 'acceptance of its values and ideology by all classes, even though they serve only its own interest in maintaining it dominance' (Lemke, 1995: 78). Neo-classical technocratic discourse engenders a type of 'conformism which is a facet of technological rationality translated into social behaviour' (Marcuse, 1968: 77). Saul (1997) understands the effect of this discourse in a similar way, as producing social passivity induced by 'the archetypes, the eternal myths, the unchangeable. Instead of giving them a new sense of power, the explanation gives comfort to passivity – particularly public passivity – facing with reigning ideologies' (pp.54–5). If Australia is to pursue a globalized civil society which is jointly constructed taking account of internal and external tensions and relations (Waterman, 1998: 227), then the Labor Party needs to be dialectical, not monologic. Through this dialectical encounter Labor needs to ask whose economic interests are being served by acquiescence,[9] and whether this is appropriate for such hybrid economies as Australia.

NOTES

1. Throughout this essay, I will refer to the Labor governments as the Hawke-Keating governments. Paul Keating was Treasurer for most of this time. He resigned as Treasurer in 1991 following a public dispute with Hawke and sat on the backbenches until he defeated Hawke in a party room ballot later in December 1991. In 1993, Keating won the 'unwinnable' election against Liberal opponent, Dr. John Hewson. However, Keating suffered a landslide loss to the Liberals led by John Howard in March 1996.
2. Statement by National Farmers Federation Industrial Director and H.R. Nicholls Society member, Paul Houlihan.
3. References taken from the Accord document and parliamentary debate are not referenced. They have been drawn from McKenna (1999).
4. Argy (1998b) refutes this strongly.
5. This is taken from McKenna (1999).
6. In a wider sense, it includes engineers, IT specialists, and applied scientists.
7. Notice that Keating's adoption of neo-classical economics and liberalism is now so complete that other neo-liberals are able to intertextually draw on him.
8. Unfortunately, critical commentary is still very marginalized. Those critical of the effect include the recently deceased anti-communist campaigner, B.A. Santamaria, the Australian Democrats, some leftist economists such as J. Quiggin and R. Green, and ageing reformers such as H. Stretton.
9. Hutton's (1996). *The State We're In* and Thurow's (1996), *The Future of Capitalism* are

examples of the many attempts to acknowledge the limitations of Keynesanism in the new social circumstances, but which questions the effect on the social fabric of neo-liberal economics. Ex-Canadian Prime Minister, Paul Hellyer (Garrett, 1999), also maintains a world wide campaign against the negative impacts of globalization.

REFERENCES

ACTU/TDC (1987), *Australia Reconstructed*. ACTU/TDC Mission to Western Europe. Canberra: AGPS.

Adorno, T.W. (1973), *The Jargon of Authenticity* (K. Tarnowski and F. Will, trans.). London.

Agger, B. (1989), *Fast Capitalism: A Critical Theory of Significance*. Urbana and Chicago.

Anthony, S. (1993), 'Industry Policy and the ACTU: Divisions Between Theory, Formal Policy and Practice', *Journal of Australian Political Economy*, No.31, pp.41–56.

Argy, F. (1998a), 'The Asian Crisis: Policy Lessons for the Future'. *The Global Trap Conference*: Available at http://conference.socialchange.net.au/globaltrap/conference/argy.html.

Argy, F. (1998b), *Australia at the Crossroads: Radical Free Market or a Progressive Liberalism?* St Leonards, NSW.

Aylmer, S. (1999a, 28 May). 'Weak Investment Threatens Growth', *Australian Financial Review*, p.1.

Aylmer, S. (1999b, 2 June). 'Current Account Deficit to Worsen', *Australian Financial Review*, pp.1–2.

Aylmer, S. (1999c, 4 May), 'Australian Dollar Rides Out Rising Trade Deficit', *Australian Financial Review*, p.1.

Bagguley, P. (1991), 'Post-Fordism and Enterprise Culture: Flexible Autonomy and Changes in Economic Organization' in R. Keat and N. Abercrombie (eds.), *Enterprise Culture*. London and New York, pp.151–70.

Battin, T. (1996), 'A Political Analysis of Australian Economic Debate: The Place of Socialist Thought' in T. Battin and G. Maddox (eds.), *Socialism in Contemporary Australia*. Melbourne, pp.107–25.

Bauman, Z. (1987), *Legislators and Interpreters*. Cambridge.

Bauman, Z. (1993), *Postmodern Ethics*. Cambridge, MA.

Bauman, Z. (1998). 'On Glocalization: Or Globalization for Some, Localization for Others', *Thesis Eleven*, No.54, pp.37–49.

Bewes, T. (1997), *Cynicism and Postmodernity*. London and New York.

Blain, N. (1993), 'Enterprise Bargaining: An Overview'. *The Economic and Labour Relations Review*, Vol.4, No.1, pp.77–97.

Blandy, R. (1993). 'Economic Rationalism and Prosperity' in S. King and P. Lloyd (Eds.), *Economic Rationalism: Dead End or Way Forward?* St. Leonards, NSW, pp.28–36.

Bonefeld, W. and Holloway, J. (eds.), (1995), *Global Capital, National Capital and the Politics of Money*. London.

Boreham, P. (1992), 'The Myth of Post-Fordist Management: Work Organisation and Employee Discretion in Seven Countries', *Employee Relations*, Vol.14, No.2, pp.13–24.

Boreham, P., Hall, R., and Harley, B. (1996), 'Two Paths to Prosperity? Work Organisation and Industrial Relations Decentralisation in Australia'. *Work, Employment and Society*, Vol.10, No.3, pp.449–69.

Bourdieu, P. (1984), *Distinction: A Social Critique of the Judgement of Taste* (R. Nice, trans.). London.

Bramble, T. (1988), 'The Flexibility Debate: Industrial Relations and New Management Production Practices', *Labour and Industry*, Vol.1, No.2, pp.187–209.

Bryan, D. (1995), 'The Internationalisation of Capital and Marxian Value Theory', *Cambridge Journal of Economics*, No.19, pp.65–89.

Buggy, J. (1992). *Working Smarter: A Practical Guide to Redesigning Work and Jobs the Participative Way*. Canberra.

Coyle, D. (1998), 'Third Way Economic Policy: An Introduction'. London. Available online.

Curtain, R. and Mathews, J. (1992), 'Two Models of Award Restructuring in Australia'.] in B. Dabscheck, G. Griffin, and J. Teciher (eds.), *Contemporary Australian Industrial Relations: Readings*. Melbourne, pp.433–50.

Dabscheck, B. (1990), 'The BCA's Plan to Americanise Australian Industrial Relations', *Journal of Australian Political Economy*, No.27, pp.1–14.

Dabscheck, B. (1995), *The Struggle for Australian Industrial Relations*. Melbourne.

Department of Foreign Affairs and Trade [DFAT] (1997), *In the National Interest*. Canberra.

Du Gay, P. (1996), *Consumption and Identity at Work*. London.

Fairclough, N. (1992), *Discourse and Social Change*. Cambridge.

Featherstone, M. (1991), *Consumer Culture and Postmodernism*. London.

Fells, R.E. (1993), 'Award Restructuring, Workplace Reform and the Changing Nature of Industrial Relations', *The Economic and Labour Relations Review*, Vol.5, No.2, pp.257–78.

Flew, T. (1989), 'The Limits to Political Unionism', *Journal of Australian Political Economy*, No.24, pp.77–99.

Friedman, T.L. (1999), *The Lexus and the Olive Tree: Understanding Globalization*. New York.

Fukuyama, F. (1995), *Trust: The Social Virtues and the Creation of Prosperity*. London.

Garrett, K. (1999), 'Global Finance: Dismantle or Reform?' Transcript of *Background Briefing*, ABC Radio (20/5/99). Available on: http://www.abc.net.au/rn/talks/bbing/stories/s27463.htm (16 June 1999).

Graham, P. (1998), 'Globalist Fallacies, Fictions and Facts: The MAI and Neo-classic Ideology', *Australian Rationalist*, No.46, pp.15–21.

Graham, P. (forthcoming), 'Hypercapitalism: The Political Economy of the Late 20th Century'. Manuscript.

Green, R. (1998), 'Asian Crisis, Global Markets, and the Future Course of Industry Policy', *The Global Trap Conference*: Available at http://conference.socialchange.net.au/globaltrap/conference/green.html.

Green, R. and MacDonald, D. (1991), 'The Australian Flexibility Paradox', *Journal of Industrial Relations*, Vol.33, No.4, pp.564–85.

Hall, S. (1996), 'The Meaning of New Times' in D. Morley and K.-H. Chen (eds.), *Stuart Hall: Critical Dialogues in Cultural Studies*. London and New York, pp.223–57.

Halliday, M.A.K. (1994), *An Introduction to Functional Grammar* (2nd ed.). London.

Halliday, M.A.K. and Martin, J.R. (1993), *Writing Science: Literacy and Discursive Power*. London.

Hamilton, C. (1997), 'Workers in the Globalised World'. *Australian Quarterly*, Vol.69, No.2, pp.24–36.

Harcourt, T. (1998), 'Globalisation and Its Labour Market Effects – What Do We Know and What Should We Do?', *The Global Trap Conference*: Available at http://conference.socialchange.net.au/globaltrap/conference/harcourt.html.

Harley, B. (1995), 'Labour Flexibility and Workplace Industrial Relations: The Australian Evidence'. *ACCIRT Monograph* No.12.

Harvey, D. (1989), *The Condition of Postmodernity: An Enquiry into the Origins of Cultural Change*. Oxford.

Heelas, P. (1991), 'Reforming the Self: Enterprise and the Characters of Thatcherism in R. Keat and N. Abercrombie (eds.), *Enterprise Culture*. London and New York, pp.72–92.

Hilmer, F. (1993), *The National Competition Policy* (the Hilmer Report). Independent Committee of Inquiry into Competition Policy in Australia (Chair F. Hilmer). Canberra.

Horkheimer, M. and Adorno, T. (1944/1998), *The Dialectics of Enlightenment* (J. Cumming, trans.). New York.

Hutton, W. (1996), *The State We're In* (rev. ed.). London.

Ikeda, S. (1996), 'World production' in T.K. Hopkins and I. Wallerstein (eds.), *The Age of Transition: Trajectory of the World-System 1945 –2025*. Leichhardt, NSW, pp.38–86.

James, C., Jones, C., and Norton, A. (eds.), (1993), *A Defence of Economic Rationalism*. St Leonards NSW.

Jameson, F. (1981), *The Political Unconscious*. Ithaca.

102 WORK AND EMPLOYMENT IN A GLOBALIZED ERA

Kalecki, M. (1943), Political Aspects of Full Employment. *Political Quarterly*, Vol.14, No.4, pp.322-31.

Karoly, L. (1993), 'The Trend in Inequality in Families, Individuals, and Workers in the United States: A Twenty-five Year Perspective' in S. Danziger and P. Gottschalk (eds.), *Uneven Tides: Rising Inequality in America*. New York, pp.19-97.

Karpin, D.S. (1995), *Enterprising Nation: Renewing Australia's Managers to Meet the Challenges of the Asia-Pacific Century*. Report of the Industry Task Force on Leadership and Management Skills (Chair D. Karpin) (April 1995). Canberra.

Kellner, D. (1989), *Jean Baudrillard: From Marxism to Postmodernism and Beyond*. California.

Kelly, P. (1994), *The End of Certainty: Power, Politics and Business in Australia* (rev. ed.). St Leonards.

Kennedy, P. (1998), 'Coming to Terms With Contemporary Capitalism: Beyond the Idealism of Globalisation and Capitalist Ascendancy Arguments'. *Sociological Research Online*, Vol.3, No.2. Available online at: http: //www.socioresonline.org.uk/socioresonline/3/2/6.html

Kenyon, P. and Lewis, P.E.T. (1997), *The Decline in Trade Union Membership: What Role Did the Accord Play?* Working Paper No 156 (February 1997). Economics Department: Murdoch University.

Krugman, P. (1998), 'Saving Asia: It's Time to Get Radical'. Issue date: 7 September 1998. Available at http://www.pathfinder.com/fortune/investor/1998/980907/sol.html

Lemke, J.L. (1995), *Textual Politics: Discourse and Social Dynamics*. London.

Lipietz, A. (1986), 'New Tendencies in the International Division of Labour: Regimes of Accumulation and Modes of Regulation' in A. Scott and M. Storper (eds.), *Production, Work, Territory: The Geographical Anatomy of Industrial Capitalism*. Boston, pp.16-40.

Littler, C.R., Quinlan, M., and Kitay, J. (1989), 'Australian Workplace Industrial Relations: Towards a Conceptual Framework', *Journal of Industrial Relations*, Vol.31, No.4, pp.500-525.

Luke, A., Nakata, M. Singh, M.S. and Smith, R. (1993), 'Policy and the Politics of Representation: Torres Strait Islanders and Aborigines at the Margins'. Paper from James Cook University of North Queensland.

Luke, T.W. (1996), 'Identity, Meaning and Globalization: Detraditionalization in Postmodern Space-Time Compression', in P. Heelas, S. Lash, and P. Morris (eds.), *Detraditionalization*. Oxford, pp.109-33.

Marcuse, H. (1968), *One Dimensional Man*. London.

Mathews, J.A. (1988), *A Culture of Power*. Sydney.

Mathews, J.A. (1989), *Age of Democracy: The Politics of Post-Fordism*. Melbourne.

Mathews, J.A. (1990), 'Theoretical Perspectives on Enterprise and Award Restructuring in Australia. *Asia Pacific Human Resources Management*, Vol.28, No.4, pp.30-39.

McKenna, B. (1997), 'How Engineers Write: An Empirical Study of Engineering Report Writing. *Applied Linguistics*, Vol.18, No.2, pp.189-211.

McKenna, B. (1999), How Labor Lost Its Labourism. A Critical Discourse Analysis of the Hawke-Keating Years: 1983 - 1996. Doctoral thesis submitted at University of Queensland (February, 1999).

McRobbie, A. (1996), 'Looking Back at New Times and Its Critics' in D. Morley and K.-H. Chen, *Stuart Hall: Critical Dialogues in Cultural Studies*, London and New York, pp.238-61.

Meynaud, J. (1968), *Technocracy* (P. Barnes, trans.). London.

Miller, P. and Rose, N. (1995), 'Production, Identity and Democracy', *Theory and Society*, No.24, pp.427-67.

Morris, P. (1989), '"Looking Forward": A New Industrial Relations for Australia', *Labour and Industry*, Vol.2, No.3, pp.364-71.

Murray, R. (1989), 'Benetton's Britain' in S. Hall and M. Jacques (eds.), *New Times: The Changing Face of Politics in the 1990s*. London, pp.54-64.

Nevile, J. (1995), 'What Happened to Income Distribution in Australian in the 1980s and Why', in J. Nevile (ed.), *As the Rich Get Richer: Changes in Income Distribution in*

Australia. CEDA Study: Growth 43. Sydney: Committee for the Economic Development of Australia.

Norton, A. (1995), 'Comment: Economic Rationalism and Democratic Debate', *Australian Journal of Social Issues*, Vol.30, No.2, pp.228–31.

Nunes, N., Crockett, G., and Dawkins, P. (1993), The Impact of Competition and Trade Unions on Workplace Reform and Organisational and Technological Change. *Australian Economic Review*, 2nd Qtr, pp.71–83.

O'Brien, J.M. (1992), 'Regulating Decentralised Industrial Relations: The Niland Prescription' in B. Dabscheck, G. Griffin, and J. Teicher (eds.), *Contemporary Australian Industrial Relations: Readings.* Melbourne, pp.324–39.

OECD (1997), *Employment Outlook* (July 1997). Paris.

Ong, A. (1991), 'The Gender and Labor Politics of Modern Postmodernity', *Annual Review of Anthropology*, No.20, pp.279–309.

Pearson, C.A.L. (1993), 'Workplace Reform and Implications for Productivity: A Workshops Field Study', *Asia Pacific Journal Of Human Resources*, Vol.31, No.2, pp.87–103.

Pusey, M. (1996), 'Economic Rationalism and the Contest for Civil Society', *Thesis Eleven*, No.44, pp.69–86.

Quiggin, J. (1996), 'The Market for Labour Reform and the Market for Tomatoes, *Journal of Economic and Social Policy*, Vol.2, No.1, pp.84–95.

Quiggin, J. (1997a), 'Social Democracy and Market Reform in Australia and New Zealand'. Paper (27 September 1997). Department of Economics, James Cook University.

Quiggin, J. (1997b), 'Economic Rationalism', *Crossings*, Vol.2, No.1, pp.3–12.

Quiggin, J. (1997c), 'Work for All – What's Stopping Us', *Australian Options*, No.25, February.

Quiggin, J. (1997d), 'Estimating the Benefits of Hilmer and Related Reforms', *Australian Economic Review*, Vol.30, No.3, pp.256–72.

Quiggin, J. (1998), 'Micro Gains from (pp.324–39). Micro Reform', *Economic Analysis and Policy*, Vol.28, No.1, pp.1–16.

Randall, K. and Williams, P. (1986, 30 October), 'Labor's New Business Deal', *Business Review Weekly*, pp.16–21.

Rees. S. (1995), 'Comment: Reply to Gow', *Australian Journal of Social Issues*, Vol.30, No.4, pp.462–4.

Reich, R.B. (1992), *The Work of Nations: Preparing Ourselves for 21st Century Capitalism.* New York.

Rifkin, J. (1995), *The End of Work: The Decline of the Global Labor Force and the Dawn of the Post-market Era.* New York.

Rimmer, M. and Watts, L. (1994), 'Enterprise Bargaining: The Truth Revealed at Last', *The Economic And Labour Relations Review*, Vol.5, No.1, pp.62–80.

Rose, N. (1992), 'Governing the Enterprising Self', in P. Heelas and P. Morris (eds.), *The Values of the Enterprise Culture: The Moral Debate.* London and New York, pp.141–64.

Saul, J.R. (1997), *The Unconscious Civilisation.* Ringwood Vic.

Saunders, P. (1993), 'Deregulation and Inequality'. Study of Social and Economic Inequality Working Paper Number 10, Centre for Applied Economic Research, University of New South Wales.

Sherden, W.A. (1998), *The Fortune Sellers: The Big Business of Buying and Selling Predictions.* New York.

Singleton, G. (1990), *The Accord and the Australian Labour Movement.* Carlton.

Skinner, W. (1988). 'The Productivity Paradox', *Harvard Business Review*, July–August, pp.55–9.

Sklair, L. (1995), *Sociology of the Global System*, 2nd ed. Baltimore.

Stegman, T. (1993), '"Jobsback" and the Future of Wages Policy', *The Economic And Labour Relations Review*, Vol.4, No.1, pp.50–61.

Stewart, R. (1990), 'Industrial Policy' in C. Jennett and R. Stewart (eds.), *Hawke and Australian Public Policy: Consensus and Restructuring.* South Melbourne, pp.105–36.

Strange, S. (1994), 'Rethinking Structural Change in the International Political Economy: States, Firms, and Diplomacy' in R. Stubbs and G.R.D. Underhill (eds.), *Political Economy and the Changing Global Order.* New York, pp.103–15.

Stretton, H. (1987). *Political Essays*. Melbourne.
TCFUA (1995). *The Hidden Cost of Fashion*. Report of the National Outwork Campaign by the Textile, Clothing and Footwear Union of Australia (March 1995). Sussex St. Sydney.
Thurow, L. (1996), *The Future of Capitalism: How Today's Economic Forces Will Shape Tomorrow's World*. St Leonards, Australia.
Tomlinson, J. (1996), 'Citizenship and Sovereignty'. *Australian Journal of Social Issues*, Vol.31, No.1, pp.3–18.
Waterman, P. (1998), *Globalization, Social Movements and the New Internationalisms*. London and Washington.

5

Cross-Cultural Diversity, Leadership and Workplace Relations in Australia

DIANNE LEWIS, ERICA FRENCH
and THIPAPHONE PHETMANY

Until recently, Australians considered themselves as little more than expatriates on an outpost of Great Britain. Until the mid-1960s an official policy of racial discrimination known as the 'White Australia Policy', aimed at excluding non-Caucasian people, specifically of Asian nationality, ensured that Australia and its workforce remained predominantly white and Anglo-Saxon. However, in the 1970s attitudes towards Asian immigration began to change and today most Australians recognize themselves as living in a multicultural society. Universities now actively recruit Asian students and many families have come to live and work in an environment that they feel will provide more scope and opportunities for themselves and their children than exist in their own home countries.

This situation has enriched Australian society, but has also created a number of issues for managers and employees. One issue is the challenge for managers in coping with the increasing cultural diversity in the workplace; and, as the global trend continues – even accelerates – in the new millennium, the development of skills in managing diverse cultures will become more and more of a priority for Australian managers.

The specific cultural diversity issue considered in this essay is the relationship between perceived leadership behaviour and subordinate job satisfaction in two different cultural groups. The essay is a combination of both theory and practice, based on the literature on leadership and job satisfaction, cross-cultural and multicultural issues, and managing diversity, as well as on an empirical case study carried out in four Australian manufacturing organizations. The term 'leadership' is used in preference to 'management', as managing cross-cultural issues is considered part of the leadership function of management.

The results of our research support the findings of Erez and Earley, 1993; Hofstede, 1980, 1991; and Rokeach, 1973, which show that cultural values impact on human behaviour. The research challenges the validity of the leadership and job satisfaction theories in cultures other than the ones in which they originated. Changes in business environments such as globalization, international mergers and acquisitions, and diverse cultural workforces have made the universal assumptions of these theories questionable. In addition, the increased recognition of multicultural workforces as inherent assets has called for organizations to have a better understanding of the cultural diversity of their workforces. More importantly, it has called for leaders to develop diversity expertise.

In the essay we differentiate between diversity and multiculturalism, give some background on Australia's multicultural society and workforce, present a short review of the literature on the relationship between job satisfaction and leadership, and justify why we have chosen to study these two aspects of diversity management, particularly in connection with multicultural and cross-cultural groups. To narrow the study further, we concentrate on transactional and transformational leadership, and on two cultural groups – Vietnamese and Australian. We then justify the need for a study such as ours, briefly describe our case – its aims, methods, findings and conclusions; discuss the significance of our research for Australian managers as they face an increasing multicultural workforce in the new millennium; and suggest areas for future research. Terms are defined as they occur.

DIVERSITY AND MULTICULTURALISM

Diversity exists in a group or organization when its members differ from one another along one or more important dimensions. Narrow definitions of diversity emphasize race, ethnicity and gender, while broader definitions imply that the term diversity refers to all individual differences among people. Broadly defined, diversity is 'a mixture of people with different group identities within the same social system' (Nkomo and Cox, 1996). It must be stressed, however, that diversity is not characterized by difference, type or item (Thomas, 1996). Diversity refers to the collective, all-inclusive mixture of differences and similarities along any given dimension.

Early approaches to managing diversity employed segregation and/or assimilation; while approaches today, apart from the legislated ones of EEO (Equal Employment Opportunity), Affirmative Action and Anti-discrimination, seem to be developing into two different streams – 'valuing' and 'utilizing'. The basic premise of the valuing approach to managing diversity is mutual accommodation and adaptation for reasons of best management practice. This approach involves varying aspects of understanding difference in order to include everyone in the process (Thomas, 1996). The utilizing approach is a recognition of diversity as an inherent resource that can be exploited in order to gain a competitive advantage. In both these streams – valuing and utilizing – diversity has become a characteristic of a large number of business organizations as they move towards globalization and organizational development and restructuring (Cox and Blake, 1991; Church, 1995; Fernandez, 1991, 1995). While diversity is very broad, this essay will deal with only one aspect of it – cultural diversity.

MULTICULTURAL AUSTRALIA

The notion that Australia has only recently faced multicultural issues is incorrect. Prior to 1788, when the 'First Fleet' arrived at Botany Bay from Great Britain to establish a penal colony, there were more than 200 indigenous tribes inhabiting the continent. This 'First Fleet' added people from 26 nations. The gold rush era in the mid-1800s continued the multicultural advance, as did the post-World War II immigration period. The 'managing diversity' practices at this time involved policies of exclusion, segregation and assimilation. The result was a multicultural Australia distinguishable by its segregated society and a workforce with group concentration that provided unfair access to the benefits and burdens of society. Today, new social policies and management practices have emerged, although the difficulties and challenges remain the same (French, 1999).

Three waves of non-British immigration have offered Australia a rich tapestry of cultural diversity. These waves were the result of international events (including war, border changes, poverty and destruction), Australian policy, industrial demand for labour, and Australia's small population. The first wave, in the nineteenth century, culminated in the gold rush era and consisted of Chinese, German and Jewish people. The second wave, in the post-war era, was predominantly European, including Italian, Greek, Maltese, Yugoslav, Dutch, Hungarian and Polish. The third wave, beginning in the 1960s to the present, began under the umbrella of what is now known as multiculturalism. Diversification increased, with people from Turkey, India, Sri Lanka, Vietnam, and Cambodia settling in Australia (Shaw, 1985).

In 1947 only 10 per cent of people living in Australia were born overseas; in 1991 the percentage was estimated at 20 per cent (Shaw, 1995); and today over 40 per cent of the Australian workforce was born overseas or has at least one parent born overseas. Of these, nearly 30 per cent are from a non-English speaking background (Cope and Kalantzis, 1997).

> Bar the unusual case of Israel, no other country in the world has had a larger immigration program over the past half century; no country's immigration population is so diverse, ethnically and linguistically. Meanwhile, the Australian economy is especially export oriented... And eight of our ten top export destinations are in the...non-Anglophone countries of Asia and the Western Pacific. The key areas of growth, moreover, are in highly communication and culture-sensitive industries – tourism, education and human services. All this means that Australian businesses have had to take cultural differences very seriously indeed.
>
> (Cope and Kalantzis 1997: 5)

Future trends in multiculturalism in Australia are uncertain because, unlike America, which has growing African-American and Hispanic populations, Australia's population mix is a result mainly of immigration. However, everything continues to point to the continued growth in Australia's cultural diversity, first due to its policy of multiculturalism, but also due to the fact that ethnicity does not change with nationality; for example, a Serb remains Serbian whether they live in Serbia, Albania, or Australia.

Today's multicultural Australia and organizations that function within it face new issues as they seek to mould a unique connection between people of different cultures and experiences, needs and desires. The 'managing diversity' practices called for now involve understanding, acceptance and integration. Multiculturalism in Australia is a policy based on individual rights and responsibilities, which recognizes the right of all Australians to enjoy their cultural heritage and the right to equal opportunities for everyone, regardless of their background. The term multiculturalism was coined in Australia in the 1980s and developed out of policies initiated by the Whitlam Labor government of 1972–75. A policy of multiculturalism has been endorsed by subsequent governments and replaces the previous official policies of exclusion and assimilation (Shaw, 1995).

Turning diverse cultural workforces into an opportunity is likely only when they are properly managed and led (DiTomaso and Hooijberg, 1996; Klagge, 1995); and in a multicultural nation such as Australia, the effectiveness of organizations will be strengthened and the door of international business opportunities can be opened wider only when leadership has acquired diversity skills (Clegg and Gray, 1996; Karpin, 1995; Office of Multicultural Affairs, 1993). This essay will deal with only two cultural groups – Vietnamese and Australian.

JOB SATISFACTION, LEADERSHIP AND DIVERSITY MANAGEMENT

The two bodies of knowledge, leadership and job satisfaction, have long been truly central parts of the interdisciplinary field of literature that includes management, organizational psychology, organizational behaviour, sociology, social science, and educational administration (Bass, 1981, 1990a; Gruneberg, 1976; Yukl, 1981). They have been intertwined through common conceptual frameworks and, for the most part, have reflected practicality through a focus on the interaction and influence process between an individual and a group, and between superiors and subordinates. While there are many skills required in diversity management, we chose to investigate only leadership and job satisfaction because of the many questions that still remain about the relationship between leadership, job satisfaction and cultural diversity.

The study of leadership has evolved over several decades, moving from research trying to identify 'traits' to more sophisticated studies looking at transactional and transformational leadership. Transformational leadership is supposedly the type of leadership necessary to bring about major change in an organization and in which a leader develops followers so that they are able to handle a greater responsibility; to have greater heights of awareness of the good of the group; and to be concerned with achievement and self-actualization (Bass, 1985). According to Bass, there are basically three attributes of transformational leadership:

Charisma: The ability to instil pride, faith and respect; a gift for seeing what is really important, transmitting a sense of mission.

Individualized consideration: The delegation of projects to stimulate learning experiences, provide coaching and teaching, and the treatment of each follower as an individual.

Intellectual stimulation: The attribute of a leader who arouses followers to think in new ways and emphasizes problem-solving and the use of reasoning before taking action.

Transactional leadership, on the other hand, is what Burns (1978: 4) says political leaders use 'with an eye to exchanging one thing for another'. According to Bass (1985), transactional leadership comprises two attributes:

Contingent reward: Rewards given if followers perform in accordance with contracts or expend the necessary effort.

Management by exception: An attribute of a leader who avoids giving directions if the old ways are working and allows followers to do their jobs as always if performance goals are met.

A transactional leader, therefore, would not attempt to change a culture, whereas a transformational leader would (Bass, 1985, 1990b).

Leadership has been the focus of more research than almost any other topic in the field of management research. As long ago as 1974 Stogdill reported over 3000 empirical studies conducted on it, conceding that 'the endless accumulation of empirical data has not produced an integrated understanding of leadership' (Stogdill, 1974: xvii). The situation is not very different today and much of the literature on transformational leadership seems to have reverted to 'trait' theory. Lewis notes:

The so-called 'qualities' listed by many authors are no more than traits in disguise and all the 'progress' made in leadership theories could be in danger of collapsing if the literature tries to define leadership in terms of the personal qualities of such leaders.

(Lewis, 1996: 25)

Job satisfaction studies have emerged since the 1930s as part of the Human Relations School of Management (Gruneberg, 1976), where the study of job satisfaction has advanced from a content perspective to a process one. It attempts to understand job satisfaction ranging from what causes individuals' feelings of satisfaction or dissatisfaction to how individuals form these feelings towards such things as a superior, or to extrinsic and intrinsic elements of work. Extrinsic job elements are defined by Warr, Cook and Wall (1979) as physical conditions and hours of work; while intrinsic job elements are defined as the amount of variety in the job and recognition of a job well done. Studies on job satisfaction were reported as exceeding 4000 as long ago as 1969 (Locke, 1969). Gruneberg stated that:

Despite this vast output many workers...are dissatisfied with the progress that has been made in understanding job satisfaction, and despite the tremendous amount of inform-ation available, nothing still yields so much controversy as does the question of the nature of job satisfaction.

(Gruneberg, 1976: x)

Studies of leadership using the transactional and transforma-tional leadership paradigm in relation to variable outcomes such as subordinate job satisfaction have been examined repeatedly during the past few decades. They have been conducted in a variety of organizational settings with subjects such as military officers (Bass, 1985); political leaders (Bass, 1985); graduate students (Bass, 1985); nurse subordinates (Bycio, Hackett and Allen, 1995); and sales managers (Dubinski et al., 1995). In addition, research on the two leadership models has been reported in different nations apart from the country where the models were formulated; for example, in Canada (Howell and Avolio, 1993), New Zealand (Singer, 1985), Australia (Parry, 1994), Taiwan (Chu, 1993), Japan (Yokochi, 1989) and Singapore (Koh, Steers and Terborg, 1995). All these studies have tried to fit the universal model to a local situation, and while they have all contributed to our knowledge and understanding of the relationship between leadership and job satisfaction, they still leave gaps and unanswered questions about the effects of culture on leadership and job satisfaction. We have used these gaps as justification for our research.

Studies of diversity management have not, as yet, been well linked to theories of leadership. Di Tomaso and Hooijberg (1996) suggest this is the result of a theory of diversity being still very much in the development stages. They argue that as yet diversity literature has been influenced by the consulting literature, which has tended to give diversity a training focus. Diversity is currently conceptualized as 'interpersonal and intergroup interaction, combined with the practice oriented work on human resources and employment' (DiTomaso and Hooijberg, 1996: 164). Hence the leadership and diversity linkage has been a practical one.

Leadership has been regarded as an important diversity skill through influences such as recommending, supporting, and mentoring others in determining policies, encouraging acceptance of difference and providing examples of behaviour in commitment, communication, decision-making and conflict management (Gardenswartz and Rowe, 1993; Sonnenschein, 1997; Thomas, 1996). However, more recently the leadership role in diversity management has expanded to include a strategic perspective based on productivity and/or best practice justifications (French, 1999). As the leadership and diversity management nexus changes, more work needs to be done in order to expand the current understanding of the role of leadership in diversity management. DiTomaso and Hooijberg (1996) suggest that indeed more work needs to be done in expanding the links between diversity and leadership theories and also in deconstructing current leadership models to identify their cultural, emotional and perceptual limitations.

JUSTIFICATION FOR THE RESEARCH

There are a number of reasons why our research on cross-cultural leadership in Australia is justified:

Importance of Subordinate Job Satisfaction

First, our research draws a link between leadership style and job satisfaction, and published research listed above shows the importance of job satisfaction to a number of work-related issues. Most studies looking at the relationship between leaders and subordinates in the past few decades have focused on subordinates' job satisfaction, with a concern for both organizational efficiency and individual well-being (Bass, 1990b, Howell and Avolio, 1993, Singer, 1985, Chu, 1993, Koh, Steers and Terborg, 1995, Yokochi, 1989). Even though the costs and benefits of job satisfaction/dissatisfaction are still under debate due to a difficulty in numerical measurement, it is widely recognized that job satisfaction/dissatisfaction of an individual has an effect on an organization's efficiency, productivity, employee–employer relations, absenteeism and turnover (Agho, Mueller and Price, 1993; Martin and Miller, 1986). Just as importantly, job satisfaction/dissatisfaction is recognized as having an immeasurable effect on the individual's health and well-being (Clegg and Wall, 1981; Gruneberg, 1980; Steiner and Truxillo, 1980; Warr, Cook and Wall, 1979). Thus, the importance of the relationship between leadership style and job satisfaction warrants the further investigation of issues not adequately covered in the published literature.

A Lack of Research on Cultural Issues and Leadership

Second, the research fills a gap in the literature on cross-cultural and multicultural leadership. Most of the research on the relationship between leadership and job satisfaction has indicated that transformational leadership has had add-on effects to transactional leadership in the prediction of subordinate job satisfaction. However, these studies have almost invariably been conducted within cultures valuing what Hofstede (1980) terms 'individualism' and 'low power distance', as it was in these types of cultures that the leadership theories originated. Canada, New Zealand, Australia, Taiwan, Japan and Singapore, where studies have been conducted and reported, are all examples of such cultures. Little research has been reported from cultures such as Vietnam, which values 'collectivism' and 'high power distance'.

In explanation of these terms, 'individualism' refers to the loosely knit social framework in which members are supposed to take care of themselves and their immediate families only. By contrast, 'collectivism' refers to the tight knit social framework in which families' members, relatives, clan, and other groups look after one another (Hofstede, 1980). 'Low power distance' refers to cultures that are characterized by the norm value that the unequal power between members of society should be minimized. By contrast, 'high power distance' refers to cultures that are characterized by the norm value that the unequal power between members of society should be accepted and there is no need for power justification (Hofstede, 1980). Furthermore, no research has been reported in nations where the subjects are from two or more cultures. Our case study used Australians (classified as belonging to an 'individualist' and 'low power-distance' culture) and Vietnamese (classified as belonging to a 'collectivist' and 'high power-distance' culture).

Increased Questioning of the Universal Assumption of American-Based Theories in the Context of Diverse Cultures

Third, assuming cultural values impact on human behaviour in some way, there is a need for cross-cultural validation of leadership theories involving job satisfaction (Erez and Earley, 1993; Hofstede, 1980, 1993; Smith and Peterson, 1988; Triandis, 1994). Boyacigiller and Adler write:

> Cultural values of the United States underlie and fundamentally frame management research, thus imbuing organizational science with implicit, and yet inappropriate, universalism.
>
> (Boyacigiller and Adler, 1991: 262)

As culture is 'the collective programming of mind that distinguishes the members of one human group from another' (Hofstede, 1980: 25), members of different nations could have different values. Values, 'beliefs about what is ultimately worth having or doing and how one ought to behave' (Lewis, 1992: 49), are usually programmed into us early in our lives. Milner (1996: 5) says that 'The values and concepts that operate in Australian society...are often different from those influential in Asian societies' and it is these differences that cause much confusion between Australia and Asia, particularly in global advertising. According to Milner, 'cultural differences that act as obstacles to 'global' advertising concern matters such as humour, attitudes to time and authority, sensitivity about health and sexual matters, the prevalence of individualism, and the acceptance or otherwise of ambiguity' (Milner, 1996: 6).

Many forces combine to form people's values, some of which are individual, some societal. Thus it is unlikely that the U.S. management theories and practices such as leadership and job motivation could be transferred freely and without change or adaptation.

Societal factors influencing low power distance values among Australians would be, again according to Hofstede (1980), small inequality in the distribution in wealth; a population that is well-educated in order to master the technology of an advanced society; a history of independence based on negotiation; and a stable and balanced political system. By contrast, societal factors influencing high power distance values amongst Vietnamese would be large inequalities in the distribution of wealth, leading to large inequalities in power; fewer years spent at school and a different system of learning (often rote); a history of colonialism and servitude to the wealthy; and an unstable and unbalanced political system that has arisen out of French colonial rule, leading to the splitting of the country, to militant nationalism and to a long war involving foreign intervention.

Hofstede (1980) found that individualism was negatively correlated with power distance. Societal differences affecting individualism in Australian society would be a high per capita income; a representative political system and a society that encourages freedom of speech and of the media; social mobility and the development of a strong middle class; a nuclear family structure; a tradition of individualist thinking that arose from the myths of the bushranger, the swagman and 'mateship'; and an education system that is widely available to everyone. By contrast, Vietnamese have a smaller per capita income; less say in political matters and a weaker middle class; an extended family structure with a tradition of collectivist thinking and action; and a traditional education system for a minority of the people.

Increased Recognition of Cultural Diversity and Multicultural Workforces and the Need for Effective Leadership with Diversity Skills

A final justification for our research is that the recent change in business environments, such as cultural diversity of the labour force, globalization, organizational development and restructuring, and in particular, an increased recognition of multiculturalism as a valuable resource of a nation such as Australia, has called for leadership that has diversity expertise (Clegg and Gray, 1996; Karpin, 1995; Office of Multicultural Affairs, 1993; Shaw, 1996).

Revolutionary changes to today's organizations and their resulting structures, strategies and behaviours have been variously heralded as having arrived, in the process of arriving, or being developed. Such changes include the globalization of the economic and business markets, the 'meltdown' of international, social, cultural, economic and organizational borders and an increasing push for social justice within the workforce, for customers and the environment (French, 1999). These changes have contributed to repeated calls for changes to management approaches that will reflect the increased need for competitive advantage, productivity and quality as well as commitment to equity and acceptance of diversity. Leaders must be able to do more than provide a role model for diversity acceptance as currently suggested. Leaders will be expected to develop, implement and justify specific activities relative to organizational needs, employee expectations, and stakeholder requirements based on business, social, organizational and individual outcomes.

DESCRIPTION OF RESEARCH

Aims of the Research

The purpose of the research was to investigate the relationship between leadership behaviour and subordinate job satisfaction, and preferences and differences in preferences for particular leadership behaviours among the Australian and Vietnamese cultural subordinate groups. Case study methodology was used because it offered a suitable exploratory method for a new area of research that investigated complex relationships.

Methodology

The choice of research methodology should be based on a consideration of the most appropriate way of achieving the desired objectives of the research (Aaker and Day, 1990; Lewis, 1995; Marshall and Rossmann, 1995; Yin, 1994; Yukl, 1989). Yukl maintains that 'the purpose of the research should dictate the methodology and choice of samples, not the other way round' and that it is important to select methods that are 'appropriate for the type of knowledge sought, rather than merely using whatever method seems most convenient' (Yukl, 1989: 278). In our case, the aims suggested case study methodology, which is, according to Yin:

> An empirical inquiry that investigates a contemporary phenomenon in its real life context, when the boundaries between phenomenon and context are not clearly evident and in which multiple sources of evidence are used.
>
> (Yin, 1989: 10)

A case study approach has a number of strengths. According to Eisenhardt (1989: 548), one of the strengths is that it is 'particularly well suited to new research areas or research areas for which existing theory seems inadequate'. Another crucial strength is that it enables organizations to be studied in relation to their specific contexts (Yin, 1994). A review of the literature on leadership and job satisfaction showed that cultural factors were inadequately addressed. Case study methodology would thus be appropriate to this research, since it would allow the researcher to investigate the relationship between leadership styles and subordinates' job satisfaction in organizations that employ diverse cultural workers. The case study usually requires a researcher to reconcile data from many sources and link it to empirical reality. As a result it often leads to testable, relevant and quite creative theory-building (Eisenhardt, 1989; Glaser and Strauss, 1967).

Research Methods

It is not possible to give specific details here of the research methods used – and nor is it the main purpose of the essay – and the following description is a brief overview only. The case study included Australian and Vietnamese subordinate work groups and managers of four medium-sized manufacturing organizations employing 100 to 300 people (one organization was used as a pilot study.) The subjects were drawn only from manufacturing organizations that shared a similar environment and were, as far as possible, representative of the Australian and Vietnamese cultures; that is, individualist and low power distance, and collectivist and high power distance cultures respectively. Managers involved in the interviews were, again as far as possible, representative of the top management of the organizations.

In the ambit of the case study both qualitative and quantitative methods were used in order to ensure a richness of data. Quantitative data were collected from subordinates through existing survey questionnaire instruments (MLQ and Extrinsic and Intrinsic job satisfaction questionnaires developed by Bass, 1985 and by Warr, Cook and Wall, 1979 respectively). The MLQ was used to measure transactional and transformational leadership behaviours and subordinates' satisfaction with their superior. The Extrinsic and Intrinsic Job Satisfaction questionnaire was used to measure subordinates' satisfaction with extrinsic and intrinsic elements of work. The data were then analysed by the Pearson Correlation Coefficient and the Mann-Whitney-Wilcoxon Rank Sum Test in addition to the basic descriptive analysis. Qualitative data were collected from the managers through open-ended interviews. And while the data collected from the survey questionnaires were used mainly in responding to the research problems, data collected from the interviews were used as an additional contributor to the completeness of the research by engaging in the verification of quantitative findings. The quantitative data were analysed statistically and the qualitative data by data reduction, data display and conclusion drawing (Miles and Huberman, 1984).

Findings

The two leadership approaches, transactional and transformation-al, were tested for their relationship to subordinate job satisfaction. It was identified that neither transactional nor transformational leadership behaviour alone was required when working with multicultural workforces such as the Australians and the Vietnamese; but rather a mix of certain elements of each. In addition, the different ethnic work groups required leaders to display certain behaviour attributes to differing degrees.

Within the Australian cultural work group, both transforma-tional and transactional leadership behaviours impact only on subordinate satisfaction with a leader and not with any other elements of job satisfaction such as extrinsic or intrinsic elements of work. Within the Vietnamese work group both transactional and transformational leadership behaviours have an effect on *all* aspects of job satisfaction. This implies that both transactional and transformational leadership behaviours fit the Vietnamese work group (assumed to be a 'collectivist' culture) better than they fit the Australian work group (assumed to be an 'individualist' culture).

Both work groups indicated a preference for their superiors to display more of the contingent reward and charisma attributes of both transactional and transformational leadership styles.

Nevertheless, while the Vietnamese prefer the individualized consideration attribute of transformation leadership to be displayed by the leader, this is not the case for the Australians, who tend to have a higher preference for the management-by-exception attribute of transactional leadership. In addition, the findings show that cultural difference influenced the perception of the two cultural work groups, particularly towards the individualized consideration and intellectual stimulation attributes of transformational leadership.

While surveys of the two cultural groups of subordinates showed different preferences in leadership style, interviews with senior managers revealed little recognition of *any* difference between multicultural subordinates.

SIGNIFICANCE OF THE RESEARCH

Questions the Universal Assumptions of American Theories

While the findings are preliminary, they support critiques made by researchers who question the universal assumptions of American-based theories (Hofstede, 1980; Erez and Earley, 1993; Triandis, 1994). In general, the findings imply neither transactional nor transformational leadership behaviour alone is required when working with multicultural workforces such as the Australian and Vietnamese. Rather, a mix of the attributes of the two leadership behaviours is required, because different work groups prefer leaders to display different behaviour attributes to differing degrees.

Broadens the Current Two Leadership Theories and Job Satisfaction

By adding a new dimension, culture, to the leadership and job satisfaction theories, the study has broadened those theories and has helped increase knowledge and understanding in the area of multicultural leadership. Culture is a variable not taken into consideration in the American studies.

Has Direct Implications for Supervisory Leadership

Findings from the study have direct implications for supervisory leadership practices and their implications should be useful for designing supervisory leadership training for organizations and leaders who wish to develop diversity skills for the increasing multicultural workforce of the new millennium.

As the study has shown that Australian and Vietnamese workers respond to different attributes of transformational and transactional behaviour, there is a need to increase the multicultural leadership skills of supervisors. Leadership can be learned, and leadership needs training (Bass, 1990b). In order to achieve this training, it is important that training activities be supported by senior management. Our research, however, showed that there is little recognition by top managers of the difference between their multicultural subordinates in terms of the subordinates' job satisfaction and the different style of leadership the subordinates preferred.

The result of this 'blindness' to identity difference (in this case cultural) is equal treatment where management policies encourage supervisors to make decisions that treat all persons equally (Konrad and Linnehan, 1995). The risk of such 'equal treatment' is ironically discrimination, as treating different (and often unequal) people equally can result in inequitable opportunities and outcomes. Australia has one of the most segregated and concentrated workforces in the OECD countries, particularly in relation to gender difference, but also to culture difference (Ronalds, 1991; Shaw, 1995). Where individuals are segregated or concentrated in different work areas, experiencing different opportunities and outcomes, equal treatment may not be equitable and certainly will not encourage any change to systemic discrimination, but indeed encourage it further (Konrad and Linnehan, 1995).

No-one can know (or be expected to know) everything about another person or another culture. Developing the skills that will enable effective interpersonal, inter and intra-group relationships is really a life-long process. The consulting approach to the diversity literature suggests that individual diversity skills include communication, understanding, empathy, recognizing and overcoming prejudice. Organizational skills include encouraging and accepting change, cross-cultural communication, equity in policy and practice, training and mentoring others, including cross-cultural team-building.

Our research showed that managers did not recognize the need for the subordinates' immediate supervisors to be flexible in their leadership approach. For these organizations, therefore, the process to improve leadership practice should begin by increasing this awareness and recognition and be followed by designing training activities involving attributes of transactional and transformational leadership behaviours. Managers and supervisors need to be equitable through 'identity conscious' rather than 'identity blind' decision-making and actions in order to ensure fair treatment for different individuals.

FUTURE RESEARCH

Future research could take several important directions, not only in Australia, but also in any part of the world where there are multicultural workforces.

- Replications of the study in different national cultures could give greater validity and reliability to our findings and to those of all future findings, and would add strength to the argument that there is a need for managers to consider different cultural workgroups differently. Possible cultures for study are white British and Indians and Pakistanis in the United Kingdom, white Americans and Hispanics in the United States, and Israelis and Arabs and non-Israeli-born Jews in Israel. The more studies that are done, the greater the validity of the theories and the more global the application of them.

- Further research should replicate this study using larger samples from wider organizational settings. The replications would help verify or modify the results.

- A qualitative study using focus-group interviews should also be considered. This would help give a better understanding of how different cultural groups view leadership behaviour.

- Future investigation may also need to control for variables such as gender and age, which might be extraneous. More sophisticated analysis tools could be useful here.

- The findings of our research could form tentative findings for a comparative cultural study.

- Future research design could focus on more diverse cultural groups in the same organizations. They might be categorized into the same cultural dimension whose beliefs and values are similarly shared, such as those of low, medium and high individualism and power distance cultures. A measuring instrument of culture such as that devised by Hofstede (1980) could be used.

- Longitudinal studies measuring the subordinates' satisfaction before and after their supervisory leadership training would help to clarify the question of whether appropriate multicultural leadership behaviour can be learned.

• While our study did not measure motivation and the effects of good diversity management on productivity, it is possible that there is a positive correlation, which could be the focus of future research.

CONCLUSION

We do not claim that we have developed any 'grand theory' (Kuhn, 1970) from the research. Rather, the findings are preliminary and support critiques made by such cultural advocates as Hofstede (1980), Erez and Earley (1993) and Triandis (1994) on the universal assumptions of American-based theories. By adding a new dimension, culture, to the leadership and job satisfaction theories, the study has broadened those theories and helped increase knowledge and understanding in the area of multicultural leadership. Just as importantly, the findings have direct implications for supervisory leadership practices. The implications should be useful for designing supervisory leadership training for leaders who wish to develop diversity skills.

Australia's unique diversity heritage offers a significant opportunity for leading the way in diversity management. To do so, traditional authoritarian and bureaucratic styles of management must metamorphose. New styles and models must be developed to reflect the needs of a culturally diverse workforce and to recognize it as a valuable resource. We trust our study has gone a small way towards alerting managers to the changing cultural situation in their workplaces and to the implications it has for management in the new millennium.

REFERENCES

Aaker, D.A. and Day, G.S. (1990) *Marketing Research*, 4th edition, Singapore: John Wiley & Sons.
Agho, A.O., Mueller, C.W. and Price, J.L. (1993) 'Determinants of Employee Job Satisfaction: An Empirical Test of a Causal Model', *Human Relations*, Vol.46, No.8, pp.1007–25.
Bass, B.M. (1981) *Stogdill's Handbook of Leadership: A Survey of Theory and Research*, New York: Free Press.
Bass, B.M. (1985) *Leadership and Performance Beyond Expectations*, New York: Free Press.
Bass, B.M. (1990a) *Bass and Stogdill's Handbook of Leadership*, 3rd edition, New York: Free Press.
Bass, B.M. (1990b) 'From Transactional to Transformational Leadership: Learning to Share the Vision', *Organizational Dynamics*, Vol.18, No.3, pp.19–31.

Burns, J. (1978) *Leadership*, New York: Harper & Row.
Boyacigiller, N.A. and Adler, N.J. (1991) 'The Parochial Dinosaur: Organizational Science in a Global Context', *Academy of Management Review*, Vol.16, No.2, pp.262–90.
Bycio, P., Hackett, R.D. and Allen, J.S. (1995) 'Further Assessments of Bass's (1985) Conceptualization of Transactional and Transformational Leadership', *Journal of Applied Psychology*, Vol.80, No.4, pp.468–78.
Chu, I.Y-K. (1993) *The Relationship of Teachers' Job Satisfaction and their Perceptions of Principals' Leadership Styles in Private Vocational High Schools in a Selected Metropolitan Area of Taiwan (China-Kao-Hsiung)*. Unpublished doctoral dissertation, University of Northern Iowa.
Church, A.H. (1995) 'Diversity in Workgroup Settings: A Case Study', *Leadership and Organizational Development Journal*, Vol.16, No.6, pp.3–9.
Clegg, S.R. and Gray, J.T. (1996) 'Leadership Research and Embryonic Industry', in K.W. Parry (ed.), *Leadership Research and Practice: Emerging Themes and New Challenges*, Melbourne: Pitman Publishing, pp.29–40.
Clegg, C.W. and Wall, T.D. (1981) 'A Note on Some New Scales for Measuring Aspects of Psychological Well-being at Work', *Journal of Occupational Psychology*, Vol.54, pp.221–5.
Cope, W. and Kalantzis, M. (1997) *Productive Diversity: Management Lessons from Australian Companies*, Occasional Paper No.20, Sydney: Centre for Workplace Communication and Culture.
Cox, T.H. and Blake, S. (1991) 'Managing Cultural Diversity: Implications for Organizational Competitiveness', *Academy of Management Executive*, Vol.5, No.3, pp.45–56.
DiTomaso, N. and Hooijberg, R. (1996) 'Diversity and the Demands of Leadership', *Leadership Quarterly*, Vol.7, No.2, pp.163–87.
Dubinsky, A.J., Yammarino, F.J., Jolson, M.A. and Spangler, W.D. (1995) 'Transformational Leadership: An Initial Investigation in Sales Management', *Journal of Personal Selling and Sales Management*, Vol.15, No.2, pp.17–31.
Eisenhardt, K. (1989) 'Building Theory from Case Study Research', *Academy of Management Review*, Vol.14, No.4, pp.532–50.
Erez, M. and Earley, P.C. (1993) *Culture, Self-identity and Work*, New York: Oxford University Press.
Fernandez, J.P. (1991) *Managing a Diverse Workforce: Regaining the Competitive Edge*, Lexington: Lexington Books.
Fernandez, J.P. (1995) 'Diversity Delivers Competitive Advantage', *Executive Excellence*, May, p.20.
French, E. (1999) 'Managing Workforce Diversity in Organisations', in Davidson, P. and Griffin, R. (1999) (eds.) *Management: Australia in a Global Context*, Australia: John Wiley & Sons, Chapter 5.
Gardenswartz, L. and Rowe, A. (1993) *Managing Diversity: A Complete Desk Reference and Planning Guide*, Chicago: Irwin/Pfeiffer and Company.
Glaser, B.G. and Strauss, A. (1967) *The Discovery of Grounded Theory*, Chicago: Aldine.
Gruneberg, M.M. (ed.) (1976) *Job Satisfaction: A Reader*, London: Unwin Brothers Ltd.
Gruneberg, G.M. (1980) 'The Happy Worker: An Analysis of Educational and Occupational Differences in the Determinants of Job Satisfaction', *American Journal of Sociology*, Vol.86, No.2, pp.247–71.
Hofstede, G. (1980) *Culture's Consequences: International Differences in Work-related Values*, London: Sage Publications.
Hofstede, G. (1991) *Cultures and Organizations: Software of the Mind*, New York: McGraw-Hill.
Hofstede, G. (1993) 'Cultural Constraints in Management Theories', *Academy of Management Executive*, Vol.7, pp.81–94.
Howell, J.M. and Avolio, B.J. (1993) 'Transformational Leadership, Transactional Leadership, Locus of Control, and Support for Innovation: Key Predictors of Consolidated Business – Unit Performance', *Journal of Applied Psychology*, Vol.78, No.6, pp.891–902.
Karpin, D. (1995) *Enterprising Nation: Renewing Australia's Managers to Meet the Challenges of the Asia-Pacific Century*, Report of the industry task force on leadership and management skills, Canberra: Australian Government Publishing Service.
Klagge, J. (1995) 'Universalism and Diversity: A Two-headed Opportunity for Today's Organizational Leaders', *Journal of Leadership and Organization Development*, Vol.16, No.4, pp.45–7.

Koh, W.L., Steers, R.M. and Terborg, J.R. (1995) 'The Effects of Transformational Leadership on Teacher Attitudes and Student Performance in Singapore', *Journal of Organizational Behavior*, Vol.16, No.4, pp.319–33.

Konrad, A.M. and Linnehan, F. (1995) 'Formalized HRM Structures: Coordinating Equal Employment Opportunity or Concealing Organizational Practices?', *Academy of Management Journal*, Vol.18, No.3, pp.787–820.

Kuhn, T. (1970) *The Structure of Scientific Revolutions*, 2nd edition, Chicago: University of Chicago Press.

Lewis, D.S. (1992) 'Communicating Organisational Culture', *Australian Journal of Communication*, Vol.19, No.2, pp.47–57.

Lewis, D.S. (1995) 'Researching Strategic Change – Methodologies, Methods and Techniques', in Hussey, D.E. (ed.) *Rethinking Strategic Management: Ways to Improve Competitive Performance*, Singapore: John Wiley & Sons, pp.269–316.

Lewis, D.S. (1996) 'New Perspectives on Transformational Leadership', in Parry, K. (ed.) *Leadership Research and Practice: Emerging Themes and New Challenges*, Australia, Pearson Professional.

Locke, E.A (1969) 'What Is Job Satisfaction?', *Organizational Behavior and Human Performance*, Vol.4, pp.309–36.

Marshall, C. and Rossman, G.B. (1995) *Designing Qualitative Research*, 2nd edition, London: Sage Publications.

Martin, G.A. and Miller, G.A. (1986) 'Job Satisfaction and Absenteeism', *Work and Occupations*, Vol.13, No.1, pp.33–46.

Miles, M.B. and Huberman, A.M. (1984) *Qualitative Data Analysis: A Source Book of New Methods*, London: Sage Publications.

Milner, A. (1996) 'Introduction', in A. Milner, and M. Quilty (eds.), *Communities of Thought'*, Melbourne: Oxford University Press, pp.1–28.

Nkomo, S.M. and Cox, T. Jr. (1996) *Diverse Identities in Organizations*, in Clegg, S.R., Hardy, C., and Nord, W.R. (eds.) *Handbook of Organization Studies*, London: Sage Publications.

Office of Multicultural Affairs (1993) *Australian Business and Cultural Diversity*, Canberra: Australian Government Publishing Service.

Parry, K. (1994) 'The Situational Contingencies of Transformational Leadership', *Management Papers*, University of Southern Queensland, Vol.3, No.4, pp.33–62.

Rokeach, M. (1973) *The Nature of Human Values*, New York: Free Press.

Ronalds, C. (1987) *Affirmative Action and Sex Discrimination: A Handbook on Legal Rights for Women*, NSW, Australia: Pluto Press.

Shaw, J. (1995) *Cultural Diversity at Work Utilising an Unique Australian Resource*, Sydney, Australia: Business Professional Publishing.

Singer, M.S. (1985) 'Transformational vs Transactional Leadership: A Study of New Zealand Company Managers', *Psychological Reports*, Vol.57, pp.143–6.

Smith, P.B. and Peterson, M.F. (1988) *Leadership, Organizations and Culture*, London: Sage Publications.

Sonnenschein, W. (1997) *The Practical Executive and Workforce Diversity*, Illinois USA: NTC Business Books.

Steiner, D.D. and Truxillo, D.M. (1989) 'An Improved Test of the Disaggregation Hypothesis of Job and Life Satisfaction', *Journal of Occupational Psychology*, Vol.62, pp.33–9.

Stogdill, R.M. (1974) *Handbook of Leadership: A Survey of the Literature*, New York: Free Press.

Thomas, R. Roosevelt Jr., (1996) *Redefining Diversity*, Broadway, New York: American Management Association.

Triandis, C.H. (1994) 'Cross-cultural Industrial and Organisational Psychology', in Dunnette, M.D. and Hough, L. (eds.), *Handbook of Industrial and Organizational Psychology*, Consulting Psychologists Press: Palo Alto, CA, pp.103–72.

Warr, P., Cook, J. and Wall, T. (1979) 'Scales for the Measurement of Some Work Attitudes and Aspects of Psychological Well-being', *Journal of Applied Psychology*, Vol.52, pp.129–48.

Yin, R.K. (1994) *Case Study Research: Design and Methods*, 2nd edition, California: Sage Publications.

Yokochi, N. (1989) *Leadership Styles of Japanese Business Executives and Managers: Transformational and Transactional.* Unpublished doctoral dissertation, United States International University.

Yukl, G. (1981) *Leadership in Organizations*, Englewood Cliffs: Prentice-Hall.

6

Expatriate Academics in a Globalized Era: The Beginnings of an Untold Story?

JULIA RICHARDSON

For many centuries, the itinerant scholar, like the wandering minstrel, has been a recognised motif in literature: seeking new knowledge, or students, or seeking refuge from more hostile environments, academic and political (Welch, 1997: 323).

The literature on international human resource management leaves us with little doubt that expansion of the global economy has led to an increasing number of business organizations facing the issue of expatriate management (for example, Selmer, 1999; Brewster and Harris, 1998). At an individual level it is also clear that managers and corporate executives are more and more likely to experience international relocation (Forster, 1997). However, globalization and increased internationalization are not confined to the business professions alone. Education and education systems have also been affected by the forces of globalization, where in addition to a well-documented increase in travel by the student body, the academic profession is also experiencing growing levels of international mobility (Welch, 1997; Altbach and Lewis, 1996). However, compared with the extensive body of literature and research on expatriate managers, very little has been written about expatriate academics. Therefore although they have a long history of travel and current trends indicate a growing number are experiencing international mobility, expatriate academics remain something of an 'unknown quantity'.

Drawing on preliminary findings from a larger study being carried out as part of doctoral research, the author will put forward a number of propositions to mark the beginning of this new field of studies in the expatriate literature. The propositions are based on findings from interviews with expatriate academics in Singapore, informal discussions with expatriate academics in New Zealand and the author's own experience and observations. It is hoped that this will stimulate further interest in expatriate academics as a hitherto under-researched group and extend our understanding of expatriates in a more general sense. In the absence of a robust body of literature and research on expatriate academics, the study will also move towards adding another dimension to the existing literature on expatriate managers by exploring the extent to which it can be applied to expatriate academics. In doing so it will propose some of the differences between the experiences of expatriate academics and those of expatriate managers, the latter as reported in the current literature. Bearing in mind that the expatriate management literature is very extensive, the essay will focus on cross-cultural training, expatriate adjustment and the expatriate family. These topics have been selected because of the widespread attention they have received in the literature. However before moving on to explore these topics in more detail, it is useful to put the essay into context by briefly reflecting on how and why the academic profession has become increasingly international and the extent to which expatriate academics are an under-researched group. In addition it is also important to demonstrate how the forces of globalization have impacted on the internationalization of the academic profession.

THE INTERNATIONALIZATION OF THE ACADEMIC PROFESSION

International travel by the academic profession is by no means a new phenomenon (Schuster, 1994; Le Goff, 1993). During the fifth century BC Sophists from all over the Greek-speaking world travelled while giving lessons for pay (Ehrenberg, 1973). By the twelfth century national and international travel was an integral part of the academic profession. This was largely due to the international character of existing universities which attracted students and masters from all over the mediaeval world. Further, some universities deliberately set out to recruit foreign academics in order to strengthen their own position and status as institutions of learning. This is an important point, bearing in mind that contemporary institutions often use a similar recruitment strategy (Schuster, 1994).

The rapid development of education after the Second World War led to a dramatic increase in the number of universities in many countries (Boyer, Altbach and Whitelaw, 1994). Of particular significance was the movement from elite to mass higher education in countries like the US, UK, Canada, Australia and New Zealand. In addition, the more recent expansion of education in developing countries throughout Asia, the Middle East and South America has led to an increase in the demand for academics to fill the growing number of positions available (Gonzalez, 1992). However, growth in demand cannot always be satisfied within national boundaries. This is particularly true for developing countries with insufficient numbers of appropriately qualified and experienced staff 'in the pipeline'. Those who have the appropriate qualifications and experience may not wish to take the positions that are available because of negative perceptions associated with an academic career (Gonzalez, 1992) and instead may prefer to find employment in the business sector with the potential of much higher pay. In these situations overseas recruitment becomes a popular option. For example in countries like Indonesia, Singapore and the United Arab Emirates recruiting academics from overseas satisfies the growth in demand for faculty as well as ensuring continued development of local education systems.

With the international development of education systems a situation has also arisen where 'more academics than ever before now benefit from exchanges with colleagues in countries far from home' (Altbach and Lewis, 1996: 4). There is empirical support for this in the first international survey of the academic profession, carried out under the aegis of the Carnegie Foundation (Boyer *et al.*, 1994). This survey found that over half of respondents in ten of the countries studied had made at least one trip abroad for the purposes of research or study. Further, more than half of those who had been overseas had been for one month or more (see Table 1).

In addition to taking part in exchanges, the Carnegie Foundation study found that academics are independently seeking positions overseas, which means that an increasing number of universities have an international faculty. This same study classified 32 per cent of academic staff in Hong Kong and 42 per cent in Israel as international. However caution must be exercised here

TABLE 1

FOR HOW MANY MONTHS DURING THE PAST THREE YEARS HAVE YOU
TRAVELLED ABROAD TO STUDY OR DO RESEARCH?

	Percentages None	One month or more
Australia	38	62
Brazil	63	37
Chile	39	61
England	47	53
Germany	35	65
Hong Kong	28	72
Israel	7	93
Japan	45	55
Korea	38	62
Mexico	57	43
The Netherlands	30	70
Russia	64	36
Sweden	25	75
United States	65	35

Source: Ernest Boyer, Philip G. Altbach and Mary Jean Whitelaw. *The Academic Profession: An International Perspective,* Carnegie Foundation for the Advancement of Teaching, Princeton, 1994.

because it uses place of origin of highest degree as an index of international faculty, which would also include nationals who have been overseas students. Another index, such as birthplace, might present a different picture. For example, using origin of highest degree the Carnegie Foundation classified 20 per cent of academic staff in Australia as international, whereas using birthplace, with some allowance for age of entry to Australia, Baker *et al.* (1993) classified 41 per cent of academics as international. This indicates that any further research on this new field of studies must recognize that the problem of defining an expatriate academic must be carefully addressed.

The academic profession clearly has a long history of international mobility and with the expansion of education systems and improved travel and communication more and more academics are seeking overseas positions for research, study or work purposes. Indeed, if 'international' is synonymous with 'expatriate', empirical evidence suggests that expatriate faculty can be found in many institutions throughout the world. This makes it even more surprising that, as already suggested, expatriate academics are not a well-documented area of research.

EXPATRIATE ACADEMICS AS AN
UNDER-RESEARCHED GROUP

Expatriate management is a 'very extensive area of interest' (Forster, 1997: 414). However much of what we know about expatriates 'is still largely based on the expatriate assignment of corporate executives' (Inkson et al., 1997: 353). In comparison, expatriate academics remain a group about which very little is known (Welch, 1997). This is ironic considering that a number of the academics who have contributed so extensively to our knowledge of expatriate managers are, or have been, expatriates at some point in their academic careers (such as Forster, Selmer, Osland, Inkson, Hiltrop, Enderwick). Similarly, although the higher education literature demonstrates a significant interest in the international mobility of tertiary students, 'the internationalisation of academic staff has been less well analysed, despite scholars from many regions becoming increasingly mobile' (Welch, 1997: 324).

This is not to suggest that expatriate academics have been ignored altogether, it is rather that what has been done has not directly addressed their experiences as expatriates. Instead other issues have been the focus of attention, such as: migrant academics as insiders or outsiders in university communities (Saha and Atkinson, 1978); teaching in different cultures (Eastman and Smith, 1991; Hofstede, 1991; Lindsay and Dempsey, 1983); the role of Fulbright Scholars (Gullahorn and Gullahorn, 1960) and international networks and flows of academic talent (Boyer et al. 1994; Karpen, 1993; Gonzalez 1992). One exception however is Napier's (1997) reflection on her experiences of being involved in a project to start up a business school in Vietnam, where she discusses the emotional and psychological challenges she and the other expatriate staff experienced. The usefulness of this article will be discussed later.

Having established the absence of an appropriately robust body of literature specifically focussing on academics' experiences as expatriates, it is useful to explore how the extensive literature on expatriate managers could be used as a loose frame of reference. To do this we must first consider what the expatriate management literature says about the themes this essay will address, i.e. cross-cultural training and support, cross-cultural adjustment and expatriate families.

REVIEW OF THE LITERATURE

What does the literature say about cross-cultural training and support systems for expatriate managers?

Throughout much of the literature there is a strong recommendation that cross-cultural training and support should be provided for expatriate managers. Recommendations have also been made that they should also be provided for the expatriate manager's family (Shaffer and Harrison, 1998). Following on from this, one of the most important themes is that cross-cultural training and support systems have a positive effect on performance during the overseas assignment because they facilitate adjustment, improved relations with host nationals, improved perceptual skills and self-development (Thomas, 1998). Further, provision of appropriate support systems has been shown to have a positive influence on organizational commitment (Yavas and Bodur, 1999; Guzzo, Noonan and Elron, 1994). However, despite gaining widespread recognition for their positive effects, empirical research also suggests that training or support are still not provided by many organizations and that any such provision is generally *ad hoc* (Thomas, 1998; Brewster and Harris, 1996; Forster and Johnsen, 1996).

As well as establishing the importance of providing cross-cultural training and support, some writers have investigated the kind of training required, e.g. cognitive or experiential, information on cultural hygiene factors or the emotional and psychological experiences of expatriation. Recent work has recommended a move away from concentrating on cultural hygiene factors to providing expatriate managers and their families with the skills to understand and manage the emotional experiences of expatriation (Forster, 1997). Generally speaking however, the consensus seems to be that it depends on context, e.g. destination location, degree of distance between host and home cultures, size and cohesiveness/homogeneity of expatriate community, employee overseas experience and assignment objectives (Thomas, 1998).

To summarize, the expatriate management literature indicates widespread agreement that cross-cultural training and support has a positive effect on expatriate managers' experiences during an overseas assignment (Stedham and Nechita, 1997; Forster, 1997; Brewster, 1995). However at the same time, it also recognizes that providing cross-cultural training and support is a highly complex and difficult task which depends as much on the context of the assignment as it does on the individual being sent.

What does the literature say about cross-culture adjustment among expatriate managers?

A review of the literature reveals a large body of research and writing on cross-cultural adjustment among expatriate managers and their families (e.g. Shaffer and Harrison, 1998; Aycan 1997; Aryee and Stone, 1996). One reason it has received so much attention is that cross-cultural adjustment leads to a more positive experience, better performance and therefore less likelihood of 'failure' – whether defined as premature repatriation or under-performance (Aycan, 1997).

Black and Stephens (1989) have identified 'three dimensions' of adjustment. They are adjustment to work, adjustment to interacting with host nationals and adjustment to the general environment. In addition to using these dimensions some researchers have sought to understand, and in some cases measure, the relationship between them. For example, to what extent does general adjustment affect work adjustment? (Gregerson and Black, 1990). Although no hard and fast conclusions have been drawn, there is some agreement that expatriate managers who are adjusted generally and interacting with host nationals are more likely to be adjusted at work (Stening and Hammer, 1992). In addition, in response to gaps left by the U and W curve, other researchers have turned to what Thomas (1998) describes as 'non-linear models' of adjustment (e.g. Fenwick and Haslett, 1994). Osland (1995, 1990) has also developed a metaphorical model, which portrays the overseas assignment as a hero's adventure. This model has proven a useful alternative serving to encourage a rich understanding of managers' experiences during overseas assignments.

There has been considerable interest in the demographic and individual factors which might affect expatriate managers' adjustment. For example age, sex, marital status, educational background, overseas experience, relational skills and certain personality traits (e.g. Birdseye and Hill, 1995; Nicholson and Imaizumi, 1993). Empirical research has shown that there are relationships between demographic and individual characteristics and ability to adjust. However, as far as marital status and family are concerned there are some contradictions (Thomas, 1998). For example, the literature seems to suggest that married expatriate managers adjust better than those who are single, possibly because of the support of the family/spouse. However it also shows that one of the main reasons for early repatriation is family/spouse inability to adjust. Having some understanding of the family and other individual and demographic factors is therefore seen as important because it helps employers to adopt more effective selection criteria for overseas assignments. For example, greater tolerance of ambiguity, cultural flexibility, willingness to communicate, well developed interpersonal skills and strong marital relationships have been identified as important criteria to look for when recruiting expatriate managers because they facilitate easier adjustment.

As already indicated, there is also general agreement that ensuring adequate pre-departure preparation by providing support and information before an assignment would have a positive effect on adjustment. This might include outlining expectations or setting up buddy systems with experienced expatriate employees in the host country.

There is clearly a large and mature literature on adjustment among expatriate managers. This is demonstrated by how adjustment has been approached, and the extent to which it can be divided into further areas of interest such as: factors contributing to adjustment – organizational, individual and environmental; the impact of adjustment on performance and intent to stay; family and/or spouse as factors influencing speed and ability to adjust; adjustment as a process. The complexity of what has been written is supported by one of the most important themes in the literature which is that adjustment is influenced by a wide range of variables: personal, organizational (home and host) and environmental (Aycan, 1997)

What does the literature say about the families of expatriate managers?

The expatriate manager's family has been a major source of interest (e.g. Shaffer and Harrison, 1998; Blonigen, 1998; Harvey, 1997). One of the most important themes is how the family, particularly the spouse, influences the manager's ability to adjust during the overseas assignment. This applies to both men and women, with married women's adjustment being 'significantly connected to how well their spouses have adjusted' (Taylor and Napier, 1996: 79). As already shown, the literature on training and support systems has addressed this issue by recommending that the family should be included in selection and training procedures in order to enhance a manager's ability to adjust. However, as stated above the literature as a whole indicates that the effect of the family's adjustment can hinder as well as help the expatriate manager's ability to adjust (Thomas, 1998).

There has also been some interest in the role played by the family when an overseas assignment is offered. This has shown that the spouse has a direct influence in the decision-making process when an overseas assignment is either accepted or declined (Mileski, 1998; Windham International, 1997). These issues are also covered in a growing literature on the subject of dual-career couples suggesting that an increase in the number of women having their own careers will have a significant impact on expatriate recruitment. This means that women will be less likely to accompany a spouse who has been sent on an overseas assignment because of their own professional commitments. Alternatively those who do go will be looking for a position which matches the one they left at home and will be less likely to settle for part-time or voluntary work which is quite often the only work available in some countries, such as Singapore and the Middle East. In order to resolve this situation Taylor and Napier (1996) have suggested that organizations might use 'trailer spouses' as a useful resource. In addition to women who are accompanying spouses, research has also shown a growing number who are themselves expatriate managers and executives. Therefore, as an increasing number of women managers and executives are being assigned to overseas positions there is an increase in the number of 'trailing husbands' (Linehan and Walsh, 1999; Taylor and Napier, 1996; Antal and Izraeli, 1993; Punnett, Crocker and Stevens, 1992).

METHOD

Defining an Expatriate Academic

The problem of defining an expatriate academic has already been alluded to and is indeed something which must be approached with caution. As a preliminary step the expatriate academics at the centre of this study are defined as 'professors and non-professorial staff, the latter only as far as [they are] part of the research and teaching profession' (Karpen, 1993: 42). They have been employed in an educational institution outside of their country of origin for

five years or less and intend to live in that country at least until the
end of their working contract. It is hoped that imposing a
maximum period of residence in the host country will help to
distinguish between expatriate academics and migrant academics.
However it is acknowledged that the distinction between
expatriates and immigrants will require greater exploration in the
larger study.

Sample

Focused in-depth interviews were carried out with 15 expatriate
academics of four different nationalities who were working in
Singapore (see Appendix 1). Subjects were approached through an
informal network of personal contacts which the author had made
during a three-year period of employment there. It is acknowledged
that this approach limits the conclusions that can be drawn.
However, these interviews represent an exploratory stage of a larger
study and are only intended to create propositions to mark the
beginning of expatriate academics as a new research topic in the
expatriate management literature. In addition to the interviews with
expatriate academics living in Singapore, the essay will also refer to
information gathered during informal conversations with expatriate
academics currently living in New Zealand. These conversations
have taken place over the past two years, many of which were
instrumental in the author's decision to pursue the larger study. The
study will also draw on the author's own experiences as an
expatriate academic in Singapore, Japan and Indonesia.

Data Analysis and Collection

Bearing in mind the stated objectives for conducting the interviews
a loose interview agenda was created which centred around some
of the main themes in the current body of expatriate management
literature. In this respect although the interviews explored how
much the literature can be applied to the experiences of expatriate
academics, they also allowed interviewees to introduce potentially
new themes.

Collection of data was iterative, with each interview feeding into
the next. For example if one interviewee raised a new issue, it
would be introduced during later interviews with other expatriate
academics. In addition, when all of the interviews were completed
some academics were interviewed for a second time to confirm the

new ideas and themes which had arisen. In this respect the interviews were more to collect background information and to establish general themes and ideas rather than as formal procedures. Eleven of the interviews were tape-recorded and transcribed. During transcription, notes were made at the side of salient themes, particularly where comments bore any resemblance to themes already identified in the literature on expatriate managers. Each interview lasted between one and four hours. Notes were made both during and after the informal conversations carried out in New Zealand.

In order to impose some structure to the analysis a flexible template approach was used (King, 1998; Crab and Miller, 1992). This template was based on the themes which had emerged during the review of the literature on expatriate managers. In using this approach a common problem was that many issues had to be assigned to more than one of the categories on the template; in this situation parallel coding was used to show that the topic had appeared in discussions relating to all three areas: cross-cultural training and support systems, cross-cultural adjustment and expatriate family.

DISCUSSION

How does the literature on cross-cultural training and support systems relate to expatriate academics?

The relevance of the literature on cross-cultural training and support systems appears to be mediated by two important differences between expatriate academics and expatriate managers. First, unlike many – but not all – expatriate managers, academics are not sent but elect to go overseas. Second, other than those who are taking sabbatical positions, there is usually no concept of a home and host organization for expatriate academics, whereas expatriate managers are frequently sent overseas with the expectation that they will return to the home organization.

Focussing on the provision of cross-cultural training and support systems, the expatriate academics involved in this study demonstrated the same kind of experiences as the expatriate managers in the literature. That is to say, very few had been provided with cross-cultural training or support and most of what had been provided was *ad hoc* with very little evidence of systematic procedures being in place. Although some reported having been given basic support, e.g. provision of accommodation for the first few weeks after arrival or the option of taking up residence in staff quarters on campus, most of what was available rested on the goodwill of their department and work colleagues rather than formal procedures. Many reported having attended organized induction programmes during the first few weeks of their employment in the foreign university. However these were invariably general induction programs meant for all new staff and hence did not cater for the specific needs of expatriate academics. None had been given pre-departure training, either cross-cultural or otherwise, although most had been sent books and pamphlets covering cultural hygiene factors such as living conditions and social norms. Other than occasional social evenings, to which spouses were usually invited, there appeared to have been no systematic attempt to provide training or support for the expatriate academic's family. Although most were aware of 'family support groups' within their institutions, these groups were organized to cater for all staff families (not just expatriate families). Groups which were specifically for expatriate families were organized by local embassies or clubs, for example in Singapore the British or American club. It was interesting to note that in the absence of such procedures, it was the expatriate academics who had already been there for a while who were willing to provide most support, particularly in terms of advice on professional responsibilities and domestic matters. One academic suggested that this might have been because they had already experienced the difficulties involved in taking an overseas appointment and were thus more aware that some kind of help and support was essential.

The literature strongly recommends that organizations should provide some form of cross-cultural training and support systems for their expatriate managers. However the idea that the same should apply to employers of expatriate academics had a mixed response. Surprisingly, among the expatriate academics whose experiences contributed to this study, there was a general consensus that because they had elected to take overseas positions rather than being sent, their employers were under no obligation to provide any form of cross-cultural training or support. In fact two interviewees were offended at the suggestion that expatriate academics should be provided with cross-cultural training. They believed that the university's decision to employ them indicated an underlying assumption that they would be able to adjust without the need for extra support and training.

> Look, when they took me on they must have thought I could handle it otherwise why would they bother with me? I would hope their recruitment strategy would weed out people who couldn't hack being here.
>
> (British expatriate academic in Singapore)

However this approach was limited to only two people. Most said that although it was not something they would expect, provided that it was effectively organized, it would have a positive effect on their perceptions of their employer. Again this is consistent with the major themes in the expatriate management literature which suggest that most expatriate managers and their families have a positive perception about cross-cultural training and support systems and that, if organized effectively, it also has a positive effect on their commitment to their employer.

Although none of the expatriate academics in Singapore had had any systematic cross-cultural training and support, the majority of those interviewed felt it would have had a positive effect on their ability to adjust and perform both at work and socially. Unexpectedly, the British expatriate academics in New Zealand also felt they would have benefited significantly from some form of cross-cultural training, particularly something that might have helped them to deal with culture shock. This fits well with a recent theme in the expatriate management literature which indicates that it would be a mistake to assume that managers moving to 'close' cultures need less training and support than those moving to 'distant' cultures (Selmer 1997, Forster, 1997). The British expatriate academics living in New Zealand seemed to have the same experiences as the Hong Kong Chinese managers in China who took part in Selmer's (1997) study. On the one hand they reported less 'cultural novelty' but on the other they indicated significant difficulties with the novelty they did perceive, usually because it was unexpected. There was a general sense that they had expected living in New Zealand to be quite similar to living in Britain but had found that although some aspects were the same there were subtle differences which had made adjustment very difficult. One of the most important points was that for some people they had specifically chosen to go to New Zealand because they thought it would be culturally similar to Britain. As a consequence, the unexpected differences had forced them to re-evaluate their positions. For one person this had meant making a decision to return to Britain.

With regard to the kind of cross-cultural training required, the most common theme was that they would have benefited from advice on what one person described as the 'roller coaster of an overseas appointment'. For example information about how to cope with expatriation itself, particularly culture shock and home sickness.

> It's not the differences between Singapore and home that upset me, I can deal with them because I can see them in front of me. It's the sense of isolation and wondering if I did the right thing in leaving that bothers me, I mean does everyone feel like this? I was really pleased the other day when I found out that lots of people who've been here for years have felt like me but it doesn't mean that I should go home. You should expect it when you go to live abroad.
>
> (British expatriate academic living in Singapore)

Parallels can be drawn here with the expatriate management literature which recommends a movement away from cultural hygiene factors as a basis for training and support, towards ensuring a better understanding of the emotional and psychological reactions to expatriation (Forster 1997; Brewster, 1996). From this it seems reasonable to suggest that these themes could be useful to institutions employing expatriate academics, particularly in terms of providing support during the first few months. It could also be useful for expatriate academics themselves in terms of how they might best prepare for an overseas position. For example as well as becoming familiar with the cultural hygiene factors of a country, they might also find out how to understand and cope with the psychological and emotional experiences of going to live overseas. This has been well supported by the expatriate academics taking part in this study with many suggesting that understanding the process of expatriation should be a top priority for anyone considering a move overseas.

Although the expatriate management literature is a useful reference for the kind of training and support to provide for expatriate academics it is of less use for the issue of when to provide it. Pre-departure training is strongly recommended throughout much of the literature on expatriate managers. However because the concept of 'home' and 'host' organization does not usually apply to expatriate academics, unless the overseas institution has a campus or contacts in the academic's home country, it is seldom possible for them to be given pre departure training. However, this being said, the recommendation that pre-departure training is important could encourage academics to organize their own pre-departure training, be it to enhance their knowledge of the host culture or, as suggested earlier, their ability to cope with the psychological and emotional experiences of moving overseas.

To summarize, the current body of literature on cross-cultural training and support systems for expatriate managers does provide a useful framework for understanding expatriate academics. However bearing in mind that this is a preliminary study based on expatriate academics in only two countries it would be wise to exercise caution. In the absence of any large-scale study it is difficult to ascertain just how many universities provide cross-cultural training and support systems for their expatriate staff. The author's own experience indicates that institutions in the Middle East and Japan provide extensive cross-cultural training and support systems throughout the period of employment. Further research is therefore required if we are to develop a better understanding of expatriate academics' experiences of cross-cultural training and support. However, this being said, without a sufficiently robust body of literature which specifically addresses the experiences of expatriate academics, the expatriate management literature does provide a useful starting point.

How does the literature on cross-cultural adjustment among expatriate managers relate to expatriate academics?

The expatriate management literature also provides a useful frame of reference for developing an understanding of cross-cultural adjustment among expatriate academics. Just as levels of cross-cultural adjustment have been shown to affect managers' experiences of their overseas assignment, all of the expatriate academics taking part in this study indicated that their ability to adjust had had a major influence on their professional and personal experiences during the overseas appointment. A particularly interesting point was that a number of the British expatriate academics living in New Zealand said their inability to adjust, both professionally and personally, had had a detrimental effect on their performance at work which had in turn had a detrimental effect on their home life. Further discussion revealed that this was in some part due to their having assumed that living in New Zealand would not be too different from living in Britain. However, as indicated earlier, because the differences they encountered were so unexpected, they had been difficult to come to terms with. In addition some felt that they received less support than expatriates from 'distant' cultures due to an underlying assumption that they would not need it. We can find a useful framework for understanding these experiences by drawing again on Selmer's study of Hong Kong Chinese managers in China. This study suggests that individuals who are 'conspicuously different may be positively encouraged and given the benefit of the doubt going through the arduous process of trying to adjust to the strange culture' (Selmer, 1997: 8). By comparison those who are seen as being the same or similar, for example British expatriate academics in New Zealand, may be perceived as needing less support. This could lead to further feelings of isolation and adjustment difficulties as well as increased reluctance to ask for help because of the perception that they 'shouldn't need it'. This was clearly expressed by a British expatriate academic in New Zealand.

> I didn't expect to have this kind of problem, New Zealand is the same as UK so I shouldn't need help, but I do. I can't go to ask anyone because they don't think I should need it either, now if I was from somewhere completely different it would be different. I think I would feel more justified in asking for help, but not here, well it wouldn't be right.'
> (British expatriate academic living in New Zealand)

Drawing further on the expatriate management literature, Osland's (1995; 1990) metaphorical model of the expatriate manager's assignment as a 'hero's adventure' could be usefully applied to the experiences of expatriate academics. In particular the expatriate academics whose experiences are reported in this essay indicated widespread support for Osland's notion of 'transformation' as an inevitable outcome of the expatriate experience. Like the managers in Osland's study, all the interviewed expatriate academics living in Singapore, and many of those living in New Zealand, said they had experienced deep-rooted personal change. In some cases this had had a major impact on how they viewed themselves, their professional ambitions and the likelihood of their returning to their home countries. The notion of 'transformation' being a useful framework for expatriate academics is also evident in Napier's (1997) reflections on building a business school in Vietnam where she says that some of the people she worked with changed their perceptions of either themselves or their disciplines or both. Continuing with the notion of personal and professional transformation and drawing again from Osland's metaphorical model, the notion that 'you can't go home again' (Osland, 1995: 171) also presents a useful framework for understanding the experiences of expatriate academics. Many of those who contributed to this study felt that because of the personal and professional changes they had experienced it would be very difficult, if not impossible, for them to return to their home countries. One British academic reported that she had gone back to the UK but could not settle and had immediately sought an overseas position. This theme was also reported in a study of teachers who experienced difficulties settling back into positions in British schools after having worked overseas (Black and Scott, 1997).

The notion that the family has an important influence on a manager's ability to adjust provides a useful framework for understanding the experiences of expatriate academics. In particular there is strong evidence of what Thomas (1998) describes as the 'paradox of the expatriate family'. For example many academics felt that not having a family had improved their ability to adjust because they did not have the responsibility of a spouse and children. In contrast many of those who were married felt that their ability to adjust had been greatly assisted by their families because it prevented them from focussing too much on themselves. Indeed one interviewee indicated that he had not been able to adjust at all until the second year of his appointment when his wife and children had arrived in Singapore.

> No, I didn't settle till my wife and children came. Now they are here and it's better, I am much happier, it's better like

this. I am much happier because they are with me. It's more expensive but it makes me think about them not just about me. Besides they are supposed to be with me, I get lonely.
(Indian expatriate academic living in Singapore)

However, providing further evidence of 'the paradox of the expatriate family', the same academic also agreed that the family's inability to adjust creates a greater likelihood of premature repatriation and under-performance. Indeed many interviewees illustrated this point by drawing either on their own personal experience or that of colleagues and friends.

Well for a start I know someone who left not because he didn't like it but because his wife didn't. She was bored and wanted to go home. That's the thing – your family has to like it or it's too difficult. Getting the family to like it is more important – then your problems aren't nearly as bad.
(British expatriate academic living in New Zealand)

From what has been said thus far, it is clear that the expatriate management literature does provide a useful framework for understanding cross-cultural adjustment among expatriate academics. However, as with the literature on cross-cultural training and support systems, its application is mediated by important differences between expatriate managers and expatriate academics. The most important difference was the issue of not having a home organization. Virtually all those who contributed to this study said that because the concept of a home and host organization does not apply to expatriate academics, premature repatriation means not having a job to go back to. Some argued that this would mean more effort would be put into adjusting. However it could also mean that academics who want to leave are forced to stay on simply because they have no other job to go to. For example one British interviewee said that he had been wanting to go home for most of the time he had been in Singapore but could not afford to because he did not have much hope of being able to find a job in Britain. As a result he had stayed on but said he felt he was under-performing in all aspects of his job. Drawing again on the expatriate management literature, this is an example of what Lanier (1979) describes as a 'brownout', that is to say, an expatriate who remains on an overseas assignment and under-performs rather than returning prematurely. Continuing with the theme of not having a home organization, one interviewee suggested that expatriate academics are in a more 'precarious' situation because they do not have a 'safety net' if things go wrong.

> If it doesn't work out for us, where can we go? What can we do? We have nothing to go back to, we've given up our jobs at home and come here. If [we] leave our jobs here, that's it, we're kicked out. There's no running home to what we had there.
>
> (American Expatriate in Singapore)

Although there may be some truth in this it is also true that expatriate managers who return prematurely (and those who successfully complete the overseas assignment) often find themselves in an equally difficult situation even though they do have a home organization to return to. However, the expatriate academics who took part in this study seemed to perceive expatriate managers as being very secure and generally well looked after during an overseas appointment, both in terms of financial reward and extra benefits as part of an overseas package. This could suggest another as yet under-researched area in the expatriate management literature. That is to say, the way in which different groups of expatriates perceive one another and the extent to which their perceptions are accurate.

How does the literature on expatriate managers' families relate to expatriate academics and their families?

Reference has already been made to how the expatriate management literature can be used to understand the position and influence of the expatriate academic's family. The notion that the spouse plays an important role in the decision-making process about whether or not an overseas position is accepted is equally relevant for expatriate academics as it is for expatriate managers. Both the married and the single academics who were involved in this study thought that because expatriate academics elect to take an overseas appointment it is more likely to be the result of a joint decision. Recounting their own experiences, those who were married said that the decision to move overseas had been made only after extensive discussion between themselves and their spouses. They also felt that this indicated more 'buy in' by their spouse than if they had been transferred by their employer, as may be the case for many expatriate managers. In addition most went on to suggest that the joint decision had created a greater sense of enthusiasm for the overseas appointment which had in turn had a positive effect on their willingness to adjust and 'try to make a go' of things.

The importance of finding a job for an accompanying spouse, as described in the literature on expatriate managers, was supported by both the single and married expatriate academics who contributed to this study. Taylor and Napier's (1996) suggestion that host organizations could use 'trailing spouses' as an important resource had a mixed reception. While most felt that it would be very helpful to the individuals concerned, they were unsure about the ethics of such a policy. However reluctance to allow the employer to bear responsibility for finding a job for the spouse did not undermine the recognized fact that a job should be found as soon as possible. As with much of the literature on expatriate managers, many of those who contributed to the study indicated that inability to find work, particularly for someone who had given up a professional career in the home country, had been a major barrier to adjustment. As a final point it was also interesting that eight interviewees did not like to use the term 'trailing spouse' but preferred to use the term 'accompanying spouse'. One explained that this was directly related to expatriate academics electing to take an overseas appointment and hence the spouse 'actively' going rather than 'trailing' behind someone who had been sent by an organization. We can also draw parallels here with Osland's (1990, 1995) notion of the hero's adventure because it might reveal something about how expatriate academics see themselves – that is, as going overseas as independent 'adventurers' rather than being sent.

The way in which the family affects cross-cultural adjustment has already been discussed where it is clear that the same paradox exists for expatriate academics as for expatriate managers, i.e. families can be a positive or a negative influence on adjustment and performance. In this respect the expatriate management literature is a useful frame of reference from which to develop an understanding of the experiences of expatriate academics. However it is also clear that the qualitative differences between expatriate managers and expatriate academics may mediate the extent to which the literature can be used. Lack of a home organization to which they can return if something goes wrong was seen again as a major difference separating expatriate managers and expatriate academics. With regard to the expatriate academic's family, it might mean that they are in a more dangerous position. For example some interviewees felt that expatriate managers' families were far better off because of the level of support they get from both the home and host organizations. References were made to expatriate managers and their families living in what Osland (1990) describes as 'golden ghettos' with luxury homes, house servants and other facilities.

> No, we aren't like them, we don't get what they get. I mean, I have seen them around Singapore, they get everything, not like us – we're basically the back packers of the expatriate community.
> (British expatriate academic living in Singapore)

Although this is clearly not the case for all expatriate managers, as already suggested above, it presents an interesting indication of how they are perceived by some expatriate academics. It also raises further questions about how expatriate academics perceive themselves. This could present further evidence of how the expatriate academics involved in this study saw themselves more like the 'heroes' in Osland's (1990) metaphorical model because of their having 'gone it alone'. The fact that they had gone overseas under their own volition without the support of a home organization appeared to be seen as an act of bravery which could be an example of Osland's (1990) mythical hero venturing into the unknown. From this we can begin to identify that how expatriate academics perceive themselves and other kinds of expatriates may be an area which requires further attention, particularly with regard to issues such as performance and expectations of working overseas.

The literature on the expatriate manager's family presents some important themes which could be used as a starting point for further research on expatriate academics. The spouse's influence on decision making and cross-cultural adjustment appears to be particularly relevant. This section has also raised the issue of perceived differences and how they may impact on expatriate academics' perceptions of themselves and their experiences in the overseas location. This is something which merits further attention because of its potential impact on their experiences of the overseas appointment in a wider sense. For example, if they do see themselves as 'going it alone' like a mythical hero on an adventure, are they therefore more or less likely to accept the difficulties of an overseas appointment as part of the 'adventure'? Alternatively, does seeing an overseas appointment as a period of 'going it alone' have an impact on their sense of belonging and commitment to the overseas institution? Further research on expatriate academics might ask this kind of question.

CONCLUSION

This essay has proposed that in the absence of a robust body of literature specifically focusing on expatriate academics' experiences of cross-cultural training and support, cross-cultural adjustment and the families of expatriate academics, the current expatriate management literature could present a useful starting point. The expatriate academics who have contributed to this study appear to share many experiences with expatriate managers. For example, a lack of coordinated cross-cultural training programmes and support systems, perceptions of the positive effect of providing such programmes, the impact of cross-cultural adjustment on performance and the paradoxical role of the family. In this respect it is proposed that these and the other identified areas of similarity could be used as a starting point for developing a more in-depth understanding of expatriate academics as a hitherto under-researched group. However it has also been proposed that application of the expatriate management literature be mediated by two major differences between expatriate academics and expatriate managers. First, that expatriate academics elect to take an overseas appointment rather than being sent as is often, but not always, the case for expatriate managers. Second, the concept of a home and host organization does not apply to expatriate academics in the way that it applies to most, but again not all, expatriate managers. Related to this is the perception that expatriate academics (and their families) are in a more 'dangerous' position than expatriate managers are because they do not have the 'safety net' of the home organization. These were the two most important issues arising from the interviews and discussions with the expatriate academics involved in this study. They were raised during discussion of all three themes – cross-cultural training and support, cross-cultural adjustment and the expatriate family. However bearing in mind that this is only a preliminary study further research might discover other equally important differences which would affect the extent to which the current body of expatriate management literature can be used to understand expatriate academics.

This study has also sought to extend our understanding of expatriates as a larger group. By focusing on the experiences of expatriate academics issues have been suggested which add another dimension to our understanding of the expatriate experience in a more general sense. For example the idea of 'going it alone' rather than being sent and the implications it has for performance, cross-cultural adjustment, organizational commit-ment and dynamics within the family. In this regard it is only by understanding the experiences of different kinds of expatriates that we can fully appreciate the different dimensions of expatriation both from the perspective of the individual and that of the employer, be it a business organization or educational institution.

A major objective of this study has been to highlight the need for further research on expatriate academics as an increasingly large but under-researched group. The study has also shown that a growing number of universities and other educational institutions will face the question of how to manage expatriate academics. At an individual level an increasing number of expatriate academics will also be asking questions about what they should expect during an overseas appoint-ment and how best to prepare themselves, their families or both. These questions can only be answered by developing a robust body of literature based on extensive research. Such research may reveal that current practices are indeed appropriate and that most universities are successfully managing their expatriate academic staff. It may be that the majority of expatriate academics are satisfied with all aspects of their overseas appointment resulting in very few failures – whether defined as premature repatriation or under-performance. Alternatively it may be that a large number of expatriate academics are leaving overseas appointments prematurely or are under-performing because of difficulties with cross-cultural adjustment and/or other issues. The point this essay has sought to make is that at the present time, these are things which we do not know.

In addition to the above, the essay has presented the results of one of the preliminary stages of a much larger study in progress. The larger study is seeking to better understand academics' experiences of expatriation. In presenting the preliminary results the essay has sought to stimulate further discussion and thought about expatriate academics as a new area of research in expatriate management. It is also hoped that the essay will encourage readers who are or have been expatriate academics, to reflect on those experiences as an area for future research.

REFERENCES

The author would welcome any comments about this essay, particularly from academics who have experienced expatriation. She may be contacted at the Department of Management, The University of Otago, P.O. Box 56, Dunedin, New Zealand, email: juliarichardson@ excite.com.

Altbach, P.G. (ed.) (1996) *The International Academic Profession Portraits of Fourteen Countries* Carnegie Foundation for the Advancement of Teaching, Princeton.
Altbach, P.G. and Lewis, L.S. (1996),'The Academic Profession in International Perspective' in P.G. Altbach (ed.) *The International Academic Profession Portraits of Fourteen Countries,* Carnegie Foundation for the Advancement of Teaching, Princeton, pp.3–48.
Antal, A.B. and Izraeli, D.N. (1993), 'A Global Comparison of Women in Management: Women Managers in their Homelands and as Expatriates' in E.A. Gagenson (ed.) *Women in Management: Trends, Issues and Challenges in Managerial Diversity,* Newbury Park, CA: Sage, Vol.4, pp.206–23.
Aryee, S. and Stone, R.J. (1996), 'Work Experiences, Work Adjustment and Psychological wellbeing of Expatriate Workers in Hong Kong', *International Journal of Human Resource Management,* Vol.7, No.1, pp.150–65.
Aycan, Z. (1997), 'Expatriate Adjustment as a Multifaceted Phenomenon: Individual and Organizational Level Predictors', *The International Journal of Human Resource Management,* Vol.8, No.4, pp.434–56.
Baker, M. *et al.* (1993*) The Role of Immigration in the Australian Higher Education Labour Market,* National Institute of Labour Studies. Canberra: Bureau of Immigration and Population Research, Australian Government Publishing Service.
Birdseye, M. and Hill, J.S. (1995), 'Individual, Organizational/Work and Environmental Influences on Expatriate Turnover Tendencies: An Empirical Study', *Journal of International Business Studies,* Vol.26, No.4, pp.787–813.
Black, D.R. and Scott, W.A.H. (1997) 'Factors Affecting the Employment of Teachers Returning to the UK After Teaching Abroad', *Educational Research,* Vol.35, No.1, pp.39–61.
Black, J.S. and Stephens, G.K. (1989), 'The Influence of the Spouse on American Expatriate Adjustment in Pacific Rim Overseas Assignments', *Journal of Management,* Vol.15, pp.529–44.
Blonigen, M. (1998) 'Managing Global Operations: Focus on Expatriates', *Decision Line,* Vol.7, pp.6–8.
Boyer, E., Altbach, P.G. and Whitelaw, M.J. (1994), *The Academic Profession: An International Perspective.* Princeton: Carnegie Foundation for the Advancement of Teaching.
Brewster, C. (1995) 'Effective Expatriate Training' in J. Selmer (ed.), *International Management: New Ideas for International Business,* Westport: Quorum Books, chapter 4.
Brewster, C. and Harris, H. (1996) 'Preparation for Expatriation: Evidence about Current Needs'. Unpublished paper.
Brewster, C. and Harris, H. (1998) 'The Coffee Machine System: How International Selection Really Works', *International Journal of Human Resource Management,* forthcoming.
Brewster, C. and Pickard, J. (1994), 'Evaluating Expatriate Training', *International Studies of Management and Organization,* Vol.24, No.3, pp.18–35.
Crab, B.F. and Miller, W.L. (1992), 'A Template Approach to Test Analysis Developing and

Using Code books', in B.F. Crabtree and W.L Miller (eds.). *Doing Qualitative Research*, Newbury Park, CA: Sage.

Eastman, V. and Smith, R. (1991), 'Linking Culture and Instruction', *Performance and Instruction*, Vol.30, No.1, pp.21–8.

Ehrenberg, V. (1973), *From Solon to Socrates: Greek History and Civilisation During the Sixth and Fifth Centuries BC*. London: Methuen.

Fenwick, M. and Haslett, T. (1994), 'A Cusp-Catastrophe Model of Cross-Cultural Adjustment' *Paper presented to the annual meeting of the Academic of International Business, Boston.*

Forster, N. (1997), '"The Persistent Myth of High Expatriate Failure Rates": A Reappraisal', *The International Journal of Human Resource Management*, Vol.8, No.4, pp.414–33.

Forster, N. and Johnsen, M. (1996), 'Expatriate Policies in UK Companies New to the International Scene', *The International Journal of Human Resource Management*, Vol.7, No.1, pp.179–205.

Gonzalez, A. (1992), 'Higher Education, Brain Drain and Overseas Employment in the Philippines: Towards a Differentiated Set of Solutions', *Higher Education*, Vol.23, pp.21–31.

Gregerson, H.B. and Black, J.S. (1990), 'A Multi-faceted Approach to Expatriate Retention in International Assignments', *Group and Organization Studies*, Vol.15, No.4, pp.461–85.

Gullahorn, J.T and Gullahorn, J.E. (1960), 'The Role of the Academic Man as a Cross-Cultural Mediator', *American Sociological Review*, Vol.25, pp.414–17.

Guzzo, R.A., Noonan, K.A. and Elron, E. (1994), 'Expatriate Managers and the Psychological Contract', *Journal of Applied Psychology*, Vol.79, No.4, pp.617–26.

Harvey, M. (1997), 'Dual-Career Expatriates: Expectations, Adjustment and Satisfaction with International Relocation', *Journal of International Business Studies*, Vol.3, pp.626–58.

Hofstede, G. (1986), 'Cultural Differences in Teaching and Learning', *International Journal of Intercultural Relations*, Vol.10, pp.301–20.

Inkson, K., Arthur, M.B., Pringle, J. and Barry, S. (1997), 'Expatriate Assignment versus Overseas Experience: International Human Resource Development', *Journal of World Business*, Vol.32, No.4, pp.351–68.

Karpen, U. (1993), 'Flexibility and Mobility of Academic Staff', *Higher Education Management*, Vol.5, No.2, pp.141–50.

King, N. (1998), 'Template Analysis' in G. Symon and C.M. Cassell (eds.), *Qualitative Methods and Analysis in Organizational Research: A Practical Guide*. London: Sage.

Lanier, A.R. (1979), 'Selecting and Preparing Personnel for Overseas Transfers', *Personnel Journal*, Vol.58, pp.160–63.

Le Goff, J. (1993), *Intellectuals in the Middle Ages*, Blackwells, Cambridge, MA.

Lindsay, C.P and Dempsey, B.K. (1983), 'Ten Painfully Learned Lessons About Working in China: The Insights of Two American Behavioural Scientists', *The Journal of Applied Behavioural Sciences*, Vol.19, No.3, pp.265–76.

Linehan, M. and Walsh, J.S. (1999) 'Recruiting and Developing Female Managers for International Assignments' *The Journal of Management Development*, Vol.18, No.6, pp.521–30.

Mileski, A.S. (1998), 'It's Time to Relocate Employees: Will They Accept the Transfer?', *Compensation and Benefits Review*, Vol.30, No.2, pp.51–8.

Napier, N.K. (1997), 'Reflections on Building a Business School in Vietnam', *Journal of Management Enquiry*, Vol.6, No.4, pp.341–54.

Nicholson, N. and Imaizumi, A. (1993), 'The Adjustment of Japanese Expatriates to Living and Working in Britain', *British Journal of Management*, Vol.4, pp.119–34.

Osland, J.S. (1995), *The Adventure of Working Abroad*: San Francisco: Jossey Bass.

Osland, J.S. (1990), *The Hero's Adventure: The Overseas Experience of Expatriate Business People*. Unpublished PhD thesis, Case Western Reserve University.

Punnett, B.J., Crocker, O. and Stevens, M.J. (1992), 'The Challenge for Women Expatriates and Spouses: Some Empirical Evidence', *The International Journal of Human Resource Management*, Vol.3, No.3, pp.585–92.

Saha, L.J and Atkinson, C.M. (1978), 'Insiders and Outsiders: Migrant Academics in an Australian University', *International Journal of Comparative Sociology*, Vol.19, Nos.3–4, pp.203–18.

Saha, L.J. and Klovdahl, A.S. (1979), 'International Networks and Flows of Academic Talent: Overseas Recruitment in Australian Universities', *Higher Education*, Vol.8, pp.55–68.

Schuster, J.H. (1994), 'Emigration, Internationalization and "Brain Drain": Propensities among British Academics', *Higher Education*, Vol.27, pp.437–52.

Selmer, J. (1999), 'Career Issues and International Adjustment of Business Expatriates', *Career Development International*, Vol.4, No.2, pp.77–87.

Selmer, J. (1997), 'Which is Easier: Adjusting to a Close or a Distant Culture? The Experience of Western and Ethnic Chine Expatriate Managers in the People's Republic of China'. Paper presented to the International Management Division at the Annual Meeting of the Academy of Management, Boston, MA.

Shaffer, M.A. and Harrison, D.A. (1998), 'Expatriates' Psychological Withdrawal from International Assignments: Work, Non-work, and Family Influences', *Personnel Psychology*, Vol.51, No.1, pp.87–118.

Stedham, Y. and Nechita, M. (1997), 'The Expatriate Assignment: Research and Management Practice', *Asia Pacific Journal of Human Resource Management*, Vol.35, No.1, pp.80–89.

Stening, B.W., and Hammer, M.R. (1992), 'Cultural Baggage and the Adaptation of Expatriate Japanese Managers', *Management International Review*, Vol.32, No.1, pp.77–89.

Taylor, S. and Napier, N. (1996), 'Working in Japan: Lessons from Women Expatriates', *Sloan Management Review*, Vol.37, pp.76–84.

Thomas, D.C. (1998), 'The Expatriate Experience: A Critical Review and Synthesis', *Advances in International Comparative Management*, Vol.12, pp.237–73.

Welch, A. (1997), 'The Peripatetic Professor: The Internationalisation of the Academic Profession', *Higher Education*, Vol.34, No.3, pp.323–45.

Windham International (1997), *Global Relocation Trends 1996 Survey Report*. New York: Windham International.

Yavas, U. and Bodur, M. (1999), 'Satisfaction among Expatriate Managers: Correlates and Consequences', *Career Development International*, Vol.4, No.5, pp.261–9.

APPENDIX I

DETAILS OF THE EXPATRIATE ACADEMICS INTERVIEWED IN SINGAPORE

Sex	Age	Time in Singapore	Nationality
F	41–45	5 years	USA
M	25–30	2 years	USA
F	36–40	1 year	USA
F	41–45	3 years	UK
F	31–35	3 years	UK
M	31–35	1 year	UK
M	51+	1 year	UK
M	36–40	3 years	UK
M	36–40	3 years	UK
M	41–45	4 years	UK
M	40–45	2 years	Chinese
M	41–45	3 years	Chinese
F	31–35	1 year	Chinese
M	31–35	4 years	Indian
M	46–50	3 years	Indian

7

Globalized New Public Management and its Impact on Scientific Research Activity in New Zealand

The primary purpose of this essay is to describe and evaluate the impact 'new public management' (NPM) has had on the organization and management of human resources in scientific research in New Zealand. The essay first considers the idea that there is a globalized form of public sector management, often referred to as NPM. Then developments over the last 20 years in public sector reform in New Zealand are reviewed. The impact of public sector reform on scientific research in New Zealand is considered with specific reference to organizational and human resource management restructuring. Finally there is a summary.

THE GLOBALIZATION OF NPM?

In general terms the debate about the globalization of new public management can be seen in two ways. One is the view that the specific forms of public sector restructuring and NPM around the world are less important than the overall tendency that it represents: that is, to whittle away the notion of the 'public interest' through commercialization and privatization in the interests of transnational business (Martin, 1993). The other is the view that the specific forms of public sector management that are emerging *are* important to the extent that they represent a globally converging form of NPM (Common, 1998).

When we consider the first of these positions it is possible to differentiate further between those who are somewhat critical of the increasing power of global capital (Le Heron, 1993) and, those who argue that nation-states *need* to restructure themselves in order to remain competitive and to attract global capital

(Dahrendorf, 1995). Le Heron, for example, argues that the globalization perspective has:

> its roots in the idea that capitalism is an accumulation process which has, at the most general level, two opposing tendencies; the equalization of conditions of production and consumption and the differentiated penetration of activities by capital. Both tendencies are the products of human agency, especially by key players such as large corporations and government organizations and both tendencies lie behind the perpetual search for new organizational forms and arrangements for production and consumption.

A less critical approach to the globalization of public sector management suggests that what we might be witnessing is policy convergence rather than a new form of global NPM. This discussion questions the extent to which globalization of public sector management is really happening in any converged way, and perhaps all we are witnessing are adjustments being made in the management of the state to facilitate its appropriateness in a globalized economy (Common, 1998). A further element of this debate argues that restructuring state management is about removing the barriers that exist between public and private sector management. It is, according to Hood (1994), concerned with moving away from a procedurally driven civil service ethic to an 'achieving results' ethic (see McKenna, 1990). Some writers see this as occurring in an ideologically neutral way (Castles, 1982). This view suggests that socio-economic and technological pressures are causing administrative elites to simply react to environmental changes. Writers such as Le Heron (1993) recognize that such restructuring facilitates the circulation of global capital that is then matched by new technological and organizational structures.

The position taken here is that rather than being an ideologically neutral movement the development of new public management, in whatever form, is an attempt to impose certain clear ideological positions:

- The assertion of the superiority of the market over the state, including the view that the application of methods of business management to the public sector is inherently good;

- The idea that NPM, in whatever form, is concerned with making the public sector more exposed to the 'market' and therefore, more customer-oriented;

- The notion that NPM increases the efficiency with which services are delivered to the user/customer.

NPM in all its forms is managerialist in principle, and because it promotes the ethic of competition, efficiency and the market it is obviously ideological and values driven (see Bosanquet, 1983; Brittan, 1984; Le Grand and Robinsons, 1984).

COMMERCIALIZATION, CORPORATIZATION AND PRIVATIZATION IN NEW ZEALAND

States have and are restructuring their management in the context of globalization (Dunleavy, 1994; Held and McGrew, 1993; McGrew and Lewis, 1992). This restructuring may be driven by The World Bank and/or the International Monetary Fund, or it may be driven by state governments as they seek to position themselves to be more competitive internationally. The form such restructuring takes will differ across nation-states. In New Zealand governments have, since the early 1980s, been active in reforming public sector activities to achieve greater efficiencies and in reducing government involvement in commercial activity. New Zealand governments have shown themselves to be zealous with regard to deregulation of the economy and in exposing it to market forces. It has been suggested that these 'experiments' can be categorized in three ways: commercialization, corporatization and privatization (Spicer *et al.*, 1996). Commercialization is the 'weakest' of the three attempts at economic reform and 'involves the restructuring of government departments and functions so as to introduce accountability and economic efficiency into government commercial activities'. Corporatization involves the transfer of trading activities of government departments or enterprises to state-owned corporations. Privatization is the 'highest level' of reform and involves the state selling off assets or its equity.

In New Zealand the corporatization process has been part of a larger programme of economic and public sector reforms. These reforms were stimulated by a low growth and declining economy, rising debt, large fiscal deficits, high inflation, large agricultural and business subsidies and extensive regulations (Spicer *et al.*, 1996). According to Spicer *et al.*, economic pressures were of central importance in the decision to restructure the state sector of the economy, and a key aspect of the corporatization process has been the state-owned enterprise model introduced through the State-Owned Enterprises Act, 1986. As Spicer *et al.* (1996) note:

> A distinctive feature of this process was the attention given to opening up markets to competition and to ensuring that state-owned enterprises had neither legislative nor regulatory advantages or disadvantages relative to actual or potential competitors.

The State-Owned Enterprises Act was only one of a number of pieces of legislation initiated by the 1984 Labour government aimed at liberalizing the New Zealand economy. Others included the Labour Relations Act (1987) and Employment Contracts Act (1992), which reduced the power of trade unions and individualized the employment relationship, and the State Sector Act (1988), which made state sector chief executives accountable for effective and efficient management. As in other countries reforms have not been without considerable criticism. However, the momentum of reform and change is now well under way and the commercialization of state welfare, in the form of Work and Income New Zealand (WINZ), and the increasingly competitive environment in the education sector are further examples of these continuing developments. In addition, as the next section outlines, commercialization has affected scientific research.

THE COMMERCIALIZATION OF AGRICULTURAL RESEARCH

As part of the process of the introduction of NPM in New Zealand, university research is now being driven by collaborations between university groups and commerce as government funding of research moves from a 'bulk funding' arrangement to a competitive-tendering arrangement. This process has been developing in the country for some years in the area of agricultural research. In light of the discussion on the globalization of NPM these developments are now considered. The names of the organizations are changed to a greater or lesser degree because some sensitivity is involved in the review of these developments.

The Restructuring of Research: Background

Before 1992 the research efforts of the New Zealand government were conducted through two government research departments, the Ministry of Science (MoS) and the Department of Agriculture (DoA).[1] These organizations were bulk funded by the government and operated largely autonomously conducting research that was considered to be of national benefit. However, together with other areas of state activity, research was hit by reductions in government funding during the 1980s. The cuts made in research funding during that period can be viewed as being driven primarily by the need to reduce costs; there did not appear to be a more complex strategy behind the restructuring of scientific research. It was not until the following decade that a more thoughtful strategic approach was developed. In particular, the Foundation for Research Science and Technology (FRST) was created to establish more substantive criteria for the funding of research in order to make research more clearly accountable for its outcomes.

The creation of FRST is significant in that it applies a discipline of accountability, which would be central to the work of corporate R&D departments, to research work funded by the taxpayer. This initiative, effectively introducing a form of NPM into research activity, was the stimulus for a range of organizational structural developments in government research centres. A most important structural change was the creation of Crown Research Institutes (CRIs) which came into being on 1 July 1992. Ten research institutes were established, constituted from the two research organizations, the MoS and DoA. The creation of CRIs required a new culture to be established in scientific research – a culture that was synergistic with the thrust of the globalization of biotechnological and agro-food R&D and which would facilitate greater movement towards the expansion of so-called 'near market' or commercialized R&D activity. The difficulties and issues involved in achieving this are outlined in the following sections through a case study of one CRI: Farmresearch.

The Case of Farmresearch: Organizational Issues

Farmresearch is one of the CRIs established in the restructuring of research in 1992. The institute conducts research into crop improvement, crop systems and environment, food quality and safety, germplasm enhancement, crop protection, new crops, nutrition, and health and seafood. The institute has approximately 300 staff and operates out of ten sites. The creation of Farmresearch immediately produced a range of organizational, structural and cultural issues, many of which had not been systematically thought through in advance of the restructuring. Of crucial significance was the fact that research, previously undertaken in large bureaucracies, was now to be carried out in smaller, more accountable 'business units'. This initial restructure and refocus created a number of important management-of-change issues.

- Three of the five divisional managers in Farmresearch came from MoS with the two others brought from outside. Consequently, staff who came from both the MoS and DoA were now managed by predominantly MoS managers. There was no consideration given to the implications of this for staff management and the problems it might cause.

- There was an overall flattening of the organizational structure with some loss of power for staff, particularly managers. The process of power and status reduction was not managed well.

- Redundancies were a feature of the restructuring, and a significant amount of uncertainty and insecurity were created as a consequence of the process involved leading to decreases in morale and performance.

- Little thought was given to existing research collaborations and how they could be maintained within the new structural arrangements.

- There were considerable problems concerning the compatibility of cultures as staff from the MoS and DoA came together in the new institute. Staff were also now operating in smaller groups. There was a structural shift from the bureaucratic and formal to the more personal and informal which was poorly planned and managed.

- There were changes to working conditions as staff faced reduced employee benefits that had an impact on morale and levels of motivation.

The restructuring of scientific research activity resembles those of other industries that have been restructured in order to become more 'lean' (Holbeche, 1998). However, the restructuring process was carried out in a particularly haphazard and unplanned way and the management strategy for change was certainly not thought through.

In addition, the restructuring of government science and the formation of the CRIs had a considerable impact on practising scientists. There was general mismanagement of the substantial organizational and people management changes that needed to be introduced in response to the restructuring of scientific research. At the micro-level, the conclusion is that management of change was undertaken poorly with little consideration of the enormity of the impact such changes would have. The major reason for this appeared to be the low level of competence among managers and their lack of professional management training, often a feature of such change in both private and public sectors (Carnell, 1995). The point is that if NPM is to be introduced into the public sector it is critical to prepare managers for the changes they are expected to implement.

Given the fundamental transformational change that is at the heart of NPM as it relates to the restructuring of scientific research, however, it is likely that considerable dislocation was in any case unavoidable. External exigencies, in this case the New Zealand government-driven restructuring, were forcing change internally. In a major transformational change in the private sector environment restructuring can be explained, rightly or wrongly, with clear reference to the 'threat of closure' or need to 'adjust to market conditions' arguments. Incoming senior management can move quickly and often decisively to implement a range of cultural-change mechanisms (Taylor, 1994), although this process rarely operates as easily as this suggests. In the public sector, and particularly in the area of scientific research, such a 'business-oriented' approach to change is rarely faced. The tradition and culture of government research activity provides 'jobs for life' and employment conditions that are reasonable and stable. Now however, research scientists and managers operate in a new and threatening environment, one for which they are not well prepared or equipped. The psychological contract as it existed between research scientists and government has been broken. Furthermore, the 'culture' shift to a more commercially oriented science is a difficult one to implement, requiring, among other things, a substantial redefinition of 'research' and 'science' in the minds of scientists. Indeed, many researchers see commercially-driven science work, not as 'research' but as 'development'. Consequently the magnitude of required change in this context is enormous.

The period between 1992 and 1998 saw senior management at Farmresearch implement a further range of change management initiatives that sought to align the organization with the intended strategy of producing more 'near market' R&D. Some of these changes were draconian – for example, staff who were not attracting enough commercial funding were made redundant; site reductions were planned, with four sites closed involving further redundancies and relocations.

Farmresearch, 1998–2000

Farmresearch now operates in an environment where government funding is increasingly uncertain and more directed, and where private sector funding of R&D in New Zealand remains low. These factors continue to shape the environment of Farmresearch and have required further 'reform' of organizational structure, which was divisional (see Figure 1). In 1998 another round of organizational restructuring took place in response to the politico-economic situation (Figure 2). A driver for this restructuring was the need, not simply to gain 'industry group' endorsement for research, or simply to identify end users of the research, but to involve the industry group(s) in the planning and financial support of the research programme. In addition, government funding is now related directly to funding priorities. Major areas of current funding for Farmresearch have been deprioritized, leaving a considerable gap in incomes. One further environmental factor is the expansion of competition for the available funds.

The continuing pressures of change are forcing Farmresearch to seek ever more funding from the commercial sector (an intended effect). The need to involve the commercial sector much more closely in the research planning process, a prerequisite for gaining more private sector funding, has led to the most recent strategic organizational restructuring. The objective is to increase commercial funding from 30 per cent to 50 per cent of total funding in five years. In turn, an increase in commercially relevant research will increase government funding. Indeed, the government is ready to be supportive of Farmresearch as long as it is able to show, through an increase in commercial support, the relevance

FIGURE 1
FARMRESEARCH MANAGEMENT STRUCTURE – 1992

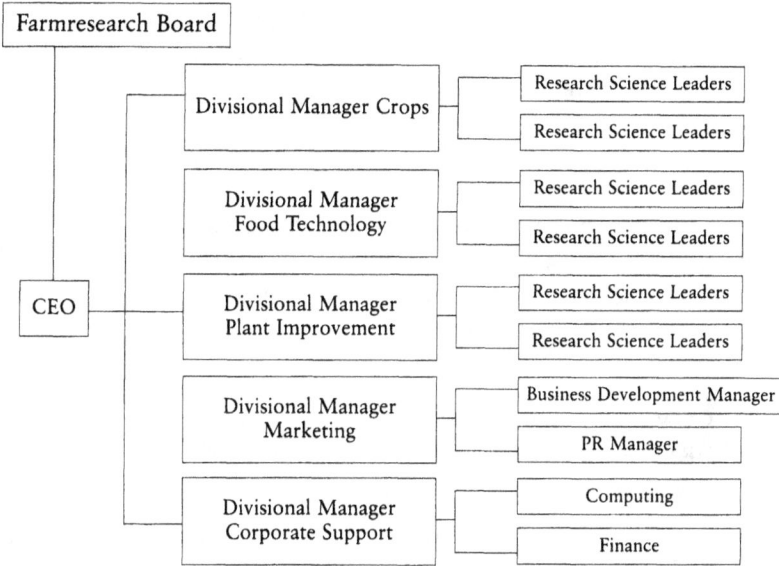

FIGURE 2
FARMRESEARCH ORGANIZATIONAL STRUCTURE – 1998

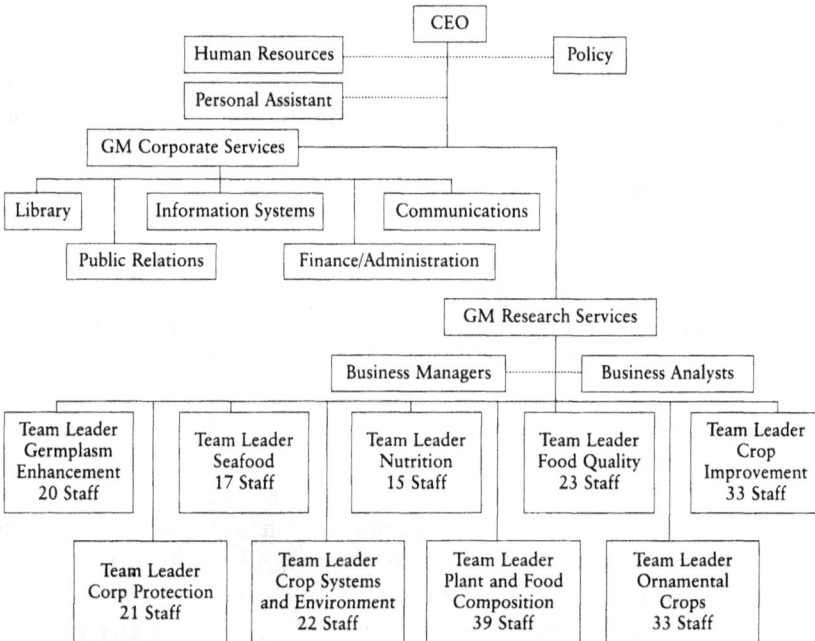

and application of its activity. In one sense, then, the cycle of funding is thus reversed, where government funding is offered to Farmresearch *after* commercial funding has been acquired. Success in achieving commercial funding indicates to government that the research is 'relevant', 'near-market' and therefore worthy of taxpayers' money. The commercial viability of research becomes the measure of government funding. The restructuring of Farmresearch in order to position it more effectively to work with industry requires the alignment of organizational structure with a commercialized strategy. The key issue in organizational restructuring then, becomes one of designing a structure and work that fits a commercialized environment.

THE COMMERCIALIZATION OF SCIENTIFIC RESEARCH: CURRENT STRUCTURAL, CULTURAL AND PEOPLE MANAGEMENT ISSUES

The restructuring of Farmresearch (Figure 2) has a clear focus on the importance of teams, rather than divisions (Figure 1). The most obvious effect of this is that groups of scientists now work in units of between 15 and 39 staff instead of the 80+ person groups of the divisional structure. The rationale for this change is that structurally smaller units and sub-units can be more responsive to commercial needs. The divisional structure was considered too cumbersome and was perceived as promoting large empire building rather than interdisciplinary team building. Furthermore, it was felt that the new structure of small cross-disciplinary teams would be more flexible and would generate more innovation. A further important element of the restructuring was the appointment of a General Manager, Science who had a commercial background and orientation.

The approach to aligning organizational structure with environmental changes is one that follows the advice of the management literature, where teams are generally viewed as enabling organizations to be more 'lean' and 'customer-focussed' (Holbeche, 1998; Haskins, 1998; Mintzberg *et al.*, 1996). However, a major problem with the manner in which the restructuring has taken place at Farmresearch is the lack of concern shown to effective implementation (Moorhead and Griffin, 1998). For the introduction of teamworking to be effective the implementation has to be extremely well planned in the light of company goals and objectives. In particular, significant amounts of time and energy need to be put into the design of teams, training those in them to operate effectively in a small team environment and the recruitment and selection of team leaders. This implementation has been undertaken too speedily at Farmresearch, leading to poor decisions over team leaders and poorly functioning teams, which has been reflected in high levels of reported conflict and lack of cross-team collaborations. There has been and continues to be a lack of effective management of change in order to realize the benefits of restructuring.

Ongoing Cultural Adjustment

The new team-based structure at Farmresearch requires team leaders to operate at the interface between science and commerce. Team leaders also interface with the GM Science. Consequently they have a crucial change agent and customer-focused role within Farmresearch. They need to articulate commercial and industry group requirements to research scientists and they need to derive funding streams. They have to build and perpetuate a business-focused culture while managing the production of science that has short-term application and that facilitates a more commercial orientation.

Early evidence suggests that one-year into the new structure, the attitudes of research scientists often remains 'pure'. There remains a substantial lack of 'buy in' to the new commercially driven situation. Changing the mindsets of Farmresearch scientists is, as should have been expected, proving a slow business. Part of the explanation may relate to the fact that seven of the new team leaders were small-team leaders in the divisional environment and one other was a divisional manager. While senior management and the Board have been keen to tinker with the structural arrangements they have been less keen to evaluate the possible 'barriers' to change that may be present in the 'mindsets' of those who have been appointed to restructured positions. Indeed, there has been a total reluctance to go outside of Farmresearch for new staff and management. Senior management at Farmresearch appear unwilling to make the kind of further dramatic change that would be associated with the appointment of outsiders, should they be available. This is likely to slow the pace of change.

HUMAN RESOURCE MANAGEMENT ISSUES

Structural reconfigurations are only one aspect of organizational change processes at Farmresearch as NPM has been implemented. Strategies for change need also to consider the specific strategies for the management of people if the change is to have any chance of success.

Strategic HRM

The literature on strategic human resource management (HRM) emphasizes the importance of aligning HRM strategy with business strategy in one of two ways – either through the matching model or the capability model (Boxall, 1995). The matching model argues that HRM strategies, policies and practice should support the strategy of the business directly. So, if an organization seeks to gain competitive advantage through innovative products or services, it needs to ensure that appropriate people are recruited, selected and trained, and that reward systems support innovative behaviours. The capability model proposes that some organizations may seek to build their competitive advantage on the people themselves. It may be the case, for example, that the advantage of professional service firms is built on the 'intellectual capital' of the partners, or their particular expertise in a specific area.

HR policies and practices that support HR strategy are important in assisting change or in cementing it. It is through strategic HRM practices that organizations can begin to develop a new culture and direct preferred behaviours. Clearly this is not a simple task as has been recognized in the literature (Mabey and Salaman, 1995). It is difficult to develop such strategies in R&D environments in particular (Randle, 1997). Managers at Farmresearch are generally underskilled in people-management strategies and practices and will need to become adept at developing appropriate people-management systems if they are to facilitate and embed 'real' change within the organization.

Of particular importance for Farmresearch to realize its strategy – to generate more commercial funding for science research – is the requirement to develop a team-based organization. The restructuring represented in Figure 3 was focussed on smaller, cross-disciplinary teams with a team leader who acted as the interface between the teams of scientists, the market and the GM

Science. The role of team leader in this new arrangement is therefore critical. While it is the responsibility of the team leader to coordinate a range of research activities within their team, the scientists in research project area sub-teams will also need to be interfacing with customers and industry groups. Such a focus of activity has clear implications for HR strategy and practice, as Table 1 identifies. The new direction and strategy for the organization will require management to reappraise HR strategy and practice in order to develop alignment in support of the strategy. Table 1 shows how, as the structure of the organization of scientific research changes, human resource requirements in support of a new structure and strategy also change. These issues are considered in more detail in the following sections.

TABLE 1
HOW CHANGES IN STRUCTURE WILL AFFECT HR PRACTICES

HR Area/ → Organizational ↓ Structure	Staffing	Rewards	Performance Management	Training & Development
Government-funded Bureaucracy	Technical skills	Seniority/ length of service	Unrelated to budgetary constraints	Little beyond updating science skills
Divisionalized Structure	Primarily technical skills	More directed towards attraction of funding	Attraction of funding	Little beyond updating science skills
Team-based Structure	Technical skills and interpersonal relationship-building competencies	Related to customer orientation and the development of business	Attracting clients and meeting deliverables	Interpersonal skills, business awareness, account management, relationship-building etc

Staffing

In the area of staffing, Farmresearch has a documented process that begins with the job description, advertising a vacancy, creating a shortlist based on CVs and then selecting based on interviewing and references. This is a system that fits well with the operation of a large bureaucracy, and although it is a process that does not necessarily conflict with the current strategy it does not support it. There has been little or no reconsideration of the staffing approach in the light of new business realities or new structures. In particular, there remains an emphasis on technical skills in the selection process and there is little or no emphasis given to interpersonal skills and customer focussed research activity or relationship building. In addition, the techniques used to recruit (primarily the interview), have not been reviewed in the light of the new organizational strategy. Furthermore, evidence from Farmresearch suggests the employment interviews tend to be rather unstructured and haphazard affairs.

The appointment of team leaders was generally undertaken with little regard for the skill requirements in the new environment, none were recruited externally and those appointed internally were not given additional training and development. While this shows a commitment to current staff in the organization, from a business point of view it is an ineffective use of human resource management tools and techniques to facilitate cultural change. Overall the recruitment and selection systems do not support the direction of change that is currently Farmresearch strategy.

Rewards and Performance Management Systems

The issue of how to reward people in R&D environments is a subject of considerable debate (Randle, 1997). When new business strategies require rewards systems to move towards performance-related pay schemes the situation in R&D environments becomes very complex. Randle (1997), for example, argues in his case of pharmaceutical research that, in a situation of

> intensifying competition and restructuring, we see a growing belief among Pharmex employees that performance indicators will be used to determine something more fundamental than the annual pay increase. The outcome of pay review, providing clear classifications of performances as 'good' or 'poor', may be used to determine who is retained and who is not.

This is similar to the situation at Farmresearch. In the government-funded bureaucracy a job for life with annual salary increments was the norm. Scientists could get on with the job of 'doing' interesting science. However, the changed environment has completely altered the appropriateness of this. If the objective of the rewards strategy is now to support the organizational strategy there needs to be the sort of focus highlighted in Table I; with rewards related to business development and meeting customer requirements. Of course, such a shift in rewards strategy presents obvious problems. For example, while salaries may not have been overly generous in a government-funded research environment, the relative freedom to pursue autonomous research agendas was a source of intrinsic reward. In a commercially focussed environment this sort of reward will no longer exist in this form. The nature of the intrinsic rewards that can be offered changes fundamentally in a commercialized environment. Such rewards may not relate to the high degree of autonomy and discretion available in choice of research, but may relate to the rewards that can be got from the pursuit and development of business and the satisfaction of customer needs. This is a very different type of intrinsic reward that may require an entirely different kind of scientist.

Where the emphasis is on the development of a commercial focus it is likely that those who have a 'need' for this, or who will be intrinsically motivated by the possibility of achieving the associated goals, should be recruited to these positions. Those interested in 'core' science will continue in 'core' science roles. The problem here is that those interested in 'core' science are often those interested in 'pure' science, and they may be difficult to manage in the new environment and may have a problem committing themselves to it. This is particularly the case if being commercially focussed requires a more short-term view of research, with companies requiring speedy returns on their investments.

Farmresearch has yet to deal with these issues appropriately and effectively. Staff below team leader level are employed on a collective contract where salaries are determined by job size (which relates to positioning of jobs in an evaluated banding structure), market rate and performance. Within the evaluated bands there are three milestones. The market rate element is related to a variety of industry surveys, while the performance element is related to an annual performance review. Theoretically the review is conducted within the context of a performance management system and performance is rated against a set of objectives that have been established in the performance planning process. From the review of performance a recommendation is made regarding whether salary should be reviewed or a bonus paid. A view is also taken as to whether the banding/milestone of the staff member should be reviewed. Once a recommendation is made from project leader to team leader there is consultation with other team leaders in order to ensure the maintenance of relativities.

Theoretically the system is well structured. Like many performance review systems there are key elements that need to exist in order for it to work well:

- The establishment of fair and equitable objectives.

- The opportunity for staff to realize the objectives.

- Line and project managers must operate the performance review process systematically and professionally.

- It should be entirely clear how bands and milestones are objectively different.

- It should be clear why bonuses are paid.

- It should be clear as to why relativities are maintained.

In addition to these issues is the question as to whether the system supports the new strategy of 'business development and meeting customer needs.

A major problem with the way the process operates at Farmresearch is that after the recommendation has been made by the line/project manager the process becomes unpredictable and lacks transparency. Furthermore, the feedback process is often non-existent. The review operates as an evaluation of performance at a specific point in time without a developmental aspect. In addition, whatever the outcome of the review in terms of recommendations it is often not traceable to the line/project managers. A further major deficiency of the system relates to the link between 'performance' and business strategy. The management of performance in the above review process is detached from the requirements of the business strategy. If management at Farmresearch are to use the process to facilitate change in the organization, these two processes must be linked. The system that operates is one that fits a more bureaucratic situation and there is no relationship between the measurement of performance and business development (increased funding) and customer satisfaction. Consequently, rewards remain distinct from clear performance indicators that add value to the business. Like the present system of recruitment and selection the performance management system does not support the business strategy in the new environment. Indeed, it may actually detract from achievement of the strategy.

There is a considerable need to align the performance management system and the rewards management system with the new direction of the business. However, such alignment is not easy to achieve. The required changes to HRM systems lag behind the structural changes that have been made. Cultural change (defined here specifically as the norms and values of staff) is also slow and will lag behind structural change. This is particularly so since little 'new blood' has been introduced into the organization. In short, we can identify at Farmresearch, as a consequence of the introduction of NPM, a number of internal changes that are occurring at varying degrees of speed (Figure 3). The speed with which the changes occur will relate to the degree of adjustment the business and its people have made. Senior management and the Board in response to political pressures have initiated structural changes. However, there has been little significant thought given over to the support of structural change through the strategic management of norms and values (meaning), or HRM systems and practices. And, in any case, the psychological transition required of staff, few of whom are new to the organization, is unlikely to occur as quickly as structural changes are made.

FIGURE 3

CHANGE MOMENTUM

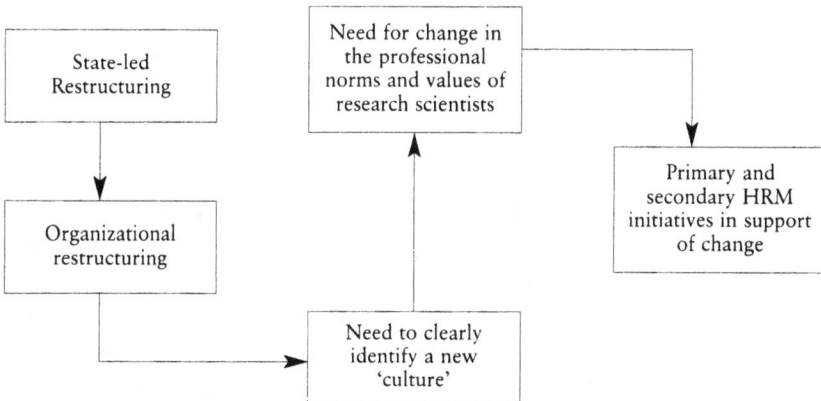

Aligning Rewards with the New Organizational Focus

Strategic HRM suggests that in order to support a commercially focussed strategy reward systems need to be aligned with the strategy. One approach currently under review at Farmresearch is to introduce profit-related bonuses at the team level. The rationale for this is that at a team level the connection between increasing profit and team effort is easier to identify than if profit-related bonuses were operated at a wider organizational level. While such a proposal has some merit it may actually deter inter-team collaboration, because teams may wish to protect a new idea, method or approach. Furthermore, there is an assumption implicit in the proposals that the scientists are ready for a commercially driven approach, which is not in reality quite yet the case. The introduction of the profit-motive into scientific research adds a dimension that most CRI staff have never before experienced and are unlikely to accept immediately.

Team leaders at Farmresearch do, however, now have their rewards more appropriately aligned with the new organizational direction. They receive a base salary and an additional performance-based component. One of the components is profit related, although other measured components are staff satisfaction, customer satisfaction, and number of cross-team projects. Detailed criteria have been introduced to measure these factors. It is as yet too early to identify whether the process is being successful. Furthermore, there will be a need to review the reward and performance management systems in place for other roles and positions in the new organization structure, for example for research project managers. There remains a great deal of work to be undertaken to align reward systems and management at Farmresearch with the new organizational focus and strategy.

Human Resource Development

Like other elements of the Human Resource Management system, human resources development (HRD) is strategically critical in the process of organizational change. Farmresearch, by the very nature of its business, has a huge commitment to staff development. However, the majority of this development is not focussed on supporting the new strategy for the business, and it is often not directed on 'skill' upgrading but is used by management as a reward, as a bribe or to gain favour.

There is a definite need to undertake a comprehensive training and development needs analysis, and to structure the use of training as a strategic tool designed to facilitate organizational change. There also needs to be some conceptualization of the relationship between staff development, business development and organizational learning. Of course, a move in this direction raises the same issues as those related to other aspects of the people management system. There is, in this new commercially focussed environment, a very obvious move away from the 'culture' of 'pure science'. The development of 'business skills' emerges as equal to, if not more important than, the 'doing of science' and there remains substantial resistance to such training within Farmresearch.

SUMMARY

This essay has attempted to trace the relationship between the introduction of NPM in the management of scientific research in New Zealand and its implications for organizational restructuring and changes in HRM systems. NPM in New Zealand has been introduced through privatization, deregulation, commercialization and corporatization, and of course these activities have been a feature of global developments in the management of the public sector over the past 20 years. What the introduction of NPM does is to require micro-level restructurings and redesigned organizational practices. The primary concern of this essay has been to describe the restructuring of scientific research in New Zealand in order to highlight the complexities and difficulties involved in moving from publicly funded to commercially funded research, and the implications of this for issues of organizational design and human resource management. The introduction of NPM in any societal context will create micro-management issues and problems. This case study of scientific research in New Zealand highlights the difficulties of managing changes at the micro-level as the processes of globalization increasingly require that research is accountable to the forces of global business, rather than the state.

NOTE

1. The names of these government departments have been changed.

REFERENCES

Bosanquet, N. (1983), *After the New Right*. London: Heinemann.

Boxall, P. (1995), 'Business Strategy, Human Resource Management and Executive Leadership' in P. Boxall (ed.), *The Challenge of Human Resource Management*. New Zealand: Longman Paul.

Brittan, S. (1984), 'The Politics and Economics of Privatisation', *Political Quarterly*, Vol.55.

Carnell, C. (1995), *Managing Change in Organizations*. London: Prentice Hall.

Common, R.K. (1998), 'Convergence and Transfer: A Review of the Globalisation of New Public Management', *International Journal of Public Sector Management*, Vol.11, No.6, pp.440–50.

Dahrendorf, R. (1995), 'Preserving Prosperity', *New Statesman and Society*, Vol.15 (29 December).

Dunleavy, P. (1994), 'The Globalization of Public Services Production: Can Government Be 'Best in the World'?, *Public Policy and Administration* Vol.9, No.2, pp.36–64.

Haskins, M. E., Liedtka, J. and Rosenblum, J. (1998), 'Beyond Teams: Toward an Ethic of Collaboration', *Organizational Dynamics*, Vol.2.

Held, D. and McGrew, A. (1993), 'Globalization and the Liberal Democratic State', *Government and Opposition*, Vol.28, No.2, pp.261–85.

Holbeche, L. (1998), *Motivating People in the Lean Organisation*. Oxford: Blackwell.

Hood, C. (1994), *Explaining Economic Policy Reversals*. Buckingham: Open University Press.

Le Grand J. and Robinson, R. (eds.) (1984), *Privatisation and the Welfare State*. London: Unwin.

Le Heron, R. (1993), *Globalized Agriculture*. Oxford: Pergamon Press.

Mabey, C. and Salaman, G 1995), *Strategic Human Resource Management*. Oxford: Blackwell.

Martin, B. (1993), *In the Public Interest?* London: Zed.

McGrew, A. and Lewis, P (1992), 'Conceptualising Global Politics', in McGrew, A., Lewis, P. et al., *Global Politics: Globalization and the Nation State*. Cambridge: Polity Press.

McKenna, S. (1990), 'The Business Ethic in Public Sector Catering', *The Service Industries Journal*, Vol.10, No.2, pp.377–98.

Mintzberg, H., Dougherty, D., Jorgansen, J. and Westley, F. (1996), 'Some Surprising Things About Collaboration: Knowing How People Connect Makes It Work Better', *Organizational Dynamics*, Vol.3.

Moorhead, G. and Griffin, R.W. (1998), *Organizational Behavior*. Boston: Houghton Mifflin.

Randle, K. (1997), 'Rewarding Failure: Operating a Performance-related Pay System in Pharmaceutical Research', *Personnel Review*, Vol.26, No.3.

Spicer, B., Emanuel, D. and Powell, M. (1996), *Transforming Government Enterprises*. Wellington: The Centre for Independent Studies.

Taylor, B. (ed.) (1994), *Successful Change Strategies*. Hemel Hempstead: Director Books.

8

Globalization, Economic Crisis and Employment Practices: Lessons from a Large Malaysian Islamic Institution

PAWAN BUDHWAR and KHAIRUL FADZIL

The last two decades have witnessed a rapid increase in the globalization of business. Developments in the fields of information technology, manufacturing technology, transportation, trade liberalization, emergence of new markets and increase in foreign direct investments have contributed significantly in this regard. The concept of a 'global village' has now become a reality. Frenkel and Peetz (1998: 282) define globalization as the processes that reduce barriers between countries, thereby encouraging closer integration of economic, political and social activity. Globalization is known to have a large number of implications: it increases level of competition, affects employment, distribution of income, and labour standards (ILO, 1998; Lee, 1997), it increases foreign direct investments, international trade, growth of multinational institutions, cross-national mergers and acquisitions, changes in institutional rules governing ownership and investment (Frenkel and Peetz, 1998), results in liberalization of markets, privatization of productive assets and deregulation of financial assets (Lee, 1996). Globalization also has significant effects on the terms and conditions, industrial relations and work organization (see Bacon and Blyton, 1999; Frenkel and Peetz, 1998). It also gives rise to labour inequalities (Wood, 1998).

Nevertheless, it is clear that as a result of globalization, businesses the world over seem to have become more interdependent then ever. It is also true that the present globalized businesses are more susceptible to economic disturbances. The so-called 'butterfly effect' has now become a regular feature. The recent Asian economic turmoil, the existing Russian political and economic crisis and the economic crisis in Brazil are some of its examples. In the present globalized world, the external environmental threats and opportunities for business are many and their nature is complex. In order to survive and achieve competitive advantage, organizations are now required to regularly change (perhaps in the form restructuring, re-engineering or downsizing) to adapt to the rapidly changing environment.

Most of the industrialized countries are already deeply enmeshed in globalization and are taking steps both to maximize its benefits and make the adjustments it demands. But there are wide differences in the readiness of developing countries to face the global economic integration (Kleinknecht and Wengel, 1998). This is mainly because they are increasingly heterogeneous in their degree of development, productive capacity, human resource base and competitiveness. Some of the developing countries (such as in East Asia) which have improved their local conditions for entrepreneurship and have expanded their domestic capacities to produce and export, have moved quickly into the mainstream global trade and investment flows. In fact, the great leap forward made in the Asia Pacific region, with long-term growth figures of up to 7 per cent per annum, gave new vigour to the process of globalization (Rosewarne, 1998).

However, it seems that these countries (such as the Dragon, Tiger and ASEAN nations) have progressed in this regard much faster then expected and without adequately preparing themselves for it – developing appropriate credit controls, mechanisms for repayments, transparency in the working of financial institutions and control over nepotism (Breman, 1998; Rana, 1997). Such factors are crucial for the smooth functioning of economies in transition (for example, from state-regulated to market-oriented economies). If not properly adhered to, then they could be disastrous. A good example of this is the East Asian economic crisis of 1997.

In such business conditions, among other factors, the effective utilization of human resources (HRs), the role of internal labour markets (ILMs) and organizational culture become critical for the success of organizations. Further, research shows that a number of both external factors and organizational contingencies strongly influence an organization's human resource management (HRM) policies, ILMs and culture (Hendry and Pettigrew, 1992; Pettigrew et al., 1988). These three topics form a significant part of an organization's internal interactive process and reflect employees' cultural characteristics. At times, religion constitutes a significant part of this cultural 'baggage' (Baligh, 1998; Tayeb, 1997).

Recently, a new emphasis regarding the role of religious principles in the successful management of organizations is emerging in the literature (see Friedman, 1999; Lipford *et al.*, 1993; Yarwood, 1993). The influence of Islam seems to be more dominating than other religions. Since Islam is prominent in over 50 countries and seems to play a significant role in the formation of management practices (especially related to finance and accounting) in many Muslim countries (Conway, 1995; Presley and Sessions, 1994), it could be of interest to people and organizations who wish to do business with them, such as multinationals, trade partners and international joint ventures.

The existing literature also shows an increasing trend of successful organizations (mainly in Muslim-dominated countries) run on Islamic principles (Guan, 1998; Haron, 1996). There are also some indications that such organizations function successfully and out-perform others not only under normal conditions but even in turbulent times (for example, in the recent Asian crisis). Why does this happen? It seems that HRM policies and practices, ILMs, and the organizational culture of an organization that has developed on the basis of Islamic principles in a primarily Muslim country strongly reflect Islamic values held by their people. This helps to bind the people together. The advent of Islam, therefore, seems to result in a greater systematization of various socio-economic processes (Baligh, 1998; Singh, 1993; Tayeb, 1997).

Research in the field of globalization and internationalization of business suggests the need to give due consideration to the local/regional forces which dictate norms and practices at the work place (see for example Tayeb, 1999). There seems to be some kind of parallel development taking place between the increasing levels of globalization of business and the flourishing of Islam world-wide. On the one hand, MNCs are diffusing best practice across national borders (Mueller, 1994); on the other hand, a diverse work force with different religious backgrounds (which is on a continuous increase as a result of globalization) bring their beliefs into the job with them (Ettorre, 1996). It is now increasingly acknowledged that an environment of tolerance and respect towards such diversity results in more productivity and high morale

(Digh, 1998). With more than 5 million adherents, Islam is expected to soon surpass Judaism as the second most commonly practised religion in the US. It is one of the fastest expanding religions world-wide.[1] In view of such developments, HR professionals should be familiar with the fundamental tenets of Islamic principles and should consider both Muslim employees and customers when designing their policies and programmes (Minehan, 1998).

An attempt has been made in this essay to further elaborate and empirically test the above briefed assumptions. The main aims are threefold:

- To examine and discuss how and why a large Malaysian financial institution run on Islamic principles prospered even in the recent economic crisis.

- To highlight the key role that both external factors (Malaysian work culture and Islamic principles) and internal factors (such as ILMs, organizational culture and HRM) can play in enabling firms to continuously improve their performance and achieve a competitive advantage.

- To highlight the main implications of the growth of Islam for the globalization of business.

The main research was conducted in one of the major Islamic financial institutions of Malaysia. However, relevant literature is also used to draw conclusions.

CONTEXT: FROM MIRACLE TO CRISIS

In the early 1950s, the Asian population was considered as the poorest in the world. Most of the indicators of economic and social development showed Asia even behind Latin American countries. A large population base, a small domestic market and poor purchasing power were some of the significant problems for Asia's poor economic performance (Tan, 1992). However, things changed rapidly and until very recently, Asia (especially the Asia Pacific region) was considered as the fastest growing region in the world. For example, in the last 35 years, the GDP of Taiwan increased 19-fold, Singapore and South Korea 17-fold, and Hong Kong 12-fold. Japan outperformed all these nations (Lee, 1996). During this time the ASEAN nations showed a strong march towards globalization, marked by a 17 per cent increase of both merchandise exports and imports (WTO, 1996: 22). East Asia also accounted for nearly a quarter of total world FDI inflows in 1994 (UNCTAD, 1995). The development economists were so impressed by East Asia's success that they named this phenomenon the 'Asian Miracle'. Globalization of business made a strong contribution to this. Despite the homogeneity of the region, the economic success has been more or less uniform. What other factors contributed to this? A number of debates took place as to why East Asia was so successful. Broadly speaking, some of the main factors being highlighted in the literature in this regard are: Confucius cultures, Asian values, social structure and overseas Chinese networks, political stability and 'soft authoritarianism', emphasis on export orientation, investment in education, the role of conglomerates and enterprise groups and sound macro economies (for details on Asian Miracle see Anwar, 1997; Wee and Tan, 1997).

However, the expansion of the East Asian economies was suddenly halted by the recent economic crisis. The economic turmoil which swept the South East Asian region over the last two years or so has affected Malaysia's economy as a whole. Beginning with economic turmoil in South Korea, it led to the currency attack on the Thai baht in mid 1997. The crisis quickly spread to other countries of the region. The Philippines' peso, Indonesia's rupiah and Malaysia's ringgit were badly affected. However, the Singaporian dollar was said to be the least affected by the turmoil. Much of the blame has been laid on strict IMF policies for the economic restructuring of the East Asian economies. High interest rates, loan restrictions, transparencies and other tighter-control policies required by the IMF are seen as unsuitable for these countries.

Economists have drawn many assumptions as to the causes of the turmoil. Prominent among these are corruption, irresponsible domestic governance, property speculation, undisclosed debts, nepotism/favouritism, willingness of both the domestic and foreign banks to over-lend, poorly enforced financial regulations, 'cosy' government business relations, over-ambitious domestic projects, poor business decision making, currency speculation, over-diversification, excess consumer spending (on imported items), withdrawal by foreign investors, rogue traders, financial liberalization and low interest rates. A number of these factors are related to the globalization of business (for more details on Asian crisis see Burkett and Hart-Landsberg, 1998; Chang *et al.*, 1998; Lo, 1999; Patibandla and Prusty, 1998).

In the case of Malaysia, the turmoil was the result of an attack on the ringgit by currency speculators which led to its devaluation. This consequently influenced overseas loan repayments and weakened the confidence of the stock market (Jomo, 1998). The reaction did not stop there. As more money had to be used for these unexpected consequences, the government had to cut back on spending. The Malaysian economy is mainly generated and assisted by government projects (Pearson and Entrekin, 1998). If the government is forced to abort or suspend projects, companies in all sectors of the economy are affected.

Before the crisis, in 1996 the GDP of Malaysia was stable at 8.6 per cent. Malaysia emphasized important aspects of globalization such as continuous expansion of international trade and inward investment. The Malaysian government encouraged an export-oriented industrialization and urged its firms to emulate Japan and has courted Japanese investment and technological cooperation (Frenkel and Peetz, 1998). Between the time period of 1991–95, Malaysia's exports as a percentage of GDP was 85.2, imports as a percentage of GDP was 86.5, inward FDI as a percentage of gross fixed capital formation was 21.3 and outward FDI as a percentage of gross fixed capital formation at 5.7 (World Bank, 1997). But the crisis hit Malaysia hard and in 1998 the economy experienced a contraction of 3.8 per cent and 6.0 per cent during the first and second quarters respectively (Central Bank of Malaysia, 1998). This gave a sudden shock to businesses. The high interest rates, currency devaluation and demand reduction lead to an increase in the non-performance loans and bankruptcies. The consequences of the economic slowdown have direct implications for most organizations and their employees.

Companies facing high operating costs together with reduced income might focus on employees to cut their costs. Reducing remuneration benefits such as bonus and commission along with reduced working hours, salaries, retrenchment reorganization or rightsizing are seen as some of the short-term measures against the crisis (Chow, 1998; Rajkumar, 1998). This resulted in a strong reduction in the demand for labour and an increase in the level of redundancies and unemployment. Malaysia's unemployment rate went up to five per cent in 1998 and is expected to go up to six per cent by the end of the year 2000 (Berita Harian, 1998).

For countries with a good welfare system, the economic pressures faced by the unemployed workers are lessened by unemployment benefits. But for countries such as Malaysia and other developing nations, the unexpected economic meltdown has hit individuals very hard, as there is hardly any state welfare system to look after workers during the times of economic crisis (Myerson, 1996). There is then a strong need for individuals to have some sort of savings plans. Any organization fulfilling such requirements (along with other factors which can increase employees' loyalty and improve employee relations) is deemed to be successful. It seems that organizations run on Islamic principles (especially the one under investigation) provide such benefits to their employees and have developed a unique set of ILMs.

In brief, the study of ILMs is important to an organization as it provides alternatives to improve the organizational function and its efficiency, optimize the organization's operational costs and enable it to cope with a competitive business environment. The ILM is usually associated with job tenure, internal mobility, job grades, rules governing promotion, deployment, transfers and lay-off (Turner, 1994). ILM and HRM are closely linked to each other (for details see Jacoby, 1985).

Empirical studies by Pfeffer and Cohen (1984) and Baker et al. (1994) suggest that ILMs can lead to an adequate supply of highly trained workers and minimize the effect of demotivation due to the rise in resentment and grievances among workers. This results in low turnover and high stability in the organization. The development of ILMs is then seen as one of the vital criteria in developing an organization. The existing literature suggests that ILMs are mainly determined by external economic conditions, unions, organizational characteristics (such as size, sector, presence of formal HRM department) and transaction cost theory (for details see Pfeffer and Cohen, 1984; Soeters and Schwan, 1990; Turner, 1994). Apart from those mentioned, it seems that the basic principles on which the very foundations of an organization are based (Islamic principles and Malaysian value system in the present research organization) also contribute to the development of ILMs.

In order to better understand the organization under study, it is necessary to consider the Malaysian work culture, particularly in the Islamic context. This is because national culture is known to influence HRM policies and practices and ILMs, which in turn influence organizational culture (Hofstede, 1993).

MALAYSIAN WORK CULTURE AND ISLAMIC PRINCIPLES

Generally, most Malaysian organizations operate on standard rules and procedures in managing their human resources, but as for rules governing employees' behaviour they have little control over this (Burns, 1998). Malaysia has a close link with the Western human resource code of practice, mainly due to its links with Britain established during the colonial period of the eighteenth and nineteenth centuries. However, as the Japanese surpassed the Western world in economic terms during the third quarter of this century, Malaysian companies have also adopted some Japanese HR philosophies, especially in relation to flexibility, teamwork and total quality management. Hence, Malaysian work culture can be described as a mix of Western and Japanese HR systems (Mansor and Ali, 1998; Pearson and Entrekin, 1998).

'Hiring and Firing' is not common in Malaysia. Until the recent economic crisis, Malaysian firms seldom terminated the service of an employee just because the organization had undergone restructuring or other changes unless the employee had committed a crime or other clearly specified disciplinary action. As a result, there is a lot of internal movement of staff within an organization. As a consequence, this has resulted in the growth of strong ILMs in Malaysian organizations. In addition, most Malaysian organizations practise 'a job for life' approach by regarding employees as an organization's greatest asset. Moreover, part-time employment is not common in the Malaysian labour market (Tsuruoka, 1993).

Islam, the dominant religion in Malaysia, influences management practices (Yong, 1996). Islam is not merely a religion. It is a way of life. The *Quran* (the Holy book of Islam) lays out principles for its followers on how to approach everyday life. These include attitude, working life, leadership etc. The challenges for management of any Islamic institution is to meld the principles with most management styles which are otherwise based on the Western system (*The Economist*, 1993). Most of the literature on the Islamic system makes a cross-reference to the financial system which has been growing at a rapid pace in recent years. Actually, the Islamic system goes much further than this. Islam emphasizes ethical, moral, social and religious principles to ensure 'equality' and 'fairness' for the whole of the society (Iqbal, 1997). Sherif (1975) identified nobility, patience, self-discipline, sincerity, truthfulness, and trust as major Islamic values. Similarly, Endot (1995) found 11 basic values of Islam: trustworthiness, responsibility, sincerity, discipline, dedication, diligence, cleanliness, cooperation, good conduct, gratefulness and moderation. Apart from these, Islam also encourages consultation at all levels of decision making, and loyalty to one's family and at the work-place to one's superior (for more details see Tayeb, 1997). These criteria apply not only to the economic and financial aspects of business but to the way people are managed and should also be incorporated in the management of its stakeholders.

During the early establishment of Islamic financial services, there were arguments about their poor performance in relation to liquidity and instrumentation. For example, in the area of 'interest free' credit, 'shared risk' between banks and individuals or organizations (Angell, 1995). However, now they seem to be attracting more businesses, and this sector has been growing globally at a rate of over 15 per cent annually for the past five years (Timewell, 1998). Instead of focusing on the economic details, this research primarily concentrates on the role of Islamic values on the management of human resources and the implementation of Islamic principles within the organization under study.

Islamic practices require a true Muslim to base their career and lifestyle on its principles. For example, the issue of *riba* presents a problem for an organization such as the one under study. Riba literally means 'an excess' and is interpreted as 'any unjustifiable increase of capital whether in loans or sales' (for details see Shepherd, 1996). This can be categorized as *interest* in capitalist nations. It has proved to be a challenge to follow the norms of a global economy that relies on the principle of interest in its day-to-day management. Matters dealing with loans, savings and profits mostly involve issues related to interest. It is not true that Islam is against profitability, but the way profit is made needs to be clearly defined.

Every prohibition by Islam has its explanation. Regarding the matter of *riba*, the prohibition is based on the arguments for social justice, equality and property rights. Islam encourages its followers to earn a profit as it is a symbol of successful entrepreneurship, but forbids the charging or gaining of interest (Angell, 1994). This represents a cost that is accrued irrespective of the outcome of business operations and may not create wealth if there are losses in the business. In linking social justification and prohibition, Islam demands that borrowers and lenders should share rewards as well as losses. In this sense, the process of the accumulation and distribution of an economy's wealth is to be conducted in fairness (Iqbal, 1997). Serious attempts have been made to inculcate this principle in the culture of the organization under study.

Generally, economic factors play an important role in every individual's life, irrespective of race or religion. Islam puts a much broader perspective on this. There is a verse in the Quran which says:

> individual is encouraged to strive for success as if he or she would live for thousand of years while at the same time, being devoted to religion as if he or she would die the next day.

According to this, individuals should balance their everyday necessities and needs and their devotion to religion. There is a requirement within Islam to ask for its *ummah* (that is, to work collectively as a nation of Islam) to find a source of income which is *halal*, that is, a source of lawful action which is within acceptable Islamic principles. Therefore, to be in an organization that practises Islamic principles in its day-to-day operations is highly sought by a good Muslim. Monetary reward is not the ultimate purpose in life. Other expectations such as self-fulfilment and self-satisfaction play important roles.

The implementation of Malaysian values such as flexibility with Islamic practices which emphasize ethical, social and moral issues can build a strong culture for any organization. This can also contribute to the development of a unique ILM. This in turn can create a competitive advantage for the organization by differentiating it from other organizations (Barney, 1991; Porter, 1985). From the perspective of employee relations, culture can provide a strong foundation for the HRM function. As adaptability of HRM policies within the organization is optimized, employees will become more aware of the organization's mission and vision, and managing changes will be much easier as employees and employer share common values. A strong culture (emphasizing the well-being of its employees) along with the firm's HRM and ILM commitments can prepare an organization to face any challenges (such as those arising from the recent economic crisis, which has resulted in large-scale reengineering and restructuring in Malaysian organizations).

METHODOLOGY

An interview-based case study method was adopted for this research. The organization for this study ('TH' is its research name) was selected due to its unique contribution to the Malaysian economy and its international operations. It is an Islamic financial institution set up by the government to handle matters pertaining to *Hajj* participation by Muslims. At the same time, it manages their savings by investing them in the businesses acceptable within Islamic principles. There are two reasons why such an institution is important to Malaysia. First, the Muslim community comprises 61 per cent of the 24 million people in Malaysia. Second, performing *Hajj* in Mecca is an obligation for every Muslim at least once in their lifetime. Due to the nature of the organization, the entire work force of TH is Muslim.

Data Collection

Primary data was collected by interviewing 11 employees of TH. They belonged to the management, supervisory and operational levels. The selection of interviewees was based on their functional specialization, length of service and involvement directly or indirectly in the recent restructuring. Two interviewees each were from the finance, personnel and administrative/quality departments and one each was from the investment development, deposit and *Hajj* services department. To assess the union–employer relationship, two representatives from the trade union were also interviewed. On average, the interviews lasted under two hours. They were recorded and, later, transcribed. Secondary data was collected from the organization's annual reports, policy documents and related books.

A semi-structured interview schedule was used. The main topics of discussion during the interviews consisted of the history and organization of TH, economic crisis and restructuring, culture, employee relations, HRM practices, impact of the economic crisis on management practices and ILMs and organization details. Consultations with experts in the field were also sought to form the interview-schedule. It was piloted and required changes were made. As the Malaysian government requires and encourages the use of Malay (the national language) in any correspondence with all government organizations, the interview-schedule was therefore translated into Malay. The interview data was content analysed.

HISTORY OF THE ORGANIZATION

TH was initially created by the government to specifically act as a trust in which Muslims can build up their savings to be used for pilgrimage to the Holy Land of Mecca in Saudi Arabia. It was first incorporated as *Perbadanan Wang Simpanan Bakal-Bakal Haji* (Malayan Muslim Pilgrims' Saving Corporation) in 1962. Prior to that, all matters concerning the pilgrimage to Mecca were handled by the Pilgrims' Control Office (set up in 1951). Although this body was set up to handle pilgrimage matters, it lacked the essential feature of handling the pilgrims' savings. Therefore, in 1969, through the merger of the Corporation and the Pilgrims' Control Office and with the enactment of Malaysian Law Act 8, Lembaga Urusan Dan TH Act 1969, saw the birth of The Hajj Trust and Management Board.

Basically, TH was established for two main reasons:

- To render the best services to Malaysian Pilgrims throughout the performance of *Hajj*. *Hajj* can only be performed during the month of *Zulkaedah*, the eleventh month in Islamic calendar, while *Umrah* can be performed in any month.

- To give maximum return on pilgrims' savings by investing in activities accepted by Syariah laws. The Appendix describes the five main Syariah laws.

TH has four main categories of employees: the top management, management and professionals (such as accountants, finance managers, HR manager), support staff (such as clerks, typists) and others (includes for example drivers, dispatch persons). Table 1 shows changes in the proportion of TH's employees over the past six years.

TABLE 1
TH's WORKFORCE STATISTICS

Type of Employees	1992	1993	1994	1995	1996	1997
Top Management	3	3	3	3	3	3
Management and Professionals	69	68	66	66	78	80
Support	962	941	931	916	889	915
Others	16	26	24	20	19	19
Total	1050	1038	1024	1005	989	1017

Source: TH's Annual Reports

TH, during the past few years, has re-positioned itself to be more of a proactive player in the Malaysian economy. Beginning with agricultural based investment, it has diversified its portfolio management into other sectors of the economy such as travel, catering, properties, information technology, construction, project management and engineering maintenance. In addition to investment in Saudi Arabia, mainly in properties (for the benefit of pilgrims performing *Hajj* or *Umrah*), TH has also expanded into Indonesia and the Philippines by purchasing land for plantation.

TH's Restructuring Process

The restructuring process took place in 1995; its main aim was to improve TH's response to changes in the market place (both local and global). The high growth of Malaysian GDP during the period and the increased awareness of Muslim confidence in Islamic banking principles caused the government to reposition TH. The enactment of the 1995 Act gave TH more room to manoeuvre its strategic matters with minimum interference of the government. The changes were to ensure TH's effectiveness in the economy. Therefore, in 1995, the structure of the organization was changed. The whole process took almost two years to complete.

During this time, apart from replacing the position of MD by a CEO, three new departments have been created. These are the Saudi Arabia Office, the Computer/IT division and the Depositors Service department. Technological advancement and increases in the number of pilgrims necessitated these changes. Management felt that the previous structure was no longer effective for the smooth running of pilgrimage affairs. In addition, TH also invested in Saudi Arabia, mainly in buildings for the benefit of pilgrims. This Saudi Arabia office could closely manage TH's assets there and at

TABLE 2
TH's DEPOSITORS, 1992-95

Depositors	1992	1993	1994	1995
Cumulative	2,200,202	2,347,684	2,536,582	2,737,567
New	147,621	167,621	188,898	200,985

Source: TH's Annual Reports

the same time, build up a good relationship with the Saudi Arabian government.

As TH's deposits have been continuously increasing annually (see Table 2), it was felt that TH should become more customer oriented. In this regard, the Depositors' Services department was created. It consists of three sections, namely, the Branch Operation, Savings and Withdrawals, and Marketing. The first two sections were originally under the Finance department but were transferred to this new department to ensure effectiveness and efficiency. The transfer also gave TH the opportunity to improve its communication within and between departments and consequently reduce any confusion between them. As competition increased due to the introduction of Islamic banking system in local banks, the Marketing section was created to facilitate strategies to boost TH's image in the market. The other new department of Computer/IT division was created in response to the current technological innovation and the government inspiration to establish Malaysia as the centre of IT excellence (the Malaysian government is promoting the multi-media super corridor (MSC) as part of its vision for the next century).

The challenges imposed by the political, sociological and business environment inspired TH to improve the way it operated. For this reason, not only the names of the three main departments (that is, 'Finance', 'Investment' and 'Administration' were changed to 'Finance & Asset Management', 'Investment Development' and 'Administration and Quality' respectively) were changed, but their functional scope was also increased. For instance, the Finance & Asset Management department now involves not only financial matters but also share, investment and property management. Other significant changes in the department were the transfer of the withdrawal and saving and computer section to the new depositors services department and the creation of a separate new division. The Investment Development department is now responsible for the development of TH's investments such as in land, engineering, domestic and overseas, and has a much clearer vision of executing its responsibilities. Finally, the Administration and Quality department is now actively involved in the strategic direction of TH. Management perceived that one of TH's strength is its people and that developing their skills and efficiency is vital for its success. Therefore, the Quality department was merged with the Administration department to combine the aspects of quality and people together.

The restructuring process contributed to:

1. *Increased organizational efficiency:* Now there is more clarity in the responsibilities of the departments and divisions.

2. *Improved customer satisfaction:* Now there is greater transparency in responding to customer needs. This has resulted in an increased number of customers over the years. In 1995 there were 2,737,567 depositors and they increased to 3,300,000 in 1997.

3. *Improved employee relations:* Employees have a clearer vision of day-to-day operations and management. This has also increased employees' productivity and reduced conflicts that resulted from miscommunication within departments and divisions. Consequently, the operational cost of managing TH's human resources has been reduced. However, this did not affect employees' job security, satisfaction and confidence in the organization.

The restructuring process basically had no adverse impact on TH's employees in terms of their job security and operations but for the management it gave them the opportunity to reposition and tackle current business pressures. In fact, productivity has increased as communication and performance have improved. In short, TH gained more momentum after the restructuring process. Increased customer confidence together with the diversification strategy have helped it to maintain its competitiveness during the current crisis. This is further discussed in the following section.

ECONOMIC CRISIS AND TH

TH's performance during the crisis seems to be better than other organizations, particularly the financial institutions in Malaysia.

The public confidence in TH has not changed. This is shown by the increase in the number of its depositors. Furthermore, its annual savings have increased from RM 1.76 billion in 1996 to RM 2.14 billion in 1997. Moreover, TH is still able to give a generous dividend to its investors. Its dividend for the financial year ending 1997 was 9.8 per cent, 0.3 per cent higher than the previous year.

The secret behind TH's success during this period can be attributed to several factors. First, is the diversification of its business portfolio. Basically, TH's income was derived from its investment in companies (including its subsidiaries), banks, share transactions and properties. Although the share transaction division was badly hit, its agricultural subsidiaries experienced a good performance in 1997. It contributed a profit of RM 50 million in 1997. Second, in spite of all the restructuring and merging of financial institutions in Malaysia which have resulted in retrenchment and downsizing in many organizations, TH's employees still enjoy job security. The diversification of activities has paid off. In fact, TH can afford to increase its number of employees. By the end of 1999, it was expected to open 22 new branches. Third, a unique ILM has resulted in a motivated, well-trained and loyal work force. Employee relations are good and employee grievances are much less. Fourth, the quality of service provided to customers was not affected by the present crisis. In fact, with an increase in new branches, it is hoped that the service and quality provided to customers will be further improved.

Nevertheless, during this crisis, TH had to cut its annual budget by 18 per cent, abiding by the government's cost cutting exercise. But, with regard to training and development of staff, the only effect of the crisis has been on scholarships for overseas education. Because of the devaluation of the currency, TH had to stop sending students overseas. However, its local university students' sponsorships, in-house training, and staff education have not been affected. One exercise to cut the cost of training but without affecting the number of employees is to conduct the training within TH's training centres. TH has a number of buildings in Malaysia which are used as operation centres during the busy *Hajj* period. In less busy times, they are used as training centres rather than sending personnel to training sessions in hotels. TH is also working with a local higher education institution (the Mara Institute of Technology) to conduct a Diploma course in business management at TH's HQ. The course takes place every Saturday for a period of three years.

Also, during the crisis, transfers were not encouraged, as they increase costs. Nevertheless, if there was a need for any employee to be transferred for their career development, or to fill in gaps in other departments, divisions or branches, the transfer would still take place. Transfers during the crisis accounted for five per cent of total staff, compared to 20 per cent during normal times.

Competitors are competing with TH in giving returns on investments/dividends/bonuses to their investors. In tackling challenges presented by competitors, TH has the necessary human resources with sufficient skills to help it achieve a competitive edge over its competitors (mainly coming from local banks and investment trusts). Therefore, the present economic conditions in Malaysia do not force it to keep its best employees at any cost. Moreover, the present economic crisis requires other organizations to reduce their manpower, so that the poaching of TH's employees is minimized. Cost reduction pressures during the crisis are concentrated on reduction of the cost of travel, transfer, allowances and the day-to-day operation of departments. The cost of human resource development has not been significantly reduced. The training and development of staff is still carried out as before. This is because TH values its employees as long-term assets.

Based on the combination of both Malaysian and Islamic values, TH has tried to develop its own culture and a unique ILM. This is mainly because not all Malaysian culture is acceptable within Islam. Therefore, the development of the organizational culture is based on a combination of both Malaysian and Islamic values. Malaysian work culture can be described as related to creating a 'caring society' (by trying to avoid any retrenchment or downsizing, providing life-long employment and experience-based pay). Most organizations in Malaysia practise flexibility in task and regulation and there is also a greater use of self-managing teams to compensate for the opportunities lost.

Islam stresses fairness and equality in an individual's dealings with society. Muslims have always been required to devote themselves to religion while at the same time remaining responsible to family, community and society. They are also required to avoid any prohibitions specified by the religion such as gambling, receiving *riba*, or bribery, as these actions might challenge the social justice, equality and property rights of another individual, regardless of their race and religion. Therefore, a career that can balance and blend together the religion and appropriate lifestyle is highly desired.

TH's organizational culture blends both the Malaysian culture of flexibility with the Islamic values. But what makes TH unique is that its approaches are more those of a truly Islamic institution. One of TH's practices (which has become one of its unique remuneration packages not practised by other organizations in Malaysia) is the chance given to each of its employee (irrespective of ones position) to perform *Hajj* at the company's expense. Performing *Hajj* is not cheap. It could cost a pilgrim around RM 7,000–8,000. For a driver or security guard whose monthly salary is less than RM 1,000, the opportunity provided by the company is greatly valued. Indirectly, it also motivates employees and makes them loyal to the organization. This shows how TH tries to put an element of fairness and Islamic values into practice.

TH is adopting the concept of *Musyawarah* (in Islamic terms this refers to discussion and communication within a community). Discussion between the management and employees is seen as an important method to achieve a conclusion and resolution of any dispute. The practice can also reduce any sense of demotivation or grievance among employees. In addition, TH produces two monthly pamphlets, *Bulletin TH* and *Fitrah,* whose main objective is to educate the staff through news and articles on current management practices, self-improvement and ethical issues. TH also conducts an Islamic Talk and aerobic session every Saturday, which is compulsory for all of its staff, in order to create ethical and healthy employee relations. Furthermore, it rewards its best employees through monetary reward and a free trip to Mecca to perform *Umrah* annually. This indicates its commitment to combining both a career and devotion to religion in its working culture.

The present crisis has not affected the culture of TH, because financially the organization is still performing well. As a result it can still carry on with its culture development. Even though there is a requirement to cut the annual budget, programmes such as the Islamic talk, aerobic sessions and pamphlet circulation are not shed because the management acknowledges the importance of these strategies for the development of the organization's culture and their positive contributions to an individual's self-satisfaction and expectations. These also enhance TH's good relations between staff and management.

EMPLOYEE RELATIONS, HRM POLICIES AND PRACTICES AND ILMS

At the moment, there are 1017 people on TH's payroll. The company usually follows a formal method of recruitment (that is, formal advertisement of vacancies and formal interviews and selection procedures). For the positions of programmers and typists, a practical assessment test is generally conducted to test interviewees' knowledge in the relevant field. TH does face some problems in the recruitment of computer programmers, systems analysts and assistants due to the specific requirements in these fields. For instance, in the IT area, lack of knowledge or incompatibility with TH's existing system make it difficult to attract prospective candidates.

TH's wage structure is based on its Employment Scheme which is slightly higher than the government's salary scheme. Its wage structure is on a par with other similar companies in Malaysia. Employees' performance is usually evaluated through a number of assessment instruments. In addition to an employee's immediate supervisor, TH also uses assessment forms adopted from Public Service Department (PSD) practices. There are three separate assessment forms for different grades of employees.

The main areas of training vary and depend on the requirements of the department. Usually, staff will be sent for training if it is beneficial for the respective department. Training is given in the areas of management and both technical and non-technical work. In addition to this, employees also undertake ethical and motivational courses.

While discharging or laying off personnel, the main criteria taken into account are confirmed to CBT (Criminal and Breach of Trust). TH does not compromise with such actions. Usually the personnel concern will be asked to resign from TH. This action is seen as an alternative to sacking which can affect an individual's future job prospects. Other disciplinary cases are usually handled delicately by the management, for example, by giving advice, transfer or counselling. Besides the basic salary, TH's employment benefit is one of the most competitive remuneration packages in Malaysia. Eligible employees are entitled to housing loans, vehicle (car or motorcycle) loans and protection plans against accident. The facilities provided clearly show that TH's approach is successful in motivating and retaining employees. This is confirmed by the low employee turnover in TH (see Table 3).

TABLE 3

TH's 3-YEAR LABOUR TURNOVER STATISTICS

Mechanism of Turnover	1995	1996	1997
Resigned	11	18	9
Retired	6	5	8
Passed away	1	2	2
Discharged	1	3	–
Total	19	28	19

Source: TH's Human Resource Division

Statistics in Table 3 show that in the period 1995 to 1997, the number of employees who resigned was 0.8 to 2.0 per cent. The figure was lower for 1998–99 due to the economic crisis. This is mainly because of the existence of high levels of unemployment and competitive conditions prevailing in Malaysia. In such conditions, employees at TH will be more cautious in thinking about moving to another company which cannot provide them with a secure job as TH.

Any grievances are handled professionally at TH. The company has its own counsellor to listen to any work-related problems that employees may experience. Further, HR personnel are available for any kind of consultation. There is also a 'Suggestion Box' for any problem or any action that can improve TH's functioning. Criteria for promotion are a mixture of performance related and experience based. TH does not have a large number of internal promotions mainly because of its flat hierarchical structure, but every employee has at least an 8 per cent increase in their salary annually to compensate for the loss of promotion opportunities.

Basically, TH's HRM policies are based on Skim Saraan TH (TH Employment Scheme). All matters pertaining to HR are based on this document. The document describes the steps to be taken before any action is pursued (for example, discharging or promoting personnel). Due to company policy this document is not available for outside scrutiny.

Nevertheless, respondents were willing to talk about TH's general HRM strategy. It considers its employees as an asset. It believes that to take the organization into the next millennium, it is important to have skilled employees. Therefore, staff training is a continuous activity as it is essential to have skilled, dynamic and motivated staff. TH in 1998 has allocated about RM 1.1 million for scholarships for staff to undertake further studies and RM 0.8 million for in-house training of existing employees. Since TH has moved towards being a customer-oriented organization, the training and development of staff also need to conform to this system of values. It also has a quality circle, KMK: *Kumpulan Meningkatkan Mutu Kerja* (Work Improvement Group) where employees and management work together to discuss any actions that may improve organization performance. The responsibility for this aspect of the organization lies with the HR manager.

TH takes care of the welfare of its employees by creating better working conditions and by providing a number of facilities (such as those related to leave, loans and performing *Hajj*). As an Islamic Financial Institution, TH is moving towards creating a family institution by practising the concept of *Muhasabah* (in Syariah definition this refers to tender loving care for its community). For this reason, all TH's employees who reach retirement age are eligible to get medical treatment in one of TH's approved clinics and hospitals around Malaysia. This unique facility is not available in any other organization in Malaysia.

The permanent employment system is still the main one at TH, though some of its staff are on contracts. TH's vision of becoming a customer-orientated organization requires its employees to be computer literate and to have management skills such as the ability to analyse and solve any problem encountered in the day-to-day operation of the organization.

Like any other government organization, TH has its own trade union, KESAKTI: *Kesatuan Kakitangan TH* (TH Employees Association). The association is open to all non-management staff except for those in the HR division. The exclusion is to avoid any conflict of interest which might arise if there is any dispute between management and the union. The HR division is seen as a critical division as it controls the confidential HR policy pertaining to employee–employer relationship. Nevertheless, the establishment of the union is to formulate good working practice between management and union members. There are regular meetings conducted between the two parties every three months to discuss improvements in the functioning of TH. Any employee's problem can also be raised and management tries to resolve any matter through the concept of *musyawarah*. About 600 employees have joined KESAKTI. This figure comprises about 80 per cent of all TH employees eligible for membership. It is associated with the MTUC (Malaysian Trade Union Congress) labour movement.

The management has a positive attitude towards the union. Management see the union as a channel through which employees can raise any disagreement or grievance relating to the working conditions or individual concerns. Thus, the management acknowledges the contribution of the union towards the prosperity of TH. Nevertheless, not all demands can be fully satisfied because the management are also bound by certain organizational policies and requirements. The management will therefore seek alternatives to reduce or minimize the feeling of resentment among employees.

Management does not adopt any specific practices (such as internal recruitment and promotions, workers' participation or profit sharing schemes) to satisfy the union. In this respect, the management's stand is firm. It is bound by government regulations and procedures which limit its power to meet all union demands. Nevertheless, management is willing to discuss any comments by the union that can improve not only employee–employer relations but also the organization's performance and competitiveness. The present economic crisis has not put any pressure on TH to re-negotiate with its union due to the understanding of both parties of the need to work collectively during this critical period.

DISCUSSION AND CONCLUDING REMARKS

This essay began by discussing the ever increasing globalization of business and how the business world has become interdependent. It also highlighted the growing success of Islamic institutions being run on Islamic principles. It then moved to discuss how a large Islamic institution is still prospering in the present East Asian economic crisis. A number of factors responsible for the success of TH are identified. These include strong emphasis on customer satisfaction, quality, perception of HR as an asset, consultation-based communication, provision of job security to employees, welfare of employees, emphasis on good employee relations, continuous development of its employees, fairness and equality in its dealings, respect to superiors and an emphasis on team working. Most of these factors form the basis of Islamic work values and Malaysian work culture.

A combination of both Islamic values and Malaysian work culture contributes to the formation of some unique management practices at TH. These help TH to form a strong ILM, organizational culture and effective HRM practices and enables it to achieve a sustained competitive advantage. According to the resource based view of the firm there are four criteria which need to be fulfilled in order to achieve sustained competitive advantage (Barney, 1991). These are: (1) the resource must add positive value to the firm; (2) it must be unique or rare among current or potential competitors; (3) the resource must be imperfectly imitable; and (4) the resource cannot be substituted with another resource by competing firms. To a great extent TH is fulfilling these criteria.

For example, the services provided by TH are of great value to its customers. TH is not only efficient, but is run on the principles of equality and fairness. Most management practices of TH are almost unique, such as provision of a *Hajj* opportunity to its employees, total care of its employees not only while they are working at TH but also when they retire or even when their services are terminated. The Islamic principles of *riba, halal, ummah, musyawarah, muhasabah* and other Syariah concepts are strictly followed at TH. A combination of such practices is rarely found in present day organizations. TH's competitors (especially during the crisis) find it very difficult if not impossible to imitate or find a close substitute for such practices. This has helped TH to achieve a sustained competitive advantage (Wright *et al.*, 1994).

Considering the ever increasing popularity of Islam world-wide, Islamic economics provides an alternative to Muslims from assimilating into the emerging global culture whose core elements have a Western pedigree. It tries to create a balance between economic and social life. As shown by this case study, such a combination helps to create a sustained competitive advantage (by not only achieving economic objectives but also emphasizing the social well-being of its employees). It also provides key messages for organizations which are already operating or want to start businesses in Muslim-dominated regions. Based on the findings and analysis, the main implications of this research are:

1. Considering the ever increasing levels of globalization of business, most businesses the world over are directly or indirectly influenced by it. The way forward seems to be becoming a part of this modern revolution. However, businesses should carefully prepare themselves before doing so, otherwise more economic crises (like the East Asian one) should be expected in future.

2. It seems that Islam is rapidly spreading and will soon become a global religion. With the developments of globalization, more and more firms will be operating in Islam-dominated nations. The key to their smooth functioning will be dictated by the extent to which they develop their policies and practices according to Islamic principles (Minehan, 1998). Similarly, the number of Muslims in non-Islamic dominated nations is also on a continuous increase (for example in the US) and firms are under severe pressure to accommodate religious beliefs while developing relevant management policies and practices (Ettorre, 1996). This study provides useful information in this regard.

3. The competition and pressures created by the globalization of business can be tackled by an appropriate and suitable HRM approach (which considers the social well-being of employees and emphasizes moral and ethical teaching to its employees). This can improve not only an organization's employee relations but also its competitiveness and performance.

4. Increasingly many business practitioners and academics are turning to religious sources as a way of approaching and answering difficult questions related to business ethics (Pava, 1998). This research shows how moral and ethical issues (based on Islamic principles) are incorporated into the management policies and practices. This can be adopted in other similar organizations.

5. Culture can be used as a 'neutralizing agent' in managing human relations. A strong organizational culture, based on the principles of equality and fairness, can improve staff motivation and gradually satisfy their expectations of the organization. This element should be properly blended with other HRM elements to ensure its effectiveness to the organization.

6. To have a fully developed ILM should be the main agenda of modern organizations. An ILM emphasizing dominant religious values and national work values can help significantly to respond to any rapid changes forced by the present-day globalized economies (such as recession or mergers) and help to attract and attain good human resources and maintain good employee relations. Some of the unique aspects of ILMs of TH could be adopted by similar organizations.

7. The research contributes to the fields of globalization of business, ILMs, organizational studies, HRM and culture.

8. The approaches and findings of the organization under study can provide a learning tool for other organizations, especially the ones which operate in Islam-dominated areas.

Although the approach seems to be working for TH, it may not necessarily work in other organizations. It may not even work in other organizations in Malaysia as most of these are multi-racial/ethnic organizations. Nevertheless, the concept of developing culture and ILMs for organizational success can be applied to most organizations. This research has some limitations.

First, the study is limited to only one organization. However, its commitment to develop an organizational culture based on a combination of Malaysian and Islamic values provides a good example of a unique management approach to employee relations. The end product is a unique set of ILMs which cannot be easily imitated by competitors.

Second, the sample size is small. Nevertheless, the selection of employees from all levels of the organization and their involvement in areas such as HRM, Finance, Investment and the Union has provided valuable information for the study.

Third, the fact that TH is a single ethnic organization may prove to be a limitation in the application of this organization's approach to others. On the other hand, not much research has been undertaken on this type of organization. Therefore, it can enrich the existing knowledge in the areas of HRM, ILM, culture and restructuring particularly from an Islamic perspective. Considering the increasing trend of Islam and globalization of business, it could be of interest to both academics and practitioners.

ACKNOWLEDGEMENTS

We thank Monir Tayeb, Kamel Mellahi and an anonymous reviewer for their useful comments on an earlier version of this essay.

NOTE

1. For details see the special issue edition of *Thunderbird International Business Review*, 1999.

REFERENCES

Angell, N.B. (1995), 'Adapting Islamic Financing to Western Capital Markets', *Middle East Executive Reports*, Vol.18, No.12, pp.9 and 14.
Angell, N.B. (1994), 'Islamic and Western Banking: Part I – Major Features, Structural Forms, Comparison with Western Banks', Riba. *Middle East Executive Reports*, Vol.17, No.12, pp.9–13.
Anwar, S. T. (1997), 'Trends in International Business Thought and Literature: Reviewing East Asia's Miracle, Its Economic Dynamism and Future Issues', *The International Executive*, Vol.39, No.1, pp.83–109.
Bacon, N. and Blyton, P. (1999), The Impact of Globalization on Trade Unions and Their Member, A Varied Picture from the International Iron and Steel Industry. Paper Presented at the 14th ERU Conference, Cardiff Business School, Cardiff.
Baker, G., Biggs, M. and Holmstrom, B. (1994), 'The Internal Economics of the Firm: Evidence from Personnel Data', *Quarterly Journal of Economics*, Vol.109, No.4, pp.881–919.
Baligh, H.H. (1998), 'The Fit Between the Organization Structure and its Cultural Setting: Aspects of Islamic Cultures', *International Business Review*, Vol.7, pp.39–49.
Barney, J.B. (1991), 'Firm Resources and Sustained Competitive Advantage', *Journal of Management*, Vol.17, No.1, pp.99–120.
Benson, J. (1995), 'Future Employment and The Internal Labour Market', *British Journal Of Industrial Relation*, Vol.33, No.4, pp.603–08.
Berita Harian (1998), '10 per cent Retrenchment Due to Mergers'. 15 April, Internet Edition.
Breman, J. (1998), 'The End of Globalization?' *Economic and Political Weekly*, 14 February, pp.333–6.
Burns, R. (1998), *Doing Business in Asia*. Melbourne: Longman.
Burkett, P. and Hart-Landsberg, M. (1998), 'East Asia and the Crisis of Development Theory', *Journal of Contemporary Asia*, Vol.28, No.4, pp.435–56.
Chang, H-J., Palma, G. and Whittaker, D.H. (1998), 'The Asian Crisis: Introduction', *Cambridge Journal of Economics*, Vol.22, p.649–52.
Chow, T. (1998), 'Economic Slowdowa: Reorganisation, Rightsizing And Retrenchment', *Berita Personnel*, MIPM, March–April, pp.8–9.
Conway, P.J. (1995), 'Islam and Modernisation: A Comparative Analysis of Pakistan, Egypt and Turkey', *Southern Economic Journal*, Vol.62, No.2, pp.498–9.
Central Bank of Malaysia (1998), Kaulalumpur:Department of Statistics.
Digh, P. (1998), 'Religion in the Workplace: Make a Good Faith Effort to Accommodate', *HR Magazine*, Vol.43, No.13, pp.84–91.
The Economist (1993), 'Islam in Asia: For God and Growth in Malaysia', 329 (7839), 27 November, p.39.
Endot, S. (1995), The Islamisation Process in Malaysia. PhD thesis, University of Bradford.
Ettorre, B. (1996), 'Religion in the Workplace: Implications for Managers', *Management Review*, Vol.85, No.12, pp.15–18.
Frenkel, S.J. and Peetz, D. (1998), 'Globalization and Industrial Relations in East Asia: A Three-Country Comparison', *Industrial Relations*, Vol.37, No.3, pp.282–310.
Friedman, R. (1999), 'The Case of Religious Network Group', *Harvard Business Review*, July–August, pp.28–40.
Guan, L. K. (1998), 'Islamic Banking System: Concept & Application', *Asia Pacific Journal Of Management*, April, pp.104–5.
Grimshaw, D. and Rubery, J. (1998), Integrating The Internal And External Labour Markets. *Cambridge Journal Of Economics*, Vol.22, No.2, pp.199–220.
Haron, S. (1996), The Effects Of Management Policy On The Performance Of Islamic Banks. *Asia Pacific Journal of Management*, Vol.13, No.2, p.63–76.

Haron, S. (1995), 'The Framework and Concept of Islamic Interest-Free Banking', *Journal of Asian Business*, Vol.11, No.1, pp.26–39.

Hendry, C and Pettigrew, A.M. (1992), 'Patterns of Strategic Change in the Development of Human Resource Management', *British Journal of Management*, Vol.3, pp.137–56.

Hofstede, G. (1993), 'Cultural constraints in Management theories', *Academy of Management Executive*, Vol.7, No.1, pp.81–94.

ILO (1998), *World Employment, 1996–97*. Geneva: ILO.

Iqbal, Z. (1997), Islamic Financial Systems. *Finance and Development*, June, pp.42–5.

Jacoby, S. (1985), *Employing Bureaucracy: Managers, Unions and the Transformation of Work in American Industry, 1900–1945*, New York: Columbia University Press.

Jomo, K. S. (1998), 'Malaysian Debacle: Whose Fault', *Cambridge Journal of Economics*, 22, pp.707–22.

Kleinknecht, A. and Wengel, J. (1998), 'The Myth of Economic Globalization', *Cambridge Journal of Economics*, Vol.22, pp.637–47.

Lee, E. (1997), 'Globalization and Labour Standards: A Review of Issues', *International Labour Review*, Vol.136, No.2, pp.173–89.

Lee, E. (1996), 'Globalization and Employment: Is Anxiety Justified?' *International Labour Review*, Vol.135, No.5, pp.485–97.

Lee, K.Y. (1996), 'How Asia Become Dynamo of World Economics', *Strait Times*, 28 June, p.26.

Lipford, J., McCormick, R.E. and Tollison, R.D. (1993), 'Preaching Matters', *Journal of Economic Behavior and Organization*, Vol.21, No.3, pp.235–50.

Lo, D. (1999), 'The East Asian Phenomenon: The Consensus, the Dissent, and the Significance of the Present Crisis', *Capital & Class*, Spring, pp.1–23.

Mansor, N. and Mohd Ali, M.A., (1998), 'An Exploratory Study Of Organisational Flexibility In Malaysia: A Research Note', *The International Journal of Human Resource Management*, Vol.8, pp.506–15.

Minehan, M. (1998), 'Islam's Growth Affects Workplace Policies', *HR Magazine*, Vol.43, No.12, pp.1047–9.

Mueller, F. (1994), 'Societal Effect, Organizational Effect and Globalization', *Organization Studies*, Vol.15, No.3, pp.407–28.

Myerson, M. (1996), 'Flexi Benefits In Malaysia: The Trend In The Delivery Of Innovative Compensation', *Berita Personnel*, January–February, pp.11–12.

Osterman, P. (1984), (ed.) *Internal Labor Markets*. Mass: The MIT Press.

Patibandla, M. and Prusty, R. (1998), 'East Asian Crisis as a Result of Institutional Failure', *Economic and Political Weekly*, February 28, pp.469–72.

Pava, M. L. (1998), 'Religious Business Ethics and Political Liberalism: An Integrative Approach', *Journal of Business Ethics*, Vol.17, No.15, pp.1633–52.

Pearson, C. and Entrekin, L. (1998), 'Structural Properties, Work Practices, and Control in Asian Businesses: Some Evidence from Singapore and Malaysia', *Human Relations*, Vol.51, No.10, pp.1285–306.

Pettigrew, A., Hendry, C. and Sparrow, P. (1988), 'The Forces That Trigger Training', *Personnel Management*, December, pp.28–32.

Pfeffer, J. and Cohen, Y. (1984), 'Determinants of Internal Labor Markets in Organisations', *Administrative Science Quarterly*, Vol.29, pp.550–72.

Porter, M. E. (1985), *Competitive Advantage: Creating and Sustaining Superior Performance*. New York: Free Press.

Presley, J.R. and Sessions, J.G. (1994), 'Islamic Economics: The Emergence of a New Paradigm', *Economic Journal*, Vol.104, No.424, pp.584–96.

Rajkumar, K. (1998), Strategies to Manage Restructuring. *Berita Personnel*, April–March, pp.14–15.

Rana, P.B. (1997), 'Globalization and Currencies', *Far Eastern Economic Review*, Vol.160, No.37, p.29.

Rosewarne, S. (1998), 'The Globalization and Liberalisation of Asian Labor Markets', *World Economy*, Vol.21, No.7, pp.963–79.

Scriven, R. (1996), 'How To Develop 2020 Vision : Maximising Human Potential', *Berita Personnel*, MIPM, January–February, pp.1–2.

Shepherd, W.G. (1996), 'What Exactly is Riba?' *Global Finance*, Vol.10, No.5, p.48.

Sherif, M.A. (1975), *Ghazali's Theory of Virtue*. Albany, NY: State University of New York Press.

Singh, A. (1993), 'Islam and the Indo-Islamic Culture', *Employment News*, October 9–15, pp.1 and 4.

Soeters, J.L. and Schwan, R. (1990), 'Towards an Empirical Assessment of Internal Market

Configurations', *International Journal of Human Resource Management*, Vol.1, No.1, pp.272–87.
Tan, G. (1992), *The Newly Industrializing Countries of Asia*. Singapore: Time Academic Press.
TH Act (1995), Law of Malaysia, *Act 535*.
TH's Annual Report 94.
TH's Annual Report 95.
TH's Annual Report 96.
TH's Employment Scheme.
TH: Your Investment Partner.
Thunderbird International Business Review (1999), Special Issue: Islamic Banking. Vol.41, Nos. 3 & 4.
Tsuruoka, D. (1993), 'Strong Fundamentals: In Malaysia, Islam is a Basis for Business', *Far Eastern Economic Review*, Vol.156, No.37, pp.74–5.
Tayeb, M. (1999), 'Foreign Remedies for Local Difficulties: The Case of Three Scottish Manufacturing Firms', *International Journal of Human Resource Management*, Vol.10, No.5, p.842–57.
Tayeb, M. (1997),' Islamic Revival in Asia and Human Resource Management', *Employee Relations*, Vol.19, No.4, pp.252–63.
Timewell, S. (1998), 'A Market in the Making', *Banker*, Vol.148, No.864, pp.57–61.
Turner, T. (1994), 'Internal Labour Markets and Employment Systems', *International Journal of Manpower*, Vol.15, No.1, pp.15–26.
United Nations Conference on Trade and Development (UNCTAD) (1995), *World Competitiveness Report 1995: Transformational Corporations and Competitiveness*. New York and Geneva: United Nations.
Wee, C. and Tan, G. (1997), 'Making Sense of the Asian Success Story: An Integrative Framework', *The International Executive*, Vol.39, No.2, pp.161–84.
Wood, A. (1998), 'Globalization and the Rise of Labour Market Inequalities', *Economic Journal*, Vol.108, No.450, pp.1463–82.
World Bank (1997), *World Development Indicators*. New York: Oxford University Press.
World Trade Organization (WTO) (1996), *Annual Report 2*. Geneva: WTO
Wright, P.M., McMahan, G.C. and McWilliams, A. (1994), 'Human Resources and Sustained Competitive Advantage: A Resource-Based Perspective', *The International Journal of Human Resource Management*, Vol.5, No.2, pp.301–26
Yarwood, V. (1993), 'God's Work: Does Business Needs Religion?' *Management Auckland*, Vol.40, No.9, pp.30–38.
Yong, A.K.B. (1996), *Malaysian Human Resource Management*. Kaulalumpur: Institut Pengurusan Malaysia.

APPENDIX I
SYARIAH CONCEPTS AND THEIR DEFINITIONS

Concept	Definition
Al-Musyarakah	Shareholders will finance a project, and profits will be divided accordingly as agreed by the parties.
Al-Bai Bithaman Ajil	Financing with deferred repayments over a specific period of time.
Al-Mudharabah	An agreement by which one party provides the capital and management and the other party (ies) provide the expertise. Any losses suffered in the venture will be borne by the provider of the capital.
Al-Murabahah	Financing with a repayment agreed by both parties that includes the profit mark-up.
Al-Qardhul Hassan	Benevolent loan, where the provider of capital is guaranteed at least the principal portion.

Source: TH : Your Investment Partner

9

Global Competitive Pressures, Labour Market and Employment Issues in the Japanese Service Sector

YOKO SANO

Invigorating business and the maintenance of employment are urgent tasks for the Japanese economy today. A huge amount of public expenditure has been spent so far. However, fundamental and structural measures should be adopted at the same time. One of the main measures agreed was 'deregulation'. The central government has a schedule of deregulation in finance, industry, public bodies and also labour markets, and a large-scale amendment was passed to deregulate employment service and some labour standards regarding working hours and labour contracts in 1998.

It seems to be a global trend to encourage business activities in order to expand employment. This means that labour market flexibility should be developed, and that deregulation of employment protection legislation should be also considered. The present status of legislative labour standards still seems to be unsatisfactory to induce new business and maintain the level of employment.

As the central government schedule shows, details of the deregulation programme have already been decided. However, its enforcement has faced obstacles from interest groups. In the case of labour laws the national centres of trade unions are strong forces against deregulation, while in business circles they are in favour of deregulating labour laws including the Labour Standards Law (redundancy, working hours), the Employment Security Law (introduction of private companies) and the Labour Union Law (deduction of union fees). The Ministry of Labour plays a third party role, but there are few academic debates on these issues. The issues appear to be considerably political. Empirical or quantitative research on the effects of legislation regarding Japanese labour markets has been poorly accumulated in recent decades.

It should also be pointed out that a series of new legislation has been passed by the Diet in 1999. The Equal Employment Opportunity Law was amended to strengthen the legislation in 1999. The giant-scale home-care law was passed and enforced in 2000. The Industrial Accident Law was extended in 2000 to include cover for suicides owing to over-work as industrial accidents. In Japan, it is not unusual for at least one new labour-related piece of legislation to be passed every year.

The aim of this essay is to estimate the effects of deregulation of labour standards legislation on employment and business activities in Japan. More specifically, it attempts to assess the effects not only of deregulation but also of new regulation of labour standards. Examples are: deregulation of restrictive redundancy dismissals, and legislative enforcement against age discrimination for hiring and mandatory retirement. To estimate such effects, we conducted a survey of management attitudes towards legislative changes in order to explore how they would react if the present legislative framework was relaxed. We found that the deregulation of certain labour standards legislation and certain new legislative reinforcement supported the growth of employment and expansion of business activities.

GLOBALIZATION OF MARKETS, STRUCTURAL CHANGE IN INDUSTRIES AND EMPLOYMENT

Employment in Japan has been characterized by security and stability based on the lifetime commitment of organizations and employees, and the protection of industries by governments. Now it faces dramatic change in the form of a rising unemployment rate and a shift of employment growth to non-traditional sectors. The rate of unemployment in Japan exceeded that of the USA in December, 1998, and it is continuing to rise. A shift of employment is gradual but persistent giving rise to employment growth in service-related sectors. This is consistent with the current trend in advanced economies.

Co-operation but Anti-competition Culture

Co-operation is rooted in the Japanese culture, and, therefore, the concept of competition has not been accepted by traditional firms. Also, industrial protection has a long history in Japan. Although there are attempts to deregulate product markets, in service industries such as construction, finance, transportation, tourist and professional services deregulation is lagging behind that of other industries.

The construction industry consists of 18% of total firms in Japan (1998). However, its employment share has been 10% in the past decade. Despite the large number of firms, all of them are linked with each other by network associations, organized at many levels. All of them seem to be 'co-operative' rather than 'competitive'.

Industrial Structure of Employment

Employment is derived from production of goods and services. If production is reduced, employment would most likely be reduced. Factors which affect the relationship of production and employment are labour saving technologies and management. More important is that employment will not increase unless production grows. Figure 1 shows the industrial share of the workforce in 1999. During the past ten years (1990–99), total employment grew by 8.8%. The employment share of the manufacturing sector declined from 29% to 24%, that of the distribution sector declined from 22% to 20%, and employment share of the service sector grew from 25% to 29%.

FIGURE 1

INDUSTRIAL STRUCTURE OF EMPLOYMENT: 43,2800,000 EMPLOYEES – 100%
(Establishments with 5 employees or more, excluding government service as of February 1999)

Mining			0.1%
Construction			8.9%
Manufacturing	23.7%	Related to consumption	7.2%
		Related to raw materials	7.0%
		Related to machinery	9.5%
Energy			0.7%
Transportation			6.7%
Communication			1.3%
Distribution			20.4% 100%
Restaurants			4.6%
Finance & Insurance			3.8%
Real Estate			0.8%
Services	28.9%	Educational services	4.9%
		Medical & health service	5.3%
		Hotels & entertainment	3.1%
		Professional services	2.5%
		Socialinsurance & welfare	2.1%
		Others	11.8%

Source: Ministry of Labour, Japan. *Monthly Labour Survey*, February 1999.

What will the level of industrial employment there be in the next decade? The key factor will be the production scale on a macro-economic level adjusted by import substitution. What will determine import substitution? The main factor will be differences between domestic and foreign prices. If import prices are relatively lower, domestic producers and consumers will purchase more imported goods and services. Let us examine the future trends of business and employment by assessing price differences by industry sector from as follows.

- The *construction* sector, with nearly 10% of the total employment during the period faces a decline because of the growth of import products with low prices, although domestic quality is appreciated. Public expenditure which supported long-term demand for local construction will be reduced. On balance, demand for the workforce will face definite shrinkage.

- The *manufacturing* sector is divided into three categories: consumption-related, raw-material-related and machinery-related. Consumption-related manufacturing includes food processing, textiles and beverages, and this category shows an increasing trend towards imports which will grow depending on price differences. Raw-material-related manufacturing includes steel, cement and chemicals, and this category also suffers from the high prices of Japanese products. The category includes the pharmaceutical industry which in the past has grown rapidly, but will have to be multinationalized before long. Machinery-related manufacturing includes electrical appliances and precision industries. High technology is a growing sector and Japan is strong in global competition. However, it should be noted that its employment has been reduced and will be reduced further.

- *Energy production* includes electric power, gas and water supplies. This also is a high price sector, and the employment share is less than one per cent. A further increase in employment cannot be expected.

- *Transportation* occupies 6.7% of total employment, but most of it is located in road passenger and freight transport. Shipping and railways are a structurally declining sector. On the other hand, Japanese airlines have had the problem of government-owned monopoly, regulation of facilities and infrastructure and militant unionism. They suffer from high costs and competition from abroad. Road transport is growing and there are many private companies in the sector. Communication which has 1.3% share of employment is a growing sector backed by information technology.

- Japanese *distribution and retailing* has been notorious for its multi-layered structure and inefficient business practices. However, 'mom-and-pop' stores are being substituted by large-scale retailers which bypass intermediate wholesalers. The 20.4% share of employment in 1999, which was as high as 22.7% in 1990, will be reduced further. If deregulated further, mega shopping stores will grow and increase employment as Toys 'R Us and Office Depot did, while traditional retailers will lose employment.

- *Restaurants* have a similar problem to retailing. The number of employees in traditional restaurants is declining as fast food and family restaurant chains are increasing all over Japan.

- The *finance* sector is now undergoing restructuring and multi-nationalization. The employment share decreased slightly from 4.5% in 1990 to 4.1% in 1997, and it will most likely stay between 4% and 5% at most by the next decade. The real estate sector should grow marginally but the share is only 0.8% at present.

- The *service* sector has experienced growth in the past: medical and health services from 4.3% in 1990 to 5.3% in 1999, hotels and entertainment from 2.7% to 3.1%, but education declined from 5.0% to 4.9%. The service sector includes both private and public areas. As a whole they are regulated except for certain niche businesses, and are characterized by high prices. There is room for further expansion, with the possibility of deregulation and multi-nationalization. Therefore, the employment share should continue to rise.

On the whole, it is the service sector which will probably grow significantly in terms of employment in the next decade. On the other hand, the rest of the sectors will most likely experience a decline in employment, not only in terms of share but also in absolute numbers. Some exceptions will be information-related areas in conjunction with communication, research and development, high-tech entertainment and financial investment. However, their levels of employment will be too small to absorb employee displaced from the traditional sectors.

Thus, one of the major factors responsible for the changes is globalization of products and services markets. In order to balance the level of employment, Japan needs to focus on the encouragement of new business, introduction of new technology, and deregulation of markets, including labour markets.

A STUDY OF THE RELATIONSHIP BETWEEN LABOUR PROTECTION LEGISLATION AND LABOUR MARKET PERFORMANCE

This section provides a brief review of the literature on the relationship between labour protection and labour market performance, the scope of employment protection regulation, the measurement of employment protection legislation, and labour market flexibility and unemployment.

The Scope of Employment Protection Regulation

Robert Evans, Jr (1995) reviews the empirical literature on the effect of employment protection legislation on labour market performance in the United States. He identifies labour market regulation in the following subject areas: labour unions, anti-discrimination, safety, wages under the Fair Labour Standards Act, notice of lay-off, employment at will, immigration, social security, private pensions, unemployment insurance, employer mandates, industrial deregulation, occupational licenses, family leave and employment agencies. Dependent variables are job opportunities, wages, productivity and labour costs. The US has witnessed the greatest advance in the deregulation of labour markets, and much research on the effect has been done.

The Measurement of Employment Protection Legislation

The OECD Employment Outlook (1999) provides indicators of the strictness of employment protection regulation and practice. The indicators consist of regular procedural inconveniences, notice and severance pay for no-fault individual dismissals by tenure categories and difficulty of dismissal. After careful examination and evaluation of regulation and practice, scores are given under three categories: regular employment, temporary employment and collective dismissals. Finally, overall EPL (employment protection legislation) strictness scores are given. All of them are estimated by country (26 member countries). Detailed descriptions of employment protection regulation and practice include: (1) administrative procedures for individual notice and dismissal (notification procedures and estimated time before notice can start), (2) required notice and severance pay for individual dismissal (i.e. the case of a regular employee with tenure beyond any trial period dismissed on personal grounds or economic redundancy, but without fault), (3) notice periods and severance pay for individual dismissals at three different lengths of service, (4) conditions under which individual dismissals are fair or unfair, (5) compensation and related remedies following unjustified dismissal, (6) compensation pay and related provisions following unjustified dismissal, (7) regulation of fixed-term contracts, (8) regulation of temporary work agency employment, and (9) procedures and standards for collective dismissal.

The overall EPL strictness (scores range from 6 to 0) shows, in a word, that English speaking countries are ranked as low in strictness (US, UK, New Zealand, Canada, Ireland, and Australia in order) and that mostly southern European countries are ranked as high in strictness (Portugal, Turkey, Greece, Italy, Spain, France and Germany in order). Japan is ranked approximately in the middle at 14th (score: 2.3).

The regular employment strictness of employment protection legislation shows a similar trend. The score is 0.2 for the US (the lowest) and 0.8 for UK (the second lowest). On the other hand, the score is 4.3 for Portugal (the highest) and 3.2 for Korea (the second highest). The score is 2.7 for Japan (the eighth highest).

What is the effect of employment protection on labour market performance? Correlation between EPL indicators and unemployment rates is not significant. The only significant correlation is found between EPL indicators and employment/population ratios for prime-age males and prime-age females, and also the share of self-employment. It was also found that countries with high EPL scores have lower mobility between employment and unemployment, and therefore a high EPL disturbs the dynamism of labour markets in response to globalization and technological changes.

Labour Market Flexibility and Unemployment

What will happen to business when the present labour market legislation is more or less deregulated? Di Tella and MacCulloch (1998) estimate a relationship between labour market flexibility and the unemployment rate using 1984–90 average data of 21 OECD countries. In a unique study they use an opinion survey of a number of top and middle managers, called the World Competitiveness Report (WCR), to measure their country's competitiveness. Their work is based on replies to one of the nearly 90 questions: *'Flexibility of enterprises to adjust job security and compensation standards to economic realities.'*

Di Tella and MacCulloch analysed the panel data set of unemployment, employment, participation and labour market flexibility, and found that increasing labour market flexibility increases both the employment rate (employment/population by age group) and the participation rate (labour force/population by age group). They also found that more flexibility leads to lower rates of unemployment and long-term unemployment.

ISSUES RAISED IN CHANGING LABOUR STANDARDS

What will happen to employment and hence business opportunities if some of the labour standards are changed? Labour standards are constituted by the Labour Standards Law in Japan. Some of the present labour standards could be usefully deregulated, but some could be legislated in order to fill the requirements of labour market flexibility and fair labour standards. Labour market flexibility is hampered by excessive protection of workers. Employment-service related protection is now largely being removed. At the same time employment protection for women was removed with the 1999 revision of the Men and Women Employment Opportunity Law. However, there seem to be a number of provisions which should be re-examined. Some of them were under consideration by the *OECD Employment Outlook*. Strict protection is evident in the areas of redundancy dismissals, juvenile and child labour, job changes to competitors, employees' destruction of fixed-term contracts, length of fixed-term contracts, and arbitrary work with performance pay. Further restriction may be required in the areas of overtime work, night work, and age restriction for hiring and mandatory retirement. These issues (independent variables) are discussed below.

Redundancy Dismissals

The Labour Standards Law in Japan states clearly that employers can dismiss employees after 30 days notice, but judicial precedents added four conditions after 1974: (1) inevitable dismissals on the grounds of business continuity, (2) only after necessary measures of transfer, recruitment of leavers, etc. (3) reasonable selection of dismissed employees, and (4) understandable explanation to employees or trade unions by employers. In practice, most employers dismiss employees with more moderate measures. They recruit leavers with the offer of an extra amount of severance pay, and they sometimes appeal to employees' sympathy. However, together with a lifetime commitment 'ideology' such judicial precedents often result in employers and would-be employers tending to maintain a smaller number of people.

Juvenile and Child Labour

Child labour itself is a serious problem in some parts of the world, but it is not generally a social problem in advanced countries. In Japan children have no opportunity to earn money or to be trained as earners. Children and juveniles have not been educated to do business by themselves. Furthermore, pupils at junior and senior high schools are sometimes prohibited from engaging in part-time jobs even during vacation. Juveniles are restricted not only in job opportunities but also heavily in the area of working hours and working conditions.

Competitors' Behaviour in the Job Market

In a regionally restricted area it is fatal for some firms if their employees are 'scouted' or headhunted by competitive firms. Japanese judicial precedents have been sympathetic with original employing firms and appreciate loyalty to employers. On the other hand, any worker should have the freedom to choose between jobs. Disagreements can be avoided by agreeing on a penalty beforehand. Japanese firms often send employees on study leave abroad, generally on contracts which assure some fixed years of service after education or otherwise the employees reimburse the employer, but a recent judicial precedent indicated that this form of contract is invalid.

Employees' Withdrawal from Fixed-Term Contracts

In the case of fixed-term contracts, employers have the responsibility to provide job security within the term. However, employees are permitted to quit if they have considerable reason. Employers are damaged if employees quit unexpectedly, but this problem can be solved if special contracts provide forfeit and thus limit worker movement between employers. Employees such as highly talented engineers can move if scouting firms pay on behalf of the client firms concerned.

Length of Fixed-Term Contracts

For a long time, one year was the maximum for fixed-term contracts in Japan but the 1999 amendment relaxed this to three years in the case of workers over 60 years old and researchers. Part-time workers are all employed on fixed-term contracts and many of them, as well as their employers, want to have longer length contracts rather than repeated renewal.

Arbitrary Work with Performance Pay

Japanese workers have long been used to working long hours, almost throughout their lives. The law strictly controlled hours, time, and leave. Now traditional manual work and desk work are disappearing, and newer jobs require more flexible patterns of work. Arbitrary work was introduced as an exempted case in law. An arbitrary work system allows an employee flexible working time, and pay is determined on an individual performance basis. Employers need therefore to evaluate employees' performance accurately. Arbitrary work practice was at first applicable to sales people and researchers. Now it is going to be applied to a larger group of employees, although the majority are still not included.

Need to Restrict Overtime Work and Night Work

Japanese workers have tended to work long hours even if they are organized by trade unions. The present legislation allows overtime work as long as agreements are made between trade unions and employers. There is no limit on night work if it is within allowed overtime hours. However, consideration is not being given to the argument that regulation should set the upper limit of overtime and night work. Workers do not want to rely on trade unions to negotiate on their behalf as they prefer legislation to voluntary agreements.

Need to Restrict Age discrimination for Hiring and Mandatory Retirement

It is common practice in Japan to set an upper age limit for hiring employees, and to maintain employees until retirement age (60 or more). It sounds unfair to restrict working-rights by setting an age limit. Japanese work practices have relied heavily on the *nenko* system (age and seniority) and on in-house training. Employers are suffering from increases in labour costs associated with this and are especially concerned with the age of workers.

METHOD AND DATA

The aim of the study is to find the possible effects of deregulation and regulation of labour standards as discussed above. A common method in the past has been to study the data and find the net effect of a specific variable by controlling other variables. However, past data is not always appropriate even if available, because the business environment changes rapidly these days. It was thought that questionnaires to decision makers would provide more appropriate information under specified conditions. We conducted a questionnaire survey among business firms in January, 1998: Survey of Labour Market Changes and Legislation by Institute of Industries, Keio University in Tokyo.

Questions were carefully constructed. We used 'if' questions following the Vignet survey method. *If employment protection legislation is deregulated regarding redundancy dismissals, what effect will it have on your firm regarding business chances, number of employees, labour cost, human relations in the work place, loyalty of employees to the firm and rationalization of management?* These questions required discrete (qualitative) answers: yes or no. The Vignet method was originally planned to measure quantitative effects of independent variables on dependent variables. If we want to understand an individual's propensity to move (the likelihood of job changes), we can pose a question about how much higher pay can induce one's move from the present job to another job: 10% higher, 50% higher, double or triple, if other conditions are equal. After we observe a group of individuals, we can estimate a quantitative propensity to change jobs regarding monetary incentives for the group.

We posed seven questions regarding deregulation of present legislation and practice: redundancy dismissals, juvenile and child labour, job changes to competitors, employees' withdrawal from fixed-term contracts, length of fixed-term contracts, and arbitrary work with performance pay. We also posed three other questions regarding new regulation: overtime determined by labour and management agreement, night working hours, and age discrimination for hiring and mandatory retirement. All the questions used 'if' clauses.

The sample was drawn from the growing service sectors: (1) supermarkets, convenience stores and catalogue retailers, (2) restaurants, (3) hotels, (4) hairdressers, (5) film and video productions, (6) entertainment and sport clubs, (7) advertising, (8) software, (9) information processing, (10) professional services, (11) architecture, (12) social work, and (13) others.

The firms were drawn by random sampling of the Teikoku Data Bank list (the largest list of firms in Japan) producing 1970 companies. The sample was also selected by stratifying 48 prefectures in order to avoid regional bias. The questionnaire was returned by 562 firms (the response rate was 28.5%), and 556 firms were recognized as effective. The size of firms were: 225 firms (40.5%) for 1–10 employees, 170 firms (30.6%) for 11–30 employees, 109 firms (19.6%) for 31–100, and 52 firms (9.4%) for 101 or more employees.

The sample was divided into two sorts of areas in Japan: urban and rural. Urban areas included Tokyo-to, Kanagawa-ken, Osaka-fu, Aichi-ken, and Fukuoka-shi. Rural areas included the residue of the urban areas. Out of the effective (in regional entities) 547 firms, 257 firms (47.0%) were from the urban areas and 290 firms (53.0%) were from the rural areas.

ANALYSIS

Effects of Deregulation and Legislative Enforcement on Employment

The dependent variable is the number of employees in a firm. Independent variables are redundancy, dismissals and so forth. Table 1 shows the results of the questionnaire survey. The response was a choice of 'will increase', 'no change', 'will reduce', and 'don't know'.

We find first that a considerable part of the response indicates 'no change'. Assumed questions (with 'if') are generally difficult to evaluate, although we benefit by estimating an independent effect of any factor controlling other factors which are unchanged. Still it should be noted that assumed questions tend to induce 'no change' in answers. More important in this context is the relative importance of the questions. Table 1 shows that even the share of 'no change' varies among questions from 49.1% (redundancy dismissals) to 87.6% (child labour). As such, we can evaluate the relative importance of 'will increase' and 'will reduce'.

Regarding redundancy dismissals, more than a third of the firms clearly stated that if they can dismiss redundant employees easily, they will increase the number of employees. Arbitrary work with performance pay is a flexible work pattern separated from the regular working hour schedule. If firms can introduce this to other categories of workers in sales and research, they will increase employee numbers because it will ease human resource management and raise worker productivity as a whole.

Legislative enforcement against overtime work will also lead to an increase in employee numbers. Similarly, legislative enforcement against age discrimination will also increase employment. If retirement age is not mandatory, more and more older workers could remain. If firms recruit people from outside, they will have to employ more older persons because without an age limit, firms would try to manage everything more efficiently. Any employees who do not meet the firms' needs could be dismissed immediately.

Effects of Deregulation and Legislative Enforcement on Business Chances

A dependent variable is the business chances which are perceived by firms. It means new business opportunities, growth of business,

TABLE 1

EFFECTS OF DEREGULATION AND NEW REGULATION OF LABOUR MARKETS ON EMPLOYMENT

Unit: Number of firms in percentage (Sample base: 556 companies)

	Will increase	No change	Will reduce	Don't know	Total
Deregulation					
Redundancy Dismissals	33.5	49.1	12.5	4.9	100.0
Juvenile Labour	11.7	74.5	2.0	11.9	100.0
Child Labour	3.6	87.6	1.6	7.1	100.0
Length of Fixed-Term Contracts	9.6	77.3	6.7	6.4	100.0
Arbitrary Work with Performance Pay	22.9	60.3	7.3	9.6	100.0
Legislative enforcement					
Overtime Work in Agreement	22.1	65.8	7.9	4.2	100.0
Night work	8.9	82.9	3.6	4.6	100.0
Age Discrimination for Hiring & Mandatory Retirement	21.4	63.9	7.4	7.2	100.0

Source: Institute of Industries, Keio University, 'Survey of Labour Market Changes and Legislation', 1998 (mailed questionnaire to managers).

TABLE 2

EFFECTS OF DEREGULATION AND NEW REGULATION OF
LABOUR MARKETS ON BUSINESS CHANCES

Unit: Number of Firms in percentage (Sample base: 556 companies)

	Will increase	No change	Will reduce	Don't know	Total
Deregulation					
Redundancy Dismissals	37.6	50.1	2.9	9.4	100.0
Juvenile Labour	11.3	81.1	1.1	6.5	100.0
Child Labour	5.1	83.9	0.7	10.3	100.0
Job Changes to Competitors	19.2	63.9	5.1	11.8	100.0
Length of Fixed-Term Contracts	16.3	72.3	2.7	8.7	100.0
Arbitrary Work with Performance Pay	37.0	48.1	2.0	12.9	100.0
Legislative enforcement					
Overtime Work in Agreement	4.6	51.9	37.6	5.9	100.0
Age Discrimination for Hiring & Mandatory Retirement	28.4	56.3	5.3	10.0	100.0

Source: Institute of Industries, Keio University, 'Survey of Labour Market Changes and Legislation', 1998 (mailed questionnaire to managers).

diversification of business and restructuring. Therefore, what regulation or deregulation will have a positive effect? Table 2 shows the results of the survey for this issue.

The response was a choice of 'will increase', 'no change', 'will reduce', and 'don't know'. Although the majority supported 'no change', some independent variables showed a remarkable increase.

As in the case of employment effect, redundancy dismissals and arbitrary work with performance pay showed the most increase. If firms have easier redundancy dismissals, 37.6% of the firms expect more business opportunities. And if firms have a system of arbitrary work with performance pay, 37.0% of the firms expect more opportunities. Deregulation of employee transfers to competitors and length of fixed-term contracts will also provide more business opportunities. Likewise, legislative enforcement against age discrimination can provide more business opportunities to firms. The positive response to business chances was greater than for employment. Therefore, the age discrimination legislation seems to be considered a symbol of labour market inflexibility.

Regional Differences and Effects on Employment and Business Chances

Differences between urban areas and rural areas were found in a few cases. The differences were in redundancy dismissals, and arbitrary work with performance pay. Regarding the effect of redundancy dismissals on employment, 40.3% of the firms responded 'will increase' in urban areas, compared to 28.3% in rural areas. Regarding the effect of arbitrary work with performance pay on employment, 37.3% of the firms responded 'will increase' in urban areas, and 18.8% of the firms responded 'will increase' in rural areas.

Regarding the effect of redundancy dismissals on business chances, 47.0% of the firms responded 'will increase' in urban areas, and 33.2% of the firms responded 'will increase' in rural areas. Regarding the effect of arbitrary work with performance pay on business chances, 42.1% of the firms responded 'will increase' in urban areas, and 33.3% of the firms responded 'will increase' in rural areas.

Although a majority of firms supported 'no change' in the regional categories, both urban and rural firms followed the national average trend. Mostly they looked to be similar, but it was puzzling that firms in urban areas showed more sympathy with the deregulation of employment protection. We found an overall tendency for urban firms to be in favour of flexibility. The difference might come from differences in the Japanese economic structure: urban areas are more competitive and rural areas are more likely to be dependent on public expenditure.

CONCLUSIONS

Global competition leads to local business activities becoming more competitive. In theory, local workers are competing with foreign workers in product markets without regional movement. Actually, the degree of competition varies depending on regional features and institutional barriers in the country. Devices for the protection of labour standards have been developed in advanced countries, but they can protect workers and employers from labour market flexibility and can disturb market performance. The attitudes of service business managers showed some systematic responses to conditional questionnaires (a Vignet survey) and we can infer effects of legislative changes on employment and business chances. The kind of business was carefully selected among growing sectors: mainly small firms in the service sector both in urban and rural areas. Judging from the service business attitudes, both employment and business chances will be increased if redundancy dismissal procedures are deregulated, if arbitrary work with performance pay is introduced, and if age discrimination for hiring and mandatory retirement is regulated. It is interesting to note that the effects of deregulation of employment protection legislation on the growth of business chances were greater than on the growth of employment. An increase in business activities seems to be the origin of employment increases.

It should be noted that service business leaders were especially interested in redundancy dismissals regarding both business chances and employment. If redundancy dismissal procedures are deregulated and if employers can dismiss employees more easily, they will employ more workers.

Legislative enforcement against age discrimination has positive effects on employment and business chances as well. If employers can be less concerned about the hiring age and the retirement age, they will be more conscious about employee merit and performance. They will not have to maintain workers until retirement age.

Final remarks are on regional differences. Firms in urban areas were more concerned with the positive side of employment and business chances. On the other hand, firms in rural areas were doubtful about the effects. Firms in urban areas seem likely to be more 'competitive' than firms in rural areas, while firms in rural areas seem likely to be 'co-operative'.

ACKNOWLEDGEMENTS

The Survey of Labour Market Changes and Legislation was conducted by the 1995-98 Research Project of Deregulation of Labour Markets. I would like to thank all the members of the Project, and also Keio Gijuku Academic Development Funds and the Ministry of Education, Grant-in-Aid for Scientific Research for their support.

REFERENCES

Evans, Robert, Jr (1995) *United States Labor Market Regulation*, Keio Economic Observatory Occasional Paper, No.16, March (Keio University).
OECD (1999) *OECD Employment Outlook June 1999*. Paris: Organisation for Economic Co-operation and Development.
Di Tella, Rafael and R. MacCulloch (1998) 'The Consequences of Labour Market Flexibility: Panel Evidence Based on Survey Data', *Journal of Public Economics*, Vol.31, pp.377–99.
Sano, Yoko, Yasumi Miyamoto and Atsushi Yashiro (eds.) (1999) *Hitoto Kigyoo Ikasu Rule, Shibaru Rule* [Rules That Invigorate People and Companies]. Tokyo: Chuo Keizaisha.

10

Globalization, Economic Development and the Reliance on *Guanxi* as a Job Search Strategy for Chinese Students

CHENG SOO MAY

As Mainland Chinese university graduates enter the job market in the new millennium, they will be the generation that completes the massive transition from socialist to market-oriented education system. For decades, the job assignment system had given Chinese college students a free education and assured employment after graduation. In return, state planners got access to a steady flow of trained graduates who were required to work where they were told. However, in the early 1990s, the government saw many disadvantages in the job assignment system, admitting that 'Mandatory assignments cannot meet the needs of the market-oriented economy.' Many graduates were assigned jobs they did not want, in places they would prefer not to live. Many state enterprises had to accommodate, train and retain staff for life, even if they were surplus to the company's needs or completely unmotivated in their jobs. In 1994, a change towards self-paying education, and freedom for students to find their own work afterwards, was trialed in 40 Chinese universities. In 1997, of the 900,000 students graduating, 10,000 were self-payers. The transition was expected to be completed by the year 2000 (*The Economist*, 1997: 32.)

For the freedom to decide on their own jobs, students pay tuition fees of 1,500 yuan per year, a handsome sum in a country where average per capita income is 4,380 yuan in the urban areas, and less than half that in the rural areas. Students borrow this money either from relatives and friends, or from the government if they are confident of the rewards of being able to negotiate their own jobs and pay. Those students who cannot or do not wish to pay are still assigned to jobs in government departments or state-owned enterprises, or in remote locations (*The Economist*, 1997: 33).

In a healthy, growing economy, such educational reform was generally welcome as young graduates seized the vast opportunities created by economic liberalization. Five special economic zones and 14 coastal open cities were the principal beneficiaries of China's 'Open Door' policy towards foreign investment first initiated in 1979. While recent economic liberalization has extended to inland regions, the provinces of Guangdong and Fujian on the south-east coast of China remain important FDI destinations. By the end of 1997, there were more than 300,000 registered foreign joint ventures in China. Of these, 140,000 were in operation, employing 17.5 million workers (Cheong, 1998: 2–5).

However, with greater exposure to the international economy through its foreign investment and trade activities, China was inevitably affected by the financial turmoil in the Asian and other regions. Compounding this crisis was China's desire to join the World Trade Organization, which necessitated the reform of inefficient state-owned enterprises, duly spearheaded by Premier Zhu Rongji. In September 1997, the Chinese Communist Party had approved faster reform, leading to layoffs and urban unemployment of about 4%. Many who did not lose their jobs outright were kept on at lower or no pay. Retrenched workers, called *xia gang*, and under-employed workers together amount to nearly 30% of those of working age, according to one estimate (*The Economist*, 30 May 1998). Since 1 July 1999, subsidized housing has also been withdrawn, forcing more people into potential hardship. It was estimated that the Chinese economy would have to grow by 8% per annum in order to absorb the six million Chinese entering the workforce each year, as well as the 12 million being laid off by restructuring state enterprises (Huang, 1998: 12). Not surprisingly, massive unemployment marked the close of the century in China.

ECONOMIC REFORM AND THE END OF JOB ASSIGNMENT FOR COLLEGE GRADUATES

Amidst such a scenario, labour reforms intended to align the workforce with the market economy first introduced in 1979 were potentially problematic. The first key labour reform was introduced in the mid-1980s, and over the past decade, more than 20 pieces of legislation affecting employment relationships have been implemented. Branine (1997) evaluates a few main reforms.

The most significant was probably the introduction of the labour contract system as it revoked the long-standing tradition of lifetime employment (pp.78–81). Every labour contract has to cover performance targets, period of employment, working conditions, insurance and welfare benefits, discipline and penalties, and so on. The period of contract can be two or three years, and for up to 20 years, and has been formally approved by the local Labour Bureau in charge of labour allocation to enterprises in the area. First introduced in Shenzhen Special Economic Zone in 1983, it spread gradually to other parts of the economy. By 1996, the labour contract system had affected all employees, including managerial level employees. While foreign-owned enterprises and joint ventures implemented the system quite readily, the state-owned enterprises did so reluctantly as it was an administrative nightmare for which public sector managers groomed in the previously socialist system were not trained, nor psychologically prepared.

A second major labour reform was the decentralization of the staffing system (Branine, 1997: 82–6). Until recently, all applicants for employment were allocated to jobs by a local labour bureau regardless of preference. People could not choose or change jobs, but they had job security. In the decentralized system, job seekers can choose the jobs they prefer, except those that are in essential services or areas of shortage. For example, all education graduates have to become secondary school teachers. Local bureaus now act in an advisory capacity, in competition with private labour service agencies. Such liberalization means there are more opportunities for young job seekers, but also more risks. The better jobs found in joint-ventures and foreign-owned companies are competitive, demanding and can be insecure. Failure to perform up to expectation during the contractual period may lead to loss of employment and subsequent difficulty in getting a job in another company.

The third major reform was the liberalization of the rewards system (Branine, 1997: 88–92). Under socialism, the egalitarian principle prevailed, with all employees getting the same pay regardless of performance. Now employers are under pressure to implement performance criteria and measures to justify payment of a bonus for increased performance. Implementation is far from smooth, as wage differentials and disparities often caused the 'red eye phenomenon' (envy) and dissatisfaction among employees.

Such reforms affected employment relationships in a way that challenged the norms that have their roots in the country's socialist history and ideology. The socio-cultural values of solidarity, equality, mutual assistance, honesty, friendship and obedience to the law were strained under the much more individualistic market principles in the contemporary Chinese economy. Amidst the economic growth and opportunity, increased competition, rising cost of living, and overall uncertainty, institutional corruption became rife. Personal kinship or friendship networks (*guanxi*) were the only reliable support systems. Young college graduates hoping to enter into such an employment environment quickly learn to cultivate and utilize their networks too.

STUDIES OF THE IMPORTANCE OF *GUANXI*

Several research studies confirm the importance of *guanxi* in employment and business relationships among the Chinese.

Two studies by Farh (1998) demonstrated that *guanxi* (defined as 'cultivated relationship') and relational demography (defined as 'ascribed kinship relationships's) were both important for subordinates' trust in their supervisors, while business executives were only concerned with *guanxi* in dealing with their connections.

Another study by Tong and Yong (1998) identified three key aspects of personal relationships that influenced decision making – personal control, *guanxi* relationships, and interpersonal trust (*xinyong*). They argued that economic decisions were not based solely on market considerations. Rather, they were embedded in the context of larger social relations and institutional forces which shaped, reinforced, as well as challenged, a set of behaviours or organizational structures.

Books like Weidenbaum and Hughes' *The Bamboo Network* (1996), Brown's *Chinese Business Enterprise in Asia* (1995), and the Australian Government Department of Foreign Affairs and Trade's *Overseas Chinese Business Networks in Asia* (1995), all attest to the competitive advantages created through the networking of relationships among Chinese business people. The recurrent themes that run through these works describe the nature of Chinese *guanxi*:

- Personal and social relations are intermeshed with business and economic relations, with favours being exchanged as opportunities present themselves.

- These relations are enduring due to the inter-generational involvement in *guanxi* networks, and they are borderless due to the migratory nature of the Chinese and their businesses.

- *Guanxi* networks are strengthened by such values as face-saving and -giving, honour, trust, and reciprocity between individuals in an exchange – a sort of moral debt that binds the parties.

In contrast, the western idea of business or industrial networking refers to the bonding of firms rather than persons. It is the relationship that matters, not the individual entities involved in the relationship. Hence the relationships are always structured in some loose institutional framework, say, a registered society or a business forum, that is cooperative and enduring, rather than opportunistic. This structure ensures a degree of connectedness that outlives the presence of its individual members. These ideas have been explored extensively, such as in the works of western scholars like Axelsson and Easton (1992) who define a network as:

> a model or metaphor which describes a number of entities, which are connected. The entities are actors involved in the economic processes which convert resources to finished goods and services for consumption by end users whether they be individuals or organizations. Thus the links between actors are usually defined in terms of economic exchanges which are themselves conducted within the framework of an enduring relationship (p.xiv).

Also, Anderson, Hakansson and Johanson (1994) have contributed greatly to defining and explaining the workings of the industrial network as:

> a set of two or more connected business relationships, in which each exchange relation is between business firms that are conceptualized as collective actors. Connected means the extent to which 'exchange in one relation is contingent upon exchange in the other relation' (p.2).

While important in itself, a western business network as defined above would be less likely than a Chinese *guanxi* network to be accessed by college graduates for their job search purposes. Cultural differences also seem to affect the thinking and approaches to job searching among western and Chinese job seekers.

JOB SEARCH THEORY

The study of job search behaviour in the western human resource management literature suggests a primarily economic-rational explanatory framework being applied. For example, Lancaster (1990) assumes individuals to be rational and to use job search in such a way as to reflect both the characteristics of their present circumstances and the characteristics of potential job offers. The more intensive the search, the more probable that a job offer will be received within a short time period, and the more probable that the job offer will be acceptable.

Urwin and Shackleton (1999) extend Lancaster's theory by: (1) incorporating the effects of individual characteristics (such as previous occupation, industry) on transition into employment or inactivity; and (2) incorporating 'search methods employed' as well as search intensity. They classified search methods into three categories: professional bodies (including public and private employment agencies), formal methods (advertisements, formal written applications), and informal methods (friends, relatives, colleagues). They also studied the effects of individual characteristics on search methods employed.

Using data from the 1996 Labour Force Survey, Urwin and Shackleton found that among employees in the UK who had been in a job for less than three months, to get their current job 45% had used informal channels and another 45% had used formal channels. The researchers' interpretation of the use of informal channels was that job seekers wanted to signal their higher productivity to employers through the recommendation of their contacts. Among the unemployed, 22% had used informal methods, and 74% formal. This indicated that the unemployed, when in a situation that gives less access to informal networks, tended to use government-sponsored channels to seek employment. Interestingly, when the unemployed used informal methods, the effect was negative: they were unlikely to get a job! Therefore it seems that they used informal methods because they did not have skills to use formal methods.

Among formal methods used, some were more helpful than others. A study of school leavers entering the UK labour market between the recessionary years of 1979 and 1981 found that those who used the official Careers Service (public employment agency) were less successful than those who used more direct (but still formal) methods of search like responding to job advertisements or writing to preferred companies (Bradley, 1993). Surprisingly, in another study, Bosworth (1990) found that young job seekers, especially those who were less well qualified or from lower social classes, were more reliant on public job centres. Therein seems to lie one explanation for the vicious circle of chronic unemployment that socially disadvantaged youth tend to get into.

The theoretical framework used for the Shantou study is influenced by the above discussion, but focuses on less studied influences on job search behaviour, namely Chinese cultural factors such as regional identity and dialect, the educational specialization of students in a business school, and individual socio-psychological variables like work values and job aspirations of young job seekers.

A report by the Australian Department of Foreign Affairs (1995: 19) noted the importance of Chinese dialects thus:

> Understanding the importance of Chinese dialects and their distribution across Asia is critical to understanding ethnic Chinese business networks in the region. Dialects and sub-dialects often partly explain who does business with whom and what is traded.

Dialect has always been associated with regional origin of the Chinese, each dialect group tending to form its own clan association based on the village or region its members came from, or on family names (which were also clustered by location). Dialect may also distinguish the occupations and product lines that Chinese people were engaged in, for example Hainanese were known for their culinary skills and were often employed as cooks, while the Teochiu (as in the Shantou region) were engaged primarily in food and textile trading, and rice milling. (DFAT, 1995: 26–7). These distinctions have become blurred as the Chinese sought employment outside their dialect and sub-dialect group's traditional areas of specialization; nevertheless such occupational and business links with dialect provide a historical explanation for much of the job aspirations and job search behaviour of young college graduates. Hence work values and job aspirations are included as separate variables in this study.

The streaming of students into a management track and an international business track is a fairly recent development in the business curricula in Chinese universities, reflecting a greater awareness among educators of the globalization of the Chinese economy and the need to prepare young people for participation in it. Choice of one stream or the other may be an indication of the students' relative internationalization in thinking about their future. In this study, educational stream (along with geographical origin) is included as an antecedent to values, aspirations and job search behaviour.

A graphical representation of the conceptual framework is given in Figure 1.

FIGURE 1

CONCEPTUAL FRAMEWORK OF JOB SEARCH STRATEGIES

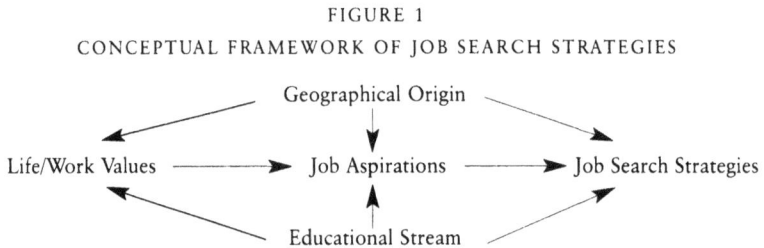

GUANGDONG'S GLOBALIZATION AND THE OVERSEAS CHINESE CONNECTION

More than 80% of the total foreign investments in China came from Overseas Chinese sources, and these employed more than 20 million people. More than two-thirds of these investments were located in south-coastal China, particularly in Guangdong province. Despite the Asian economic crisis, Guangdong province has continued to attract foreign investments, its shortfall of Southeast Asian capital inflow being replaced by increased investment from Europe, America and Taiwan (Huang, 1998: 1–11).

Huang's (1998) study of 32 Overseas Chinese Invested Enterprises (OCIEs) found several key reasons for Overseas Chinese investing in China, particularly south China:

- Ties of common ethnic origin, language and culture: To quote Lee Kuan Yew, Senior Minister in Singapore, one of the major Overseas Chinese countries to invest in China, 'People feel a natural empathy with those who share their physical attributes. This sense of closeness is reinforced when they also share culture and language. It makes for easy rapport and the trust that is the foundation of all business relations.' (*International Herald Tribune*, 1993, cited in Huang, 1998: 2)

- Rapid economic development in south China, which created vast markets for infrastructural as well as consumer products, and the availability of abundant and cheap labour (Huang, 1993: 3).

- Favourable investment conditions, particularly tax incentives and land lease policies which saw the sale of state land for private industrial and commercial development accounting for 35% of the total annual revenue in the coastal cities of south China. (Huang, 1998: 3).

Huang also found a majority of the firms to be small and medium-sized enterprises, located within a manageable distance from the investors' home bases, hence allowing the investors to exercise management and production control. Management style was largely despotic and authoritarian. Most employers believed that a paternalistic approach of providing employees with a net of security and welfare benefits would secure the workforce's loyalty and commitment to work. In an application of the Confucian concept of family, the employer also felt justified in meting out strict rules of behaviour and punishment for their violation, particularly with migrant workers from other parts of China. Accordingly, workers were allowed their clan associations or informal social networks insofar as they would assist with recruitment of workers, but strong feelings of hometown solidarity are discouraged for fear of mass industrial action against the employer (Huang, 1998: 6).

The paternalism extended towards the inhabitants of Shantou and its surrounding counties tended to be more benevolent, for historical and cultural reasons.

Shantou and the counties of Chenghai and Chaozhou are unique among Chinese cities in that they were commercial sea-ports, international trading posts and exit points for Chinese emigrés much earlier than almost any other city. Situated on the Han River delta, this cluster of sea-ports were the homes of a majority of the first-generation Overseas Chinese in Thailand, Malaysia, Singapore and Indonesia. These emigrés and their descendants have kept alive much of the Chaosan (or Teochiu, as they are called in Southeast Asia) dialect and customs, as well as preserving trading and other relations with their Mainland relatives. With these cities heavily dependent on Overseas Chinese trade and investments, *guanxi* is a particularly important feature of business life. As young people leave school or university, many are inducted into this international business network through their families' connections with overseas relatives.

Shantou University is a prime example of such links with the Overseas Chinese. It is Shantou's only university, established in 1981 with financial support from a Teochiu billionaire resident in Hong Kong, Li Ka Shing. Li's businesses are still partially funding the operation of the university and hiring (through recruitment exercises in the university) some of the top graduates for its various China-based interests including hospitals, real estate, roads and bridges. Beyond Li's patronage, many Shantou University graduates are hired into government and private organizations that service the strong trading and investment activity with the Overseas Chinese in property development, rice, live seafood, foodstuffs, textiles and clothing, shoes, electronics, handicrafts and other sectors. Indeed, Overseas Chinese Business is one of three study areas in the School of Business earmarked for special support as the university prepares itself for qualification into the final selection round of 100 top Chinese universities by the twenty-first century – a national blueprint dubbed the '211 Project'. (Pan, 1998: 38; Chen, 1998.)

Conspicuously absent from Shantou are western-owned and operated business enterprises. The only notable western investments are the Kodak industrial film manufacturing plant, and two competing dairy products manufacturers from Australia and New Zealand respectively. These firms, like most western or joint-venture enterprises in China, tend to recruit through career talks in, or upon recommendation of, local universities.

JOB SEARCHING AMONG SHANTOU UNIVERSITY GRADUATES-TO-BE

In the era of job assignment, fourth-year university students in China typically began their job placements in the final semester of a two-semester academic year. Traditionally, their school or university department would arrange for their internship at various state-owned or (since economic liberalization) private organizations, with the expectation that these placements would lead to permanent jobs for the young graduates. However, since the introduction of economic reforms which led to massive down-sizing by state-owned enterprises, and the Asian economic crisis which saw a slowdown of Overseas Chinese trade and investment into Shantou, most graduating students have had to hunt for jobs by themselves. In the relative lack of media job advertising in this town of about 10,000 people, such as is common in larger Chinese cities and other countries, these students rely more on formal job search methods like job centres and agencies, and informal methods like the recommendation of relatives, friends and teachers.

Using a semi-structured questionnaire, 90 students in two graduating business classes at Shantou University were asked to state their job aspirations and their job search strategies. (This was followed by a focus group of 25 students to get more in-depth explanations for the survey answers.) These students stated which of two business streams they were in: international business (57) and management (33). Two-thirds were male. About 80% were born and had grown up in the Shantou area, while 20% were recruited from other cities, counties or provinces. Job aspiration categories included type of job, level of job, type of employing organization, and pay level. Job search categories included:

- introduction by family members or friends
- introduction by teachers
- employment fairs
- electronic job registers
- written applications to preferred companies ('cold call')

Analysis of Work Values

Young graduating college students in China are apparently no different from their counterparts elsewhere in aspiring primarily towards economic rewards, as that first job often symbolizes the beginning of financial independence. Of the 90 students surveyed, 51% want a first job that 'pays well'. This is consistent across educational stream and geographical origin. Other aspirations are

TABLE 1

LIFE/WORK VALUES BY EDUCATIONAL STREAM

	Manage-ment	%	Int'l Business	%	Total	%
	33		57		90	
If you had to choose, what is the one most important thing you would look for in a job?						
• Pays well	16	48%	30	53%	46	51%
• Time to do what I want	3	9%	1	2%	4	4%
• Allows me to have a stable family life	10	30%	2	4%	12	13%
• Travel	2	6%	12	21%	14	16%
• Learn more things	2	6%	8	14%	10	11%
• Meet people	0	0%	4	7%	4	4%
If you had a choice, would you prefer to work in a local, national or international setting ?						
• Local (Chao-San region),	13	39%	7	12%	20	22%
• National (anywhere in China)	8	24%	26	46%	34	38%
• International (anywhere, dealing with international matters)	4	12%	21	37%	25	28%
• No preference	8	24%	3	5%	11	12%
If you had to choose, would you prefer to work with local people, other Chinese, Qiaoxiang or foreigners?						
• Local people (from Chao-San region)	10	30%	4	7%	14	16%
• Other Chinese (from other provinces)	2	6%	13	23%	15	17%
• Qiaoxiang (Overseas Chinese)	6	18%	10	18%	16	18%
• Foreigners	5	15%	22	39%	27	30%
• No preference	10	30%	8	14%	18	20%
If you had a choice, would you prefer to for a work boss/leader who is local, from another province, a Qiaoxiang, or a foreigner from overseas?						
• Local	10	30%	9	16%	19	21%
• From another province	6	18%	25	44%	31	34%
• Qiaoxiang	9	27%	9	16%	18	20%
• Foreigner	4	12%	11	19%	15	17%
• No preference	4	12%	3	5%	7	8%
Reasons affecting your choice of workmates or boss/leader:	(multiple)		(multiple)		Total	%
• Language ability	24	73%	27	47%	51	57%
• Cultural familiarity	31	94%	21	37%	52	58%
• Curiosity about other cultures	17	52%	33	58%	50	56%
• Curiosity about life outside of China	12	36%	37	65%	49	54%

TABLE 2

LIFE/WORK VALUES BY GEOGRAPHICAL ORIGIN OF STUDENTS

	Chao-San Region	%	Other Provinces	%	Total	%
	68		22		90	
If you had to choose, what is the one most important thing you would look for in a job?						
• Pays well	35	51%	11	50%	46	51%
• Time to do what I want	4	6%	0	0%	4	4%
• Allows me to have a stable family life	10	15%	2	9%	12	13%
• Travel	10	15%	4	18%	14	16%
• Learn more things	7	10%	3	14%	10	11%
• Meet people	2	3%	2	9%	4	4%
If you had a choice, would you prefer to work in a local, national or international setting ?						
• Local (Chao-San region),	17	25%	3	14%	20	22%
• National (anywhere in China)	24	35%	10	45%	34	38%
• International (anywhere, dealing with international matters)	17	25%	8	36%	25	28%
• No preference	10	15%	1	5%	11	12%
If you had to choose, would you prefer to work with local people, other Chinese, Qiaoxiang or foreigners?						
• Local people (from Chao-San region)	12	18%	2	9 %	14	16%
• Other Chinese (from other provinces)	10	15%	5	23%	15	17%
• Qiaoxiang (Overseas Chinese)	14	21%	2	9%	16	18%
• Foreigners	17	25%	10	45%	27	30%
• No preference	15	22%	3	14%	18	20%
If you had a choice, would you prefer to work for a boss/leader who is local, from another province, a Qiaoxiang, or a foreigner from overseas?						
• Local	18	26%	1	5%	19	21%
• From another province	19	28%	12	55%	31	34%
• Qiaoxiang	15	22%	3	14%	18	20%
• Foreigner	10	15%	5	23%	15	17%
• No preference	6	9%	1	5%	7	8%
Reasons affecting your choice of workmates or boss/leader:	(multiple)		(multiple)		Total	%
• Language ability	40	59%	11	50%	51	57%
• Cultural familiarity	36	53%	16	73%	52	58%
• Curiosity about other cultures	33	49%	17	77%	50	56%
• Curiosity about life outside of China	30	44%	19	86%	49	54%

somewhat more dispersed. Management (MG) stream students, most of whom also happen to have been born and had grown up in the Chaosan district, cited aspirations like 'stable family life' and 'time to do what I want' more often than students from the International Business (IB) stream, most of whom have also come to Shantou from other provinces. It appears that Chaosan students have self-selected a more stable, predictable stream of study in anticipation of secure, well-paying management jobs. On the other hand, IB students seem to be aspiring for adventure, citing 'travel' and 'learn more things' more often than their MG friends.

This observation is corroborated by the findings that more IB students are willing to work anywhere within China (46%) or internationally (37%) than MG students (24% and 12% respectively). IB students are somewhat more internationalized in their outlook, with 39% saying they would choose to work with foreigners (compared with 15% of MG students). But when it comes to choosing a boss, they are still more comfortable with a Chinese from their own province (44%, close to the MG students' 30%). Their relative internationalism is more apparent in the proportion that mentioned curiosity about other cultures (58%) and life outside China (65%).

More Chaosan students tend to expect to remain in the area (25%) after graduation, than their friends who have come from other provinces (14%), implying the presence of family and social networks they are unwilling to leave. The importance of regional, and by implication, cultural and linguistic affiliations, is also shown up in the preference of Chaosan students to work with or under others from their own area (18% workmates, 26% boss), and likewise for students from other provinces (23% workmates, 55% boss). Chinese from other provinces than Guangdong often find the southern state's main dialects of Cantonese, Teochiu and Hakka difficult to understand, as their intonation system is more complicated that that of most northern dialects and of Mandarin, the official Chinese language. Chaosan people, on the other hand, can speak Mandarin, but would usually prefer to speak their own Teochiu dialect. Their international contact has mostly been with Overseas Chinese of Teochiu stock, and their proficiency in both Mandarin and English is weak relative to people in the larger Chinese cities. Hence the reasons cited by the Chaosan students for their preference for Chaoson workmates and bosses (or for

Overseas Chinese who were more similar to them than compatriots from other provinces) were mostly 'language ability' and 'cultural familiarity'.

Analysis of Job Aspirations

Most of the students surveyed wanted to be managers (41%) in administration (39%) or marketing (28%), in a private business firm (family-owned 29%, or otherwise 30%), earning between 1001 and 1500 yuan a month (56%). This was significant in that university lecturers were earning that amount on average; it seemed the students were aware of the greater opportunities open to them

TABLE 3

JOB ASPIRATIONS (GRADUATION–5 YEARS): BY EDUCATIONAL STREAM

	Manage-ment	%	Int'l Business	%	Total	%
	33		57		90	
Type of job						
• administration/management	17	52%	18	32%	35	39%
• sales and marketing	2	6%	23	40%	25	28%
• teaching	4	12%	2	4%	6	7%
• other professional (journalism, research, accounting)	5	15%	7	12%	12	13%
• further education	5	15%	7	12%	12	13%
Level of Job						
• administrative assistant / professional trainee	10	30%	11	19%	21	23%
• manager / professional	11	33%	26	46%	37	41%
• entrepreneur	9	27%	16	28%	25	28%
• student	3	9%	4	7%	7	8%
Type of employing organization						
• family business firm	11	33%	15	26%	26	29%
• other private business firm	9	27%	18	32%	27	30%
• state-owned business firm	3	9%	6	11%	9	10%
• foreign-owned business firm	5	15%	12	21%	17	19%
• government department	2	6%	4	7%	6	7%
• educational institution	3	9%	2	4%	5	6%
Pay level expected						
• 500–1000 yuan/month	16	48%	6	11%	22	24%
• 1001–1500 yuan/month	12	36%	38	67%	50	56%
• 1501–2000 yuan/month	4	12%	9	16%	13	14%
• above 2000 yuan/month	1	3%	4	7%	5	6%

TABLE 4

JOB ASPIRATIONS (GRADUATION–5 YEARS) BY GEOGRAPHICAL ORIGIN

	Chao-San Region	%	Other Provinces	%	Total	%
	68		22		90	
Type of job						
• administration/management	30	44%	5	23%	35	39%
• sales and marketing	18	26%	7	32%	25	28%
• teaching	6	9%	0	0%	6	7%
• other professional (journalism, research, accounting)	7	10%	5	23%	12	13%
• further education	7	10%	5	23%	12	13%
Level of Job						
• administrative assistant / professional trainee	18	26%	3	14%	21	23%
• manager / professional	25	37%	11	50%	36	41%
• entrepreneur	18	26%	8	36%	26	28%
• student	7	10%	0	0%	7	8%
Type of employing organization						
• family business firm	18	26%	8	40%	26	29%
• other private business firm	20	29%	7	32%	27	30%
• state-owned business firm	7	10%	2	10%	9	10%
• foreign-owned business firm	12	18%	5	25%	17	19%
• government department	6	9%	0	0%	6	7%
• educational institution	5	7%	0	0%	5	6%
Pay level expected						
• 500–1000 yuan/month	19	28%	3	15%	22	24%
• 1001–1500 yuan/month	40	59%	10	50%	50	56%
• 1501–2000 yuan/month	6	9%	7	35%	13	14%
• above 2000 yuan/month	3	4%	2	9%	5	6%

as market activity intensified, and they had developed higher aspirations than what their lecturers' generation had experienced.

In keeping with the earlier results showing IB students to be more adventurous, they were also more ambitious, in that 40% opted for sales and marketing jobs which would offer more challenge but also greater pay levels and benefits for the hard worker (56% expected to be paid more than 1000 yuan per month). In contrast, MG students preferred steady administration jobs (52%) in family firms (33%), earning less than 1000 yuan. Remembering that MG students were also mostly Chaosan-based, a picture emerged here of local youth being sent to university to learn business management in order that they may succeed to the leadership of the family business some day. Much of this mutual expectation is tied up in the obligation of the family elders to provide a means of livelihood for their young charges, who in return are obligated to take the jobs offered even if they pay less, in anticipation of being groomed to take over the business some day.

Slightly more IB students (21%) than MG students (15%), and those from other provinces (25%) than Chaosan students (18%), aspired to work in foreign-owned firms. This may be because of linguistic and cultural familiarity as mentioned earlier, and also due to the fact that there are more foreign-owned businesses outside of the Chaosan area. And these firms, when they hire graduates, tend to hire for the sales and marketing function as local market knowledge is essential.

In view of their different work values and job aspirations, the students might be expected to utilize different job search strategies. For instance, those aspiring to work in foreign companies might use strategies similar to those used by western students, such as answering job advertisements in newspapers. However, because of the paucity of foreign companies in Shantou and its surrounding counties, and also the unavailability of newspapers from other provinces, the job search strategies are somewhat limited. The conservatism of the Chaosan culture, the area's relative isolation historically and economically, and the linguistic uniqueness, have combined to make students graduating from the local university dependent mostly on introductions for their job search.

Analysis of Job Search Strategies

Introductions: The results overwhelmingly suggest that introductions were the most popular job search techniques. Regardless of gender, place of students' origin, or stream of business study, students generally expected their parents, and to a lesser extent their relatives and friends, to introduce them to prospective employers. This expectation was based on the belief that their family's and relatives' *guanxi* networks could and should legitimately be tapped for their employment search, as it was a Chinese tradition for seniors to give a helping hand to young people as they made their transition from being students to working adults.

TABLE 5

JOB SEARCH STRATEGIES BY EDUCATIONAL STREAM

	Manage-ment	%	Int'l Business	%	Total	%
	33		57		90	
	(multiple)		(multiple)		(multiple)	
Introduction by family members	25	76%	29	51%	54	60%
Introduction by friends	18	55%	26	46%	44	49%
Introduction by local Chinese teachers	14	42%	21	37%	35	39%
Introduction by foreign teachers	1	3%	15	26%	16	18%
Employment fairs	22	67%	38	67%	60	67%
Electronic job registers	11	33%	17	30%	28	31%
Unsolicited written applications	8	24%	19	33%	27	30%

TABLE 6

JOB SEARCH STRATEGIES BY GEOGRAPHICAL ORIGIN

	Chao-San Region	%	Other Provinces	%	Total	%
	68		22		90	
	(multiple)		(multiple)		(multiple)	
Introduction by family members	49	72%	14	64%	53	59%
Introduction by friends	26	38%	17	78%	43	48%
Introduction by local Chinese teachers	24	35%	11	50%	35	39%
Introduction by foreign teachers	1	1%	15	68%	16	18%
Employment fairs	42	62%	18	82%	60	67%
Electronic job registers	15	22%	13	59%	28	31%
Unsolicited written applications	11	16%	16	73%	27	30%

Chaosan-based students were more likely to ask their family members for such introductions (72%) than students from other provinces (64%). The latter, possibly because of their having left home to study in Shantou, were more likely to appeal to friends instead (78%). Consistent with the finding that many MG students aspired to join family businesses, three-quarters of them would get introductions from family members, while many also ask friends and local Chinese teachers. IB students use these same channels, but are also more forthright in asking visiting foreign teachers for recommendations, either for jobs or higher educational opportunities. This is in keeping with their more international values and aspirations.

However, some of the students felt that the obligation attached to receiving such assistance could be too daunting, as any introduction made by a senior was expected to be accepted without fuss by the young person. Their performance and attitude towards work would thenceforth be a reflection on the person who introduced them. The young person's obligation lay in not letting the introducer 'lose face', and in repaying the favour in some form later. In the case of introductions by the students' own friends, there was slightly less pressure to comply. Students felt that they could be more honest and open with peers about their job preferences, and less bound by the tradition of *renqing* (owing a favour). However, students were pragmatic enough to recognize that most of their peers did not possess the right connections to help them in their job search.

On the whole, teachers in China are still revered by students. They are seen as the fountain of wisdom and knowledge from which students are expected to draw during their university years. Depending on their position, academic status and extent of consulting activities, they are also seen to possess valuable resources like power within the university hierarchy, or connections with other universities, government departments and the business community. Those students who aspire towards further education overseas or an international business career generally seek out teachers who are consultants for trading firms with overseas connections, or visiting foreign teachers. In the study, a majority of students would rather cultivate their local teachers as they either did not have confidence in their foreign language ability or did not see any possibility of working in an internationalized context. A handful of students, however, would visit foreign teachers at home during the teachers' 'open house' days, or attend informal chat sessions at the 'English Corner' where one or more foreign teachers were often present, or offer their services as tour guides or interpreters during the teachers' visit. The kind of help usually obtained from teachers included: jobs within the same university, direct introduction to other employers for internship or employment, or reference letters to support applications for employment or further studies. Like with parents, though to a lesser extent, students also felt obligated to accept any offer, to stay on the job, and to perform well. The relative weakness of this feeling of obligation to teachers may have been due to the mobility of graduates across city or provincial boundaries, whereupon the relationship with teachers may be transient.

Employment Fairs: The overwhelming reliance on the informal method of introduction is balanced by the heavy use of employment fairs (67% overall), a formal, independent job search method. In the new era of self-selection of jobs, Chinese youth apparently want to make informed choices, and employment fairs (usually organized by government authorities) offer the information and exposure that may not otherwise be available. Some are held on an on-going basis in a local government office, allowing employers and job seekers to drop in as needed. Others are held once a year in December or January as a major recruitment exercise for graduating students. These large employment fairs are only held in large capital cities, and students travel from all provinces to attend. Some of the Shantou students attended such a fair in Shenzhen, the nearest large Special Economic Zone to Shantou (which did not have one of similar scale). While the opportunities at such fairs were attractive, students felt that it was not worth their while to attend because:

- there were too many job seekers going after too few jobs
- the management of such fairs was often haphazard and chaotic
- criteria for selection were not made known, and prospective employers, for the sake of expediency, often shortlisted job seekers from the crowd based on their appearance (!)

Somewhat more popular were the annual recruitment drives undertaken by Li Ka Shing's enterprises and other large employers which visited Shantou University to source for promising, bright young graduates. Most students viewed such recruiters with awe, and most also felt they were seeking only top students and quickly eliminated themselves. This exclusivity was reinforced by the practice of pre-selection, where only students who were recommended by their teachers could attend interviews with such recruiters on campus.

Electronic Job Registers: Shantou University's Computer Support Department ran an electronic employment register for graduating students. Its administrator reported a steady growth of registrations since its creation a year ago, receiving up to 300 resumés/curricula vitae a year. However, among the Business students surveyed, there appeared to be little awareness of the register's existence. There was no publicity, and those students who knew about it either chanced upon it or else were in the schools of Computer Science and Electronic Engineering which were involved in its creation. Business students who used the register did not rely entirely on it for job outcomes; it was at best a supplement to their other search strategies. Such a register was limited in its efficacy by its limited reach: it was accessible only to employers who subscribed to it, and only in Shantou. Moreover, students registering had to give the administrator a disk copy of their resumés for uploading; they could not input and update their resumés readily. Only 22% of Chaosan-based students used the register, and 59% of other students used similar registers available in their home provinces or larger cities.

Unsolicited Written Applications: The least popular job search technique was writing directly to preferred employers. 30% of all students were resourceful enough to find the addresses of such employers, and felt unabashed about making 'cold calls'. However, a majority of students felt uneasy about having to 'sell' their credentials and abilities so forcefully, or felt the outcomes would be limited anyway because of the *guanxi* networks that these employers were already patronising. Strangers outside of these networks would inevitably get last priority. Such an approach was seen to be useful only if the students were applying to foreign, especially western, companies. One detraction from this negative trend was the tendency of students from other provinces to use this method (73%), primarily because they were seeking jobs away from Shantou and had little choice but to write directly to companies they knew of.

CONCLUSION

To conclude, it is useful to reiterate the cultural characteristics of Shantou that may support the obvious preference for using *guanxi* in job searching. While networking is by no means unique to the students of Shantou University, its heavy use is consistent with the following features:

- Shantou and its surrounding counties have enjoyed historical significance as port cities, and still have contemporary significance as an important gateway for Overseas Chinese to return to do business on the Mainland.

- Because of its relative isolation with respect to the other important commercial centres of Guangzhou to the south and Shanghai to the north, it has been left out of most central government planning, and has received little government investment. It has thrived instead on local family business and investments from the Overseas Chinese.

- The family and kinship relationships are precipitated by a loyalty to the distinctive Teochiu dialect, the relative wealth in the community, and the unwillingness of many locals to leave the congenial sub-tropical climate and terrain for harsher parts of China.

- The linguistic and cultural distance between Chaosan people and their northern neighbours intensifies the conservatism of the locals, encouraging them to seek protection in their familiar language, cuisine and mores.

- Shantou University is possibly the best example within Shantou of an experiment in regional integration in that staff and students have come from many other provinces. Yet because of its given mission to educate local youth for China's modernization and its support by a prominent Overseas Chinese man, it is strongly Chaosanese in character as well. Its graduates are welcome within the local community, but those students with the additional cultural and linguistic affinity are likely to be able to benefit more.

However, contrary to the conventional knowledge of *guanxi*-based business relations as being built on trust and reciprocity, the findings about students using *guanxi* in job search point to a one-way, utilitarian philosophy. Because of the unequal social status of students and their *guanxi* targets, who were mostly teachers or parents and senior relatives, there was mutual acceptance of this utilitarianism. And because Shantou has been exposed to Overseas Chinese for a long time, some local students felt it was their right to obtain help from the presumably wealthier relatives overseas. It would be very interesting for further research to be undertaken in other cities and provinces to compare the importance of *guanxi* as a job search strategy. While often assumed to be a common feature of Chinese social life, many Chinese cities are increasingly being exposed to western recruitment practices which may undermine the usefulness of personal and social relationships. Moreover with graduate unemployment rising along with the employment fallout from massive restructuring of the state-owned enterprises, job seekers will have to develop a wider repertoire of strategies to compete.

ACKNOWLEDGEMENTS

The author wishes to acknowledge the Central Queensland University's financial assistance towards the completion of this research, and the helpful comments of the referees who reviewed an earlier draft of this paper.

REFERENCES

Anderson, J.C., Hakansson, H. *et al.* (1994), 'Dyadic Business Relationships within a Business Network Context', *Journal of Marketing*, Vol.58, pp.1–15.
The Economist (1997), 'Pay as You Learn', May 10, Vol.343, No.8016, pp.32–3.
Axelsson, B. and Easton, G. (eds.) (1992), *Industrial Networks: A New View of Reality*. London: Routledge.
Bosworth, D.L. (1990). 'Unemployment and the Intensity and Method of Job Search', *International Journal of Manpower*, Vol.11, No.1.
Bradley, S. (1993). 'Job Search by Unemployed School-leavers: The Use of the Careers Service during a Recession', *International Journal of Manpower*, Vol.14, No.6.
Branine, M. (1997), 'Change and Continuity in Chinese Employment Relationships', *New Zealand Journal of Industrial Relations*, Vol.22, No.1 (April), pp.77–94.
Brown, R.A. (ed.) (1995), *Chinese Business Enterprises in Asia*. London: Routledge,.
Chen, J.Y. (1998), Director of International Cooperation Department. Interview on the internationalization of Shantou University.
Cheong, Y.R. (1998), Entry Mode of Overseas Chinese FDI in China, Paper at the International Conference for Qiaoxiang Studies, Jinjiang, Fujin, 28–31 October.
East Asia Analytical Unit, Australian Government Department of Foreign Affairs and Trade (1995), *Overseas Chinese Business Networks in Asia*.
Farh, J.L. *et al.* (1998), 'The Influence of Relational Demography and Guanxi: The Chinese Case', *Organizational Science*, July/August, Vol.9, No.4, pp.471–88.
Huang, C. (1998), 'The Dynamics of Overseas Chinese Invested Enterprises in South China', Paper at the International Conference for Qiaoxiang Studies, Jinjiang, Fujin, 28–31 October.

Lancaster, T. (1990), 'The Econometric Analysis of Transition Data', *Econometric Society Monographs*, No.17, Cambridge: Cambridge Universtiy Press.
Pan, L. (1998), *The Encyclopaedia of the Chinese Overseas*. Chinese Heritage Centre, Archipelago Press.
The Economist (US) (1998), Vol.347, No.8070 (30 May), p.42 (2)
Tong, C.K. and Yong, P.K. (1998), 'Guanxi Bases, Xinyong and Chinese Business Networks', *The British Journal of Sociology*, Vol.49, No.1 (March), pp.75–96.
Urwin, P. and Shackleton, J.R. (1999), 'Search Methods and Transitions into Employment and Inactivity: An Analysis of Linked Records from the Labour Force Survey', *International Journal of Manpower*, Vol.20, No.3, pp.4–14.
Weidenbaum, M. and Hughes, S. (1996), *The Bamboo Network*, New York: Martin Kessler Books, The Free Press.

11

Conclusion:
Globalization, Work and Employment –
Asia Pacific Experiences in Retrospect

IAN G. SMITH and YAW A. DEBRAH

The foregoing contributions to this special issue reveal the degree
to which globalization has become a major influence on the labour
process, labour markets, practice of management in general and
human resource management in particular in certain Pacific Rim
communities. The business world and equally the nation-states
affected by the processes of globalization are in the midst of a
process of adjusting to the changing world order. The forms taken
by this international dimension are various, from countries in
trading blocks to companies operating as international or
multinational businesses on a global scale. Many of these internationalized businesses earn well in excess of the national income of
nation-states, and in so doing uphold the interests of shareholders
who are usually located in far-off nations living in cultures where
values and attitudes are alien to those of local host countries.
And yet these values are often imposed on the local culture,
labour market, the labour process, groups and individuals with
outcomes that are at best difficult to discern and at worst
problematic and a potential source of friction. A significant
number and variety of these outcomes deriving from globalization
have been comprehensively evaluated in this volume, with
implications for the academic debate on globalization and for
managers, trade unions and employees and nation-states and their
governments.

In broad terms the main issues presented can be categorized as
follows.

• There is potential for misunderstanding between cultures in the
  context of the work place requiring sensitive responses from

management – a subject addressed in several contributions based on experiences in Malaysia and particularly in Australia in connection with cross-cultural diversity.

- Multinational firms interact with the more general characteristics of host or local nations where discernible trends and new questions can arise in the effects on employees, trade unions and labour market structures. Such difficulties have been considered particularly in the context of Australia, New Zealand, Malaysia and Japan. These trends and the issues they uncover sometimes give the impression that the parts are greater than the sum of globalization.

- For management there is the 'confrontation' with the local labour process and the institutions of the local labour market, as evidenced in the works on Malaysia, New Zealand, Australia, and also the management of a culturally diverse company whose members, procedures and arrangements are diverse to the extent that they do not replicate at all those of the company's home nation-state.

- Changes are brought into the organization's internal activities, which have implications for elements of the management of the labour process such as the exercise of power and influence, and the management of change in general and cultural change in particular. Again the reader will have found evaluations of these matters in Australia, and New Zealand; in the context of Japan attention was concentrated on the required appropriate structural changes to the labour market which might influence some positive outcomes to be derived from globalization.

- The reactions of employees caught up in and affected by the process of globalization do not regularly figure in the globalization debate. We may therefore ask what individual expectations arise in the context of globalization and how do people react to the outcomes; these issues have been addressed in those contributions dealing with academic expatriates, cultural diversity and the behaviour of Chinese students in searching out a positive start to their careers.

- To deal with many of the above points requires new and robust developments ins general management theory and practice and human resource management.

• There is a lack of cohesion within the process of globalization and inconclusiveness in the debate on convergence versus divergence.

CULTURE VERSUS CULTURE

Like pieces of a jigsaw all the contributions help us begin to appreciate an emerging picture of the process of internalization with piecemeal changes affecting the patterns of business, political issues, economics, technical and social change to a degree which is in some instances currently ahead of our understanding of the contents and outcomes of such changes. Not least is this the case with the labour process and cultural arrangements. The roles and preferences of stakeholders including governments, communities, groups and individuals are both affected by and can affect the outcomes of globalization, particularly in terms of giving or withholding support to international organizations and their aspirations. But methods which work in one culture may readily run into problems in another and can lead to misunderstanding and dispute. This can be exacerbated by an all too common situation where the power of management in multinational organizations increases and supplants the power of institutions in the local nation-state. The desire of governments to obtain foreign direct investments is all too readily seen – as evidenced for example in the contribution by B. McKenna covering Australia's experiences – and can greatly weaken the resolve and attempts of institutions and people to resist change brought about by globalization. Accepting developments under the heading of local opportunities deriving from global forces is not always to the benefit of the nation, its institutions and workforce.

The size and geographically widespread nature of international enterprises re-enforces the need for improved management control whether in the form of 'strict' and centralized supervisory control or localized control in semi-autonomous working units. Such control can have negative impacts on the labour market and on the role of human resource management. This may materialize in the form of a reduced reliance on local resources which dilutes their power particularly in respect of trade unions and also as a more general change for local vested interests and their economic power.

Globalization is clearly a major threat *and* an opportunity and in between lie the many problems faced by internationalized organizations, local institutions and workforces.

COHESIVE FORCE OR 'MUDDLING THROUGH'?

The very real responses made by organizations, their managers, individual employees and groups of employees to the pressures of globalization are frequently *ad hoc*, sometimes lacking in strategy and at times difficult to define because they are emerging responses – no less and no more. Perhaps all this is some kind of 'settling down' process of cultural and behavioural patterns which have been severely disturbed by globalization. The 'settling down' is a complex tangle of elements ranging from individual adjustments made, for example, by expatriate employees (Richardson), to the sometimes powerful reaction of companies and trade unions (Budhwar and Fadzil, and B. McKenna) and on to the restructuring of labour market characteristics (Sano). Additionally notions of standardiz-ation in organizational management (perhaps conformity) flow from the globalization debate as uncovered by S. McKenna, although the presence of this in reality can be challenged as, for example, by Lewis, French and Phetmany who identify the need for new and, one suspects, flexible emerging management styles which are suggested by the requirement to effectively administer the cultural diversity brought about by the internationalization of organizations and work. In more extreme terms counter forces to globalization are evidenced in the required trade union responses as identified by Holland, Nelson and Fisher; the employer–union interface may yet significantly influence much of the outcome of global pressures on labour markets, although unions may find their role seriously weakened in this process as revealed by Waring, Macdonald and Burgess.

THE SUM AND THE PARTS

From an Asia Pacific context therefore, the range of issues within any process of globalization is complex and fragmented but they are individually significant, and this significance perhaps makes the individual issue (or trend, development, pressure, conflict or whatever) more dominant than the 'global' issue of globalization itself – perhaps the parts are greater than the sum. The assessment of Science Research Activity in New Zealand by S. McKenna uncovers the need to consider the serious problems of local restructuring necessitated by global developments: in other words, the issue of management response rather than globalization in its own right. In her analysis of expatriate academics and managers Richardson reveals the degree of neglect for cross-cultural training and support (again, an element of globalization rather than the overall process itself), requiring attention from those who share a responsibility for the employment experiences and the development of professional employee groupings. From the detail issues – or parts – may emerge our better understanding of the process of globalization.

DIVERSITY AND CONVERGENCE

Budhwar tells us of 'the need to understand and acknowledge the different ways of managing human resources in different parts of the world'. In their study of Australian and Vietnamese born workers and cross-cultural diversity Lewis, French and Phetmany argue that any notion of predominant-culture based leadership behaviour faces a situation where 'diverse cultural workforces have made the universal assumptions of these theories questionable'. Quiet acceptance of any universal panacea claimed to exist in globalization has not been to Australia's fullest benefit, and B. McKenna asks 'whose economic interests are being served by acquiescence?' The workings of some universal model of globalization are therefore lacking form, and definable outcomes appear to be problematical. S. McKenna underlines this in evaluating new public management – a global development which may have influenced the structure and administration of the New Zealand public sector in general and the country's scientific research programmes in particular, but largely to the extent of creating 'micro-management issues and problems' which 'highlight the difficulties of managing changes at this micro-level'. This has been a result of mounting global pressures and shrinking influence from the nation-state and its government which oversees the public sector. In S. McKenna's study the local problems of reacting to, coping with and even diluting the forces or outcomes of globalization may transcend the fuller process of globalization. In particular the arguments for a universal theory of practice for management are seriously questioned, and we may conclude that if local issues predominate within the debate on globalization and internationalization it might raise some serious doubts about any 'new order'. Internationalism has been consistently viewed as a global process of integration involving goods, services and labour, perhaps ultimately some form of global market arrangement for commodities and labour. Yet as witnessed in this volume any process of integration is difficult to identify and is at best uncoordinated and spasmodic and at worst uncertain, not least because of the conflict and confusion between local autonomy and the new standardized forms taken by globalization which in turn threaten any harmonization. Clearly cross-boundary standardiz-ation is not here and may never arrive, and some of the foregoing works give some credence to the work of Hofstede (1980) on cultural differences, particularly Budhwar and Fadzil, and Lewis, French and Phetmany.

GLOBALIZATION AND LOCAL DIFFICULTIES

If standardization for global management theory and practice does not exist there remains the need to address the measurable effects of the outcomes of globalization on local micro-level organizations – see S. McKenna, Holland, Nelson and Fisher, and Sano – resulting for example in changes to the local labour market characteristics and radically changing the employment experiences of workforces in nation-states and industries. Sano argues the case for pro-active labour market responses to exploit the opportunities offered by such changes. Deriving from the process of change at local level some commentators claim to have discerned the trends towards the comprehensive globalization of labour and identify in turn powerful implications for product, money and labour markets (Johnson, 1991). That these three markets interlink with a process of globalization results in new forms and relationships for the legal, social and economic institutions of the state (Card and Freeman, 1993). If something is happening in these markets – even merely discernible trends – the interface between globalization and the state and culture becomes a core area of study for the student of globalization as argued by Budhwar and Fadzil, for example in the context of Islamic institutions. The process of internationalization therefore inevitably runs into the 'buffers' represented by the local characteristics of nations and cultures (whether they be Australian, Vietnamese, New Zealand or Malaysian and/or Islamic) which can act as obstacles to and frustrate attempts at standardizing or universalizing the theory and practice of managing people in work at a micro-level across the macro-level global corporations (Frenkel and Royal, 1998).

Arguments exist against the above contentions, however, and Mueller (1994) points out that multinationals can cope with local difficulties and overcome the obstacles thus allowing for some standard best practice across national boundaries. In the main such influences at national and organizational level tend to be limited to employment patterns and issues of work organization. This argument is illuminated by Waring, Macdonald and Burgess in their work on the Australian coal industry where the pressures of globalization are seen to have transformed workplace organization, coal mine management strategies and trade union organization and behaviour, although the authors equally argue that the local decisions of the employer, trade union and national government can be of equal significance for employment issues and the forces of globalization, not least because of the 'historically grounded' industry perspective. To the latter we could add the Islamic perspective, for example, as discussed by Budhwar and Fadzil. Significantly Waring *et al.* identify the industrial disputes breaking out as globalization brings impoverishment of working conditions and greater managerial control. This depressing 'vision' of conflict in the midst of multinational company preferences and practices which actually overcome local, national and cultural characteristics and preferences may be a feature of an emerging global labour market which seriously dilutes nation-state policies for the institutions within the national labour market (Lee, 1996) and threatens, at the least, the vulnerable and disadvantaged within that market.

To date the debate on globalization has provided little in the way of answers and solutions for these problematic developments which are deemed to rise from the very heart of the globalization process. B. McKenna's study of the Australian responses to globalization is broadly consistent with the depressing scenario. This has occurred partly because of the changing power relationships between labour and capital within the Australian labour market brought about by the contextual characteristics of globalization and it must be added the acquiescence of government policies. Within that same labour market the coal industry studied by Waring, Macdonald and Burgess re-enforces the picture of globalization forcing in radical change to market arrangements via the linking of commodity and finance markets. The resulting changes to the labour process have not been countered at all effectively by the trade unions who have experienced great difficulty in responding to the presence of the forces of globalization.

ADVANTAGE BEFORE DISADVANTAGE?

We can note again therefore, that the 'local' responses made by nation-states to the forces and effects of internationalization are often confused and lack cohesion. Furthermore, there appears to be a general pre-occupation with 'positive' facets of globalization and difficulties or disadvantages can sometimes be overlooked, usually because economic improvement takes precedence over socio-economic impoverishment. The 'good' of globalization embraces micro-level advantages to the firm including advances in operations and the application of information technology; the benefits accruing from international trade policies; substantial opportunities to lower costs, particularly labour costs; increased output and more general productivity improvements; and the reductions in response times to changes in market demand. Not least among these 'good' facets is the opportunity to gain competitive advantage. At macro or nation-state level the advantages include the hope of economic growth and stable employment as cited by Sano although the fulfilment of such promises is often unrealized and unproven (Smith and Debrah, 2000). Yet the benefits of globalization and the resultant aspirations of the firm and the state spur on the process of change with flexibility and lean operations, two of the core resulting developments – see B. McKenna. In Malaysia, New Zealand and Australia the dream has been followed with real determination to the point in Budhwar's review of Malaysia where the effects of the globalization of business may create labour market conditions which could actually contribute to a 'sustained competitive advantage'; such an outcome may also flow from Sano's conclusions for the Japanese economy. In New Zealand S. McKenna tells us that locally developed patterns of working and organizational structuring in the public sector have been replaced by new patterns deriving from a more internationalized approach as represented by the 'new public management'.

If our understanding of the potential and real conflict inherent in the 'local versus the international' is to become more focused and informed, then attention might usefully turn to human resource management. Globalization has been claimed to provide new challenges to human resource management at the level of the firm in the areas of industrial relations policy and practice (Veersma, 1995). As a result human resource management within the context of globalization and the multinational company becomes linked with the culture and industrial relations structures of the nation-state (De Nijs, 1992), and it is through the human resource function that such links are managed. Yet any formulated structures for some universal approach for international level human resource management (as with leadership behaviour and management in general) do not exist, perhaps because of the need to cope with and reflect the local characteristics identified in much of this volume. Thus cross-border human resource management policy in multinationals is still awaited with the 'language' of the internationalization of human resource management, perhaps the only identifiable feature so far developed (De Nijs, 1995).

HRM AND CROSS-CULTURAL DIVERSITY

The works by Budhwar and Fadzil, Richardson and Lewis *et al.* in particular reveal some weaknesses in the human resource management responses to the outcomes of globalization. In the case of expatriate employees insufficient seems to be known about professional groups who, it might be assumed, are directly able to exploit opportunities provided by the processes of internationalization in the academic world. Many of Richardson's recommendations for improved understanding of expatriate academics focus on adjustment of individual and family and the issue of cross-culture training. Although such improvements are deemed to be possible by involving a comparative analysis between expatriate academics and expatriate managers, it is interesting to note that managers too experience real difficulty in terms of their personal adjustment and in terms of adjusting to their role as a manager of diverse cultures (Mueller, 1994; Ronen and Shenkar, 1985). Cultural differences represent a major challenge to the 'internationalized' manager (Johnson, 1991) as much as to anyone else affected by globalization. The conclusions of Lewis, French and Phetmany on the implications of cross-cultural diversity for supervisory management more than hint at a failure of human resource management policies and practices at the level of the firm to face up to, let alone engage with the issue of diversity. This problem is exacerbated by the failure of senior line management to recognize differences between employees of different cultural backgrounds. The complexities underlying this problem, such as management providing 'equal treatment' to different cultural groups and causing feelings of discrimination and inequity of opportunity are perplexing and in this Australian context are a 'desperate' argument for more 'sophisticated' and 'sensitive' management training and behaviour. Clearly diversity skills have become as important an element of management as are decision making, planning and controlling, while culture and any associated theories should stand alongside leadership and job satisfaction theories.

Similar complexities under the heading of culture are revealed by Budhwar and Fadzil, and although the argument takes different directions to those of Lewis, French and Phetmany, there are real lessons for management in the international context: that is, effective human resource management needs to be characterized by a positive perception of the asset value of human resources, effective communication, provision of job security, an emphasis on employee welfare, employee development and teamwork. That these elements of effective management have aligned with Islamic work values and

Malaysian work values to help foster success for one Islamic organization strengthens the argument that human resource management needs to be 'culture sensitive' and play its part in developing equally sensitive line management policies and practices. Budhwar and Fadzil do not claim that such an approach is possible in all circumstances and all organizations, but at least an example has been provided of the effect of culturally sensitive management and the benefits accruing to all stakeholders in a real world organization. McKenna's work on public management in New Zealand also re-enforces this claim that in an international context there is an increased (and a need for an improved) role for human resource management. Change strategies for moving from public to privately funded public sector management of farm research are seen to require a strategic form of human resource management, radical changes to recruitment, selection and placement, reward systems and methods, the management of performance, team leadership and training and development. These redesigned elements of human resource management are a direct result of re-structuring in the face of a global model of management supplanting the local New Zealand model. The very real problems in this process as documented by McKenna reveal more than a hint of the cultural issues which again are seen to raise obstacles to the forces of globalization.

OPTIMISM AND CAUTION

On a different note Cheng reveals one of the more positive aspects of globalization as it affects Chinese business students. The expatriation of Chinese families has provided what for some cultures may be a novel method of networking (*guanxi*) for job searches outside of China, or for seeking job opportunities created by the internalization of parts of the Chinese economy. In this case cultural arrangements in one part of China – Shantou – help facilitate the realization of the career and business aspirations of students in the face of changing socio-economic conditions. Even here, however Cheng sounds a cautionary note pointing out that *guanxi* may not continue to work to the advantage of students partly because of the growth of 'western-style' recruitment practices in China which may well replace *guanxi*. Yet again globalization raises questions about the future viability of culture-driven behaviour and practice, perhaps as Cheng hints in this case to the detriment of business graduate career choices.

This last cautionary note reminds us yet again that if there are good elements to globalization, then there are also indifferent and bad elements. The indifferent are brought about by the seemingly inevitable changes in operations and workplace relations which accompany globalization in turn bringing about non-unionism, single employee representation and the decline of trade unions and collective bargaining (Locke, Kochan and Pione, 1995). Driving on from these indifferent developments are the 'bad' elements of insecure workforces (Heery and Salmon, 2000), the erasure of established working patterns and relations (Chaykowski and Giles, 1998) and the intensification of work accompanied by stress and related problems. We may wonder how these good, indifferent and bad elements will affect the work experiences of Japan's workforce, particularly in the small and service sector enterprises if the deregulation in the labour market required for business and employment growth – and argued for by Yoko Sano – is actually introduced.

SOME PARTICULAR AUSTRALIAN CONCERNS

It appears to be in Australia where the greatest cause for concern about the indifferent and bad outcomes of globalization arises, as presented in the contributions by Holland, Nelson and Fisher, B. McKenna, and Waring, Macdonald and Burgess. Throughout these three works there is a consistency in the difficulties and threats experienced by Australian institutions in dealing with the outcomes of globalization. In the pursuit of the positive benefits to be derived from globalization managers seem not to parallel their building of competitive advantage (by improving efficiency, quality, innovation, responsiveness to customers and utilization of technology) with modifications to human resource management which recognize local institutional, cultural and ethical characteristics. Holland *et al.* emphasize the failure of Australian trade unions to fully play their role in dealing with these matters. B. McKenna reveals the weaknesses in the responses to globalization made by several Australian governments over the past two decades, governments which may have justified passivity and non-intervention by emphasizing the technical merits of globalization and failing to recognize the wider socio-economic consequences, particularly in so far as Australian workers may not have benefited from the impact of globalization. Waring, Macdonald and Burgess similarly find that in the more particular context of the Australian coal industry there is an inability on the part of the labour force representatives to develop a sufficiently coherent and robust response to international pressures, leading in the extreme to nothing less than worker exploitation.

CONVERGENCE AND DIVERGENCE

If we conclude that the forces of globalization have a tendency to be insensitive to local nation-state characteristics, we can equally conclude that the institutions and arrangements in those nation-states appear to lack an ability to challenge and turn around the outcomes of such insensitivity. The mis-management of culture and cultural diversity, the untempered impact on labour markets and employment, the failure to optimize local characteristics in the interests of business performance have at least two root causes – the impersonal process of globalization itself and local confusion and incoherence. Additionally there is a lack of consensus in the views taken by the different parties or stakeholders on the process and outcomes of globalization. Furthermore there is no possibility of making some judgement on whether there is integration and convergence towards some new world order, not least because of the confusion which appears to exist between harmonization where some degree of local nation-state autonomy may be retained, and globalization which erases the characteristics of the host nation in terms of autonomy. In the foregoing contributions perhaps some more hopeful outcomes would have been better assured by harmonization of global and national elements rather than globalization developing as a unitary process. Interestingly the debate on convergence is currently swinging towards more divergence in the context of international business developments, with Katz and Darbyshire (2000) suggesting less consistency and more *ad hoc* variety in the approach taken by multinationals towards the labour process and institutions in the local host nation-state.

CONCLUDING NOTE AND RECOMMENDATIONS

The elements of the globalization debate presented in the various contributions of this volume are characterized by many arguments and counter arguments, contradictions and anomalies with optimism and pessimism mixed in. At the core of the debate is the relationship between multinational behaviours and national characteristics, and much of this volume provides building blocks for our wider and clearer perceptions of the issues. Whatever view we may take of globalization and its impact on institutions, culture and individuals we may assert that the labour process is changing; trade union roles are increasingly problematic; labour market arrangements are changing (usually) away from regulation towards deregulation; government roles can be unclear and at times ineffective; local elements frustrate multinational aspirations (and vice-versa); and the issues of culture and cultural diversity are growing features of the globalization debate with some significant lessons for management. Globalization may have given management greater bargaining power (and perhaps an opportunity to disregard local and cultural issues), but without more sensitivity management could yet lose the goal of optimum corporate performance via globalization. The foregoing essays reveal significant changes in the labour processes of Asia Pacific countries, particularly Japan, Australia and New Zealand, and these usually mean a 'loss' to the workforce of some kind. The lessons here are for those local agencies and representatives who require sharper and more effective responses to the international organizations and pressures arriving on their shores. But if these local responses lack focus and clarity so do the forces of globalization, and herein lies an essential message of this work – that internationalism in the business world and local or national responses do not relate to one another; they are unaligned and diverge away from one another with neither consensus or problem-free outcomes.

Therefore, recommendations for further research flowing from the contents of this volume exist within and around the core requirement for more understanding of the currently largely neglected issues of integration (or divergence) between the vested interests of globalization, and the constituents of the process and the vested interests of the nation-state and its constituents. Weaving through this, and hopefully helping to build a clearer picture of events and outcomes should be conclusions and recommendations involving cultural issues and organization success, new and evolving notions of management theory and practice in the context of globalization, an assessment of appropriate human resource management responses, and a thorough analysis of managerial, trade union and government roles in the process of globalization. The individual employee responses to globalization such as those represented by the expatriate 'experience' are elements also requiring more focused study. Inevitably the requirements for such work currently leaves internationalization and the detail elements of globalization as an ongoing, perhaps even 'just emerging' subject for research over many decades ahead, and within an appropriate agenda may lie the central theme of the role of benefits accruing to and losses experienced by the various interested and involved parties.

REFERENCES

Card, D. and Freeman, R. (eds.) (1993), *Small Differences that Matter: Labour Markets and Income Maintenance in Canada and the United States*. Chicago: University of Chicago Press.

Chaykowski, R. and Giles, A. (1998), 'Globalisation, Work and Industrial Relations', *Relations Industrielles/Industrial Relations*, Vol.53, No.1, pp.3–12.

De Nijs, W. (1995), 'International Human Resource Management and Industrial Relations: A Framework for Analysis' in Harzing, A. and Van Russeyveldt, J. (eds.), *International Human Resource Management*. London: Sage.

De Nijs, W. (1992), 'Patterns of Industrial Relations, and Personnel Management in Three European Countries' in Dijck, J. and Wentink, A. (eds.) *Transnational Business in Europe: Economic and Social Perspectives*. Tilberg: Tilberg Academic Press, pp.248–58.

Frenkel, S.J. and Royal C. (1998), 'Corporate–Subsidiary Relations, Local Contexts and Workplace Change in Global Corporations', *Relations Industrielle/Industrial Relations*, Vol.53, No.1, pp.154–82.

Heery, E. and Salmon, J. (eds.) (2000), *The Insecure Workforce*. London: Routledge.

Hofstede, G. (1980), *Cultures Consequences: International Differences in Work-Related Values*. New York: Sage Publications.

Johnson, W.D. (1991), 'Global Work Force 2000: The New World Labour Market', *Harvard Business Review*, March–April, pp.115–27.

Katz, H.C. and Darbyshire, O. (2000), *Converging Divergences: Worldwide Change in Employment Systems*. Ithaca and London: ILP Press, Cornell University.

Lee, E. (1996), 'Globalisation and Employment: Is Anxiety Justified', *International Labour Review*, Vol.135, No.5, pp.485–97.

Locke, R., Kochan, T. and Pione, M. (1995), *Employment Relations in a Changing World Economy*. Cambridge, Mass.: MIT Press.

Mueller, F. (1994), 'Societal Effect, Organisational Effect and Globalisation', *Organisation Studies*, Vol.15, No.3, pp.429–46.

Ronen, S. and Shenkar, O. (1985), 'Listing Countries on Attitudinal Dimensions: A Review and Synthesis', *Academy of Management Journal*, 28 September, p.449.

Smith, I.G. and Debrah, Y. (2000), 'Globalisation and the Changing Pattern of Employment', *International Journal of Manpower*, Vol.21, No.1, Special Edition, pp.446–510.

Veersma, O. (1995), 'Multinational Corporations and Industrial Relations' in Harzing, A. and Van Russeyveldt, J. (eds.) *International Human Resource Management*. London: Sage.

Notes on Contributors

Yaw A. Debrah is a senior lecturer in Management at Cardiff Business School, University of Wales. He teaches courses in Human Resource Management and Comparative Management at both undergraduate and graduate levels, and has also has been involved in post-experience training. He has lived and worked in Africa, North America, Asia and Europe. He has published numerous articles and book chapters, and his current research interests include the impact of globalization on management, management in emerging/transition societies, human resource management in the construction and hotel industries and age discrimination in employment.

Ian G. Smith is a senior lecturer in Management in the Human Resource Management Department, Cardiff Business School, University of Wales. He is a past Chairman of the Faculty of Management at Management Centre Brussels. His research interests have concentrated on the link between human resource performance and organizational performance, and he has published extensively on the subjects of productivity and pay, reward management and wage and salary administration and benefits, and he is a past advisor to the International Organization on productivity gain sharing, to the Ministry of Defence on performance related pay systems and the Treasury on pay system design.

Peter Waring is a Lecturer in the Industrial Relations and Human Resource Management Group in the School of Management at the University of Newcastle, Australia. His current research interests include industrial relations policy, employment relations in the coal industry and individualized employment relations.

Duncan Macdonald is an Honorary Associate of the School of Management at the University of Newcastle, Australia and is currently Acting Director of the University's Employment Studies Centre. Current research interests include public sector industrial relations, the electricity industry and trade union renewal.

John Burgess is Associate Professor in the Department of Economics, University of Newcastle, Australia. His research interests include labour market policy, unemployment, gender and work, and employment and workplace restructuring.

Peter Holland is a lecturer in Strategic Human Resource Management and Employee Relations at the School of Management, University of Tasmania. His research interests are in new patterns of work, employee relations and Occupational Health and Safety.

Lindsay Nelson is a lecturer in Human Resource Management and Industrial Relations at the School of Management, University of Tasmania. His research interests are in organizational change, enterprise bargaining and Occupational Health and Safety.

Cathy Fisher is a lecturer in International Human Resource Management at the School of Management, University of Tasmania. She has also taught in the areas of accounting and management. Her research interests are in international and strategic human resource management.

Bernard McKenna is a lecturer in the School of Communication, Faculty of Business at Queensland University of Technology. As a communication specialist, he has extensive research publications and consultancies in business, technical, and scientific writing. He is currently co-authoring a book that identifies the political sea-change occurring during this globalized hypercapitalist era.

Dianne Lewis is a senior lecturer in Management at the Queensland University of Technology. Her areas of speciality are management and organization theory and the relationships between theory and practice. She publishes widely in the areas of leadership, culture, change and power, and is specifically interested in the leadership of multicultural workgroups.

Erica French is a lecturer in Management and Human Resource Management in the School of Management at the Queensland University of Technology, where her areas of speciality include equity and diversity management. She has published internationally in the areas of individual change, equity and strategic management.

Thipaphone Phetmany is Operations Manager of Enterprise Development Consultants Co. Ltd in Vientiane, Laos. Her original research for her Masters thesis on the relationship between leadership styles and job satisfaction among different cultural workgroups in Australia forms the basis of this essay.

Julia Richardson is an International Research Fellow of the American Association of University Women and is currently pursuing her doctorate in the management department of the University of Otago, New Zealand. Her areas of specific interest are expatriation particularly with regard to IHRM issues, qualitative research methods and the use of metaphor as a research tool. She has spent the past ten years working in Asia, notably Japan, Indonesia and Singapore.

Steve McKenna was until recently a Senior Lecturer at the University of Otago, New Zealand. He is now a consultant with Stansfield Consultants in Singapore. He has worked in North America, Europe and the Asia-Pacific in teaching and in managerial posts in the telecommunications, office equipment, automotive parts and hospitality industries. His research interests are primarily in the area of management learning and organizational change.

Pawan Budhwar is a lecturer in Organizational Behaviour and HRM at Cardiff Business School. His research interests are in the areas of IHRM, management in developing countries, quality of work life and companys' performance, managerial cognition, HRM in MNCs in India and comparative HRM. He has published in a number of management journals.

Khairul Fadzil completed his MBA at Cardiff Business School and is now working in Malaysia.

Yoko Sano is Professor of Human Resource Management at Tokyo International University. She has been a visiting professor in a number of universities including the University of Illinois, Australia National University; Glasgow University, Cranfield School of Management and the University of Philippines. She has published numerous papers in academic journals, and her books in English include *Human Resource Management in Japan* and *Frontiers of Human Resource Practices in Japan.*

Cheng Soo May is Associate Professor of Management at the International Graduate School of Management, University of South Australia. Her teaching and research interests include cross-cultural management, Asian business development, international human resource management, higher education research and research methodology. Colleagues keen to discuss possibilities for collaborating on research in the Asia-Pacific region are welcome to contact her at soo-may.cheng@unisa.edu.au.

Index

Aaker, D.A., 116
Academic profession, 125, 126–78;
    and internationalization, 125, 126, 222, 242, 244, 246, 253;
    and international travel, 126;
Academic expatriates, 105, 126, 129, 134, 140, 143, 145, 147, 240;
    definition, 106;
    transformation, 110, 111, 113, 118, 119, 120, 140, 141, 157;
    and cross-cultural adjustment, 131, 144, 146, 147
Adorno, T.W. 74, 75, 78
Agger, B. 72, 78
Agho, A.O. 113
Alexander, G. 8
Allen, J.S. 80
Altbach, P.G. 125, 127
Angell, N.B. 179, 180
Antal, A.B. 133
Anthony, S. 91
Anwar, S.T. 175
Arbitrary work, 206, 208, 212, 213
Argy, F. 98
Aryee, S. 131
ASEAN, 172
Asian nations;
    miracle, 174, 175
Atkinson, C.M. 129
Australia;
    multi-cultural, 105, 106, 107, 108, 109, 113, 115, 118–22;
    trade unions, 50, 53, 54, 56–60, 67, 72, 88
Australia Re-constructed (1987) 54
Australia Workplace Agreements (1992) 53
Australian Council of Trade Unions (ACTU), 54, 56, 58, 64, 67, 71–5, 86, 89, 95

Australian Industrial Relations Commission, 52, 83
Avolio, B.J. 113
Aycan, Z. 131, 132
Aylmer, S. 72, 93, 96

Bacon, N. 50
Bagguley, P. 80
Baird, L. 58
Baker, G. 177
Baker, M. 128
Baligh, H.H. 173
Barney, J.B. 180, 193
Bass, B.M. 109–13, 118, 120, 136
Battin, T. 87, 93
Bauman, Z. 82, 93
Beer, M. 57
Bewes, T. 74, 75
Birdseye, M. 131
Black, D.R. 141
Black, J.S. 131
Blake, S. 107
Blonigen, M. 132
Blyton, P. 68
Bodur, M. 130
Boreham, P. 81, 82, 89
Bosanquet, N. 170
Boxall, P. 56
Boyer, E. 127, 129
Bramble, T. 82, 89, 97
Brewster, C. 125, 130, 138
Bryan, D. 79
Buller, P.F. 58
Burgess, J. 242, 245, 246, 250, 251
Burkett, P. 176
Burns, R. 178

Call centres 56, 59, 63–5, 67
Car Plan. 87
Card, D. 59, 245

Carnegie Foundation 127–8
Carnell, C. 170
Chang, H-J. 176
Change agent 161
Charlesworth, S. 52
Chaykowski, R. 1–20
Child Labour, 211
Chow, T. 176
Chu, I.Y-K. 111, 113
Church, A.H. 107
Clark, D. 53, 54
Clark, J. 53, 54
Clegg, C.W. 113
Clegg, S.R. 89, 109, 115
Cohen, Y. 177
Common, R.K. 151, 152
Conway, P.J. 173
Cook, J. 111, 113, 118
Cope, W. 108, 247
Cox, T.H. 107
Coyle, D. 82
Crab, B.F. 135
Crockett, G. 98
Crown Research Institutes (CRI) 155, 157
Culture 82, 83, 114–18, 218
Curtain, R. 52, 90

Darbyshire, O. 251
Davis, R. 51, 54
Dawkins, P. 98
Debrah, Y. 246
Decentralization. 52, 217
Deregulation 51, 64, 71, 73, 87, 88, 153, 169, 171, 199–204, 209, 214, 250; of financial assets 199–204
Digh, P. 174
DiTomaso, N. 112
Diversity management 109–12
Dowling, P.J. 56
Dragon Economies 172
Dual Career Couples 133
Dunleavy, P. 153
Dyer, L. 57

Earley, P.C. 114, 119, 122
Eastman, V. 129
Economic turmoil (S.E. Asia) 171, 175
Ehrenberg, V. 126
Eisenhardt, K. 117
Elron, E. 130
Employment 56, 216
Employment protection (Japan); legislation 199, 204, 205, 209
Enterprise 52, 73, 81, 95
Enterprise bargaining, 52, 73, 91, 95
Entrekin, L. 178
Erez, M. 106, 114, 122

Ettorre, B. 194
Evans, R. Jr. 88, 204
Expatriates:
  academics, 105, 126, 129, 134, 140, 143–7, 240;
  managers, 129;

Fairclough, N. 73
Farm Research 249
Featherstone, M. 82
Fells, R.E. 82, 90, 91
Fenwick, M. 131
Fisher, C. 56, 242, 244
Flexibility;
  functional working time 63;
  pay 76;
  procedural 52;
  labour 75, 76;
  organizational 50
Fordism 81
Foreign Direct Investments 80, 241
Forster, N. 125, 129, 130, 137
Foundation for Research Science and Technology (FRST) 155
Fox, C. 52–4
Fragmentation 82
France 80, 205
Freeman, R. 245
French, E. 105, 107, 112, 115, 116, 242–4, 248
Frenkel 154–83, 245, 282, 310
Friedman, T.L. 80

Gardenswartz, L. 112
Global economic integration 172, 244
Globalist discourse 71, 83, 84
Globalization 51, 64–6, 71, 75–58, 84, 87, 92, 93, 99, 107, 115, 125, 126, 152–5, 166, 171–6, 192–6, 205, 222, 239–55
Globalized hypercapitalism 71, 78
Gonzalez, A. 127, 129
Gordon, D. 50
Graham, F. 75–80
Gray, J.T. 109, 115
Green, R. 82, 87, 88, 93–8
Greenfield Sites 55, 65;
  company, 55;
  replacement, 55;
  expansion, 55;
  international, 55, 65
Gregerson, H.B. 131
Griffin, R.W. 160
Gruneberg, M.M. 109–13
Guest, D.E. 50, 56
Gullahorn, J.E. 129
Gullahorn, J.T. 129

Hackett, R.D. 111
Hajj;
    performance, 181, 182, 183, 188, 193;
    Trust and Management Board, 182
Halal 193
Hall, L. 58
Hall, R. 82
Hall, S. 80
Halliday, M.A.K. 73, 75
Hamilton, C. 92
Hammer, M.R. 131
Harcourt, T. 91, 92
Harley, B. 82, 96–8
Haron, S. 173
Harris, H. 125, 130
Harrison, D.A. 130, 131, 132
Hart-Landsberg, M. 176
Harvey, D. 81
Haskins, M.E. 160
Hawke, Bob, 51, 71, 72, 73, 87, 90
Heelas, P. 82
Heery, E. 10–20
Held, D. 153
Hill, J.S. 131
Hilmer, F. 77, 78;
Hilmer Report 77
Hofstede, G. 106, 113–20, 129, 178, 244
Holbeche, L. 10–20
Holder, G. 57
Holland, P. 67, 242, 244, 250
Holloway, J. 78
Hood, C. 152
Horkheimer, M. 78
Horton, R.J. 1–20
Howard, W. 53
Howell, J.M. 111, 113
Huberman, A.M. 118
Hughes, J. 218
Human Relations School of Management, 111
Human Resource Management;
    and Industrial relations, 50, 51, 56;
    policies and practices, 56, 59, 162, 167,
       178, 190;
    and staffing, 56
Hutton, W. 101
Hypercapitalism 71, 78

Ikeda, S. 80
Imaizumi, A. 131
Indonesia 127, 134, 175, 183, 224
Industry Commission (Australia) 95
Industrial Relations Act (Australia) 1988 54
Industrial Relations Amendment Act (Australia) 1990 54

Industrial Relations Commission (Australia) 83, 95
Industrial Relations Reform Act (1993) (Australia) 53, 76
Inequality 74, 91, 92, 115
Inkson, K. 129
International Monetary Fund, 153
Iqbal, Z. 179
Islam, I. 1–20
Islamic institution 171, 178, 192, 245
Izraeli, D.N. 133

James, C. 73, 82
Jameson, F. 82
Japan 89, 111, 134, 139, 174–179, 199, 200–213, 244, 250–52
Job satisfaction 106–13, 118–20
Johnsen, M. 130
Johnson, W.D. 244, 248
Jomo, K.S. 176
Jones, C. 73

Kalantzis, M. 108
Kalecki, M. 97
Kamoche, K. 69
Karpen, U. 129
Karpin, D.S. 90, 115
Keating, Paul 52, 71–3, 76, 86–8, 96
Keennoy, T. 52, 54
Kellner, D. 78
Kelly, D. 52, 54
Kelly, P. 88
Kennedy, P. 78–80
Kenyon, P. 91
Kesatuan Kakitangar (Employee Association) 191
King, N. 135
Kitay, J. 95, 96
Klagge, J. 109
Knight, R. 5–20
Kochan, T. 251
Koh, W.L. 124
Konrad, A.M. 120
Kramar, R. 52, 155
Krugman, P. 98
Kuhn, T. 122

Labour market 51–3, 81, 83, 95, 97, 178, 199, 239–46;
    flexibility 204–12
Ladd, R. 50
Lanier, A.R. 142
Lansbury, R. 54
Lasserre, P. and Schutte, H. 3–20
Lawler, E. 58
Leadership;
    and style 72, 105–6, 118, 231, 243;

as diversity skill 106;
transactional 110, 111;
transformational characteristics 106,
110, 111;
and job satisfaction 105, 109, 248;
and cultural issues 109;
American based theories 110
Le Heron, R. 151, 152
Lee, E. 1–20
Legge, K. 50, 56
Lengnick-Hall, C.A. 58
Lengnick-Hall, M.L. 58
Lewis, D.S. 111
Lindsay, C.P. 129
Line Managers 57, 59
Linehan, M. 133
Linnehan, F. 120
Lipford, J. 173
Lipietz, A. 81
Littler, C.R. 95
Lo, D. 176
Locke, E.A. 111, 250
Locke, R. 1–20
Lucio, M.M. 50, 51, 56, 66, 67
Luke, A. 74, 93

Mabey, C. 162
Macdonald, D. 52, 82, 97, 251, 245, 246,
252
Macken, J.J. 52
Malaysia;
financial institution 171, 174, 186;
economy 175, 176, 181, 183;
culture 177, 188;
work culture 174, 177, 178, 193;
government 176, 182, 184;
unemployment 177;
ringgit 176;
Central Bank 176–7
Management control 241
Mansor, N. 178
Mantras and mantric notions 74
Marcuse, H. 75
Markets;
product 204, 213, 239, 245;
labour 172, 199, 204, 245;
global 98, 205, 245;
liberalization 76, 171
Martin, B. 151
Martin, G.A. 113
Martin, J.R. 75
Matthews, J.A. 52, 89, 90
McCormick, R.E
McDonald, T. 82
McGrew, A. 153
McKenna, B. 75, 80, 151, 152, 243, 249,
250

McMahan, G. 58
McRobbie, A. 81
Meshoulam, I. 58
Meynaud, J. 74
Miles, M.B. 118
Mileski, A.S. 133
Miller, G.A. 113
Miller, P. 93, 94,
Miller, W.L. 135
Milner, A. 114
Min Chen 2–20
Minehan, M. 174, 194
Mintzberg, H. 160
Miscellaneous Workers Union 95
Montagnon, P. 1–20
Moorhead, G. 160
Morris, P. 86
Morris, R. 51, 52
Mortomer, D. 52
Mueller, C.W. 113
Mueller, F. 173, 245, 248
Muhasabah 131, 193
Multi-cultural workforces and diversity
106, 108, 119, 121
Murray, R. 81
Muslim country 173
Musyawarah 188

Nakata, M. 74
Napier, N.K. 58, 129, 133, 144
National Economic Summit Accords
(Australia) 72
National Wage Case (1991) (Australia) 52,
81
Nechita, M. 130
Nelson, L. 242, 244, 250
Neo-classical globalist discourse 71, 72, 99
Neo-liberal 71–7, 84, 86
Nevile, J. 91, 92
New Public Management 151, 155
New Zealand government – ministry of
science – dept. of agriculture 151, 153,
169;
research and development, 158
Nicholson, N. 131
Nkomo, S.M. 106
Noonan, K.A. 130
Norton, A. 73
NSW Minerals Council 66
Nunes, N. 98

O'Brien, J.M. 92, 95, 96
Ong, A. 79
Organization for European Cooperation
and Development (OECD) 91, 92–5,
120, 204, 206, 214
Organizational contingencies 172

Osland, J.S. 129, 131, 140, 141, 144

Palmer, G. 1–20
Parry, K. 111
Patibandla, M. 176
Pava, M.L. 194
Pay review 52, 62
Pearson, C.A.L. 82, 178, 176
Peetz, D. 171, 55
Performance Appraisal 59
Performance management 164, 165, 166, 167
Performance Pay 165, 168, 206, 209, 211, 213
Peterson, M.F. 114
Pettigrew, A.M. 172
Pfeffer, J. 177
Phetmany, T. 105, 243–4, 248
Piore, M. 250
Porter, M.E. 180
Post Fordist 89, 90
Preece, D. 55, 56
Presley, J.R. 173
Price, J.L. 113
Prices and Income Accord (Australia) 1983–96 55, 76
Privatization 71, 73, 87, 151, 153, 169, 171
Profit;
    investment, 85;
Prusty, R. 176
Public Sector Management 151;
    restructuring, 169, 247;
    reform, 151, 153;
    and the state, 217, 244;
    and the market, 153
Punnett, B.J. 133
Pusey, M. 76
Pyke, D. 51, 52, 78, 88

Quran 178, 180
Quiggin, J. 98
Quinlan, M. 95

Rajkumar, K. 176
Rana, P.B. 172
Randall, K. 162, 72
Recruitment and Selection 58, 63, 161, 164, 166, 189, 249
Redundancy and dismissal 200, 205, 206, 209–14
Rees, S. 73
Regional differences 212
Reich, R.B. 79, 80
Reward strategy 164, 165
Rewards and reward systems 110, 118, 143, 162, 164, 165–9, 188, 215, 217, 225, 249

Riba 179
Richardson, J. 242, 243, 247
Rifkin, J. 74, 78, 79
Rimmer, M. 51, 52, 82
Ronalds, C. 120
Ronen, S. 248
Rose, N. 82, 93, 94, 113
Rosewarne, S. 172
Royal, C. 245

Saha, L.J. 129
Salaman, G. 162
Salmon, J. 250
Sano, Y. 199, 244, 247, 250
Saul, J.R. 74, 75, 76, 78, 99
Saunders, P. 92
Schuster, J.H. 126, 127
Schwan, R. 177
Scientific and Agricultural Research (in New Zealand) 151, 154
Scott, W.A.H. 141
Selmer, J. 129, 137, 125, 140
Shaffer, M.A. 130, 132
Shaw, J. 120, 108
Shenkar, O. 248
Shepherd, W.G. 179
Sherden, W.A. 78
Sherif, M.A. 179
Singapore 127, 134, 224
Singer, M.S. 111, 113
Singh, A. 173
Singleton, G. 91
Sisson, K. 56, 150, 173
Skinner, W. 90
Smith, I.G. 246
Smith, P.B. 114
Smith, R. 73, 129
Soeters, J.L. 177
Sonnenschein, W. 112
Spicer, B. 153, 154
Stedham, Y. 130
Steel Plan 87
Steers, R.M. 111
Stegman, T. 96
Steiner, D.D. 113
Stening, B.W. 131
Stephens, G.K. 131
Stevens, M.J. 133
Stewart, R. 74
Stills, L. 52
Stogdill, R.M. 110
Stone, R.J. 130
Storey, J. 56, 50
Strange, S. 80
Strauss, A. 117
Stretton, H. 80, 86
Stuart, M. 67

Tan, G. 174
Tayeb, M. 173
Taylor, S. 133
Tella, R.D. 205, 206
Terborg, J.R. 111, 113
Textile, Clothing and Footwear Union
    (Australia) 79, 95
Thomas, D.C. 130, 131, 141
Thomas, R. 112
Thurow, L. 78, 92
Tichy, N.M. 57
Tiger Economies 172
Tomlinson, J. 73
Total Quality Management 178
Trade Unions 50–60, 66, 71
Triandis, C.H. 119, 122
Tsuruoka, D. 178
Turner, T. 177

Ummah 180
Unitarist 50, 56, 57, 62
United Arab Emirates 127

Veersma, O. 247
Vietnamese 106, 109, 114–120, 129, 243,
    245

Wagstyle, S. 1–20
Wall, T.D. 113
Walsh, J.S. 133

Waring, P. 242, 245, 246, 251
Warr, P. 113, 118
Waterman, P. 71, 79, 99
Watts, L. 82, 89
Wee, C. 175
Welch, A. 125, 129
Wengel, J. 172
Weston, S. 50, 51, 56, 66, 67
Whitelaw, M.J. 127
Williams, P. 72
Wiseman, J. 2–20
Wood, A. 171
Work practices 208
Work and Income New Zealand (WINZ)
    154
Working conditions 64, 65, 156, 191, 217
Workplace;
    reform 50, 52;
    relationships 53
Workplace Relations Act (Australia) 53
Wright, P.M. 58, 193

Yarwood, V. 173
Yavas, U. 130
Yeung, H.W. 1–20
Yin, R.K. 116, 117
Yokochi, N. 111
Yong, A.K.B. 178

Zappala, G. 5

For Product Safety Concerns and Information please contact our EU
representative GPSR@taylorandfrancis.com
Taylor & Francis Verlag GmbH, Kaufingerstraße 24, 80331 München, Germany

www.ingramcontent.com/pod-product-compliance
Lightning Source LLC
Chambersburg PA
CBHW070355270326
41926CB00014B/2553

9 780714 681627